To: Ashle

Keep finding!

Love Always'

Jonathan

Miracles, Angels, and Messages

"Patient Zero"
A True Covid Delta Variant Story

Jonathan Powell Crooks

Jonathan Powell Crooks

JONATHAN POWELL CROOKS
EMBRACING THE PROFOUND

MIRACLES, ANGELS, AND MESSAGES

Copyright © 2024 Jonathan Crooks

Cover Copyright © 2024 Jonathan Crooks

Editing and Publishing Services provided by Edits by Stacey

Cover art and "angel" portrait created by Angelika Domschke at Kudzu Art Zone, Gallery & Art Studios Angelikart.com

Published by J. Powell Crooks LLC

All rights reserved.

No part of this book may be reproduced in any form or by any electronic or mechanical means, including information storage and retrieval systems, without written permission from the author, except for the use of brief quotations in a book review.

The book is for informational purposes only and is not intended to diagnose, treat, or cure any condition. The reader assumes all risks associated with using the information. Readers should consult a medical professional if they seek medical advice, diagnoses, or treatment. The author and publisher are not responsible for any errors, inaccuracies, or omissions in the book.

For permission requests, write the publisher at MiraclesAngelsandMessages.com

Library of Congress Control Number: 2024927427
Identifiers:
Paperback: 979-8-9909256-0-1
Hardcover: 979-8-9909256-1-8
eBook: 979-8-9909256-2.5

This work is dedicated to all those who have been the biggest influence in my life and my blessings:

Those who have gone before me:

Robert W. Crooks, Vivian S. Crooks, Patricia L. Crooks, Charles P. Crooks, Sheila M. Keasbey

Those still with me:

Vivian W. Crooks, Kristine T. Lockstedt, Gary R. Crooks, Nancy T. Chesney, Timothy G. Keasbey, Diane Keasbey, Michael Chesney, Evan Lockstedt, Michael Drago, Jessica T. Crooks, Jonathan "Henry" Lockstedt, Heidi Joy Buksbazen, Paul Buksbazen, Philip Chesney, Thatiana Chesney, Jacob "Jake" Keasbey, Rebecca M. Keasbey.

And to all those yet to come....

CONTENTS

Introduction ix
Letter to the Reader xi

1. Chapter 1 Miracles and Angels 1
2. The Back Story 5
3. Navigating the Troubled Waters 11
4. The Dawning of a New Day 68
5. Where Do We Go from Here? 89
6. One More Stop Until Homeward Bound 103
7. The Good, The Bad, and The Ugly 135
   COVID-19 Recovery Manual
8. The Inevitable Questions 173
9. Angels of Protection 182
10. "The Evidence of the Past Gives Us Hope for the Future" 202
11. Readjusting to Life 230
12. In the End 262
    Epilogue 273

Appendix 285
Acknowledgments 291
About the Author 293

INTRODUCTION

On August 11, 2021, one of my twin daughters discovered she was pregnant with my first grandchild. It should have been a joyous time. Instead, I was in a coma with twenty tubes invading my body. The ventilator was monitored by dozens of worried nurses and doctors who were concerned about kidney failure. There was also concern that I may have a mild heart attack. The bottom line was my systems were shutting down! "He's not responding...," the lead doctor called out. I had taken a turn for the worse.

I was declared "Patient Zero" at the Wellstar North Fulton Hospital on July 25, 2021. It's a rather dubious honor. It means I was the first person admitted to that hospital with the COVID-19 Delta Variant, and the doctors were at a loss as to how to treat it. They were back to square one as everything they had used on the first version of COVID did not work on Delta.

On this roller coaster ride of emotions, family, friends, and thousands of people I didn't even know from around the country, and the globe were taken to their limits while I hung onto every prayer chain post during my battle with the Delta Variant of COVID-19.

This is the true story of what happened leading to those fateful days and what happened after them. I hope that you will walk away from reading this book with a renewed sense of faith in things greater than ourselves in whatever way you may define them. Discover that miracles happen. Find angels exist in many forms. Messages are constantly being delivered if we are open enough to look for them, recognize them, and listen to them.

LETTER TO THE READER

Dear Reader,

A "medical miracle," that's what they called me. The term is not quite an oxymoron, but it's close. We refer to medicine and the medical profession to save us in dire medical distress. Therefore, to term an outcome as a "medical miracle" would indicate that the outcome was not expected. In my case, the outcome was that I survived against all odds. Having visited death's door twice over several weeks in a medically induced coma and four times in total over a sixty-day juggernaut journey, leads one to ponder where my life's story could have, and perhaps by all rights should have, ended.

This is a story of survival. It's a story of medicine, miracles, angels, messages, love, compassion, family, doctors, nurses, friends—new and old—and strangers coming together from hospitals, churches, community organizations, and lives past and present. They all banded together to find a way.

I should have died according to conventional wisdom. This story is a roller coaster ride through COVID-19, or at least the version I contracted. Medical notes will be included, as well as family memories, friends' memories, doctors' and nurses' recollections, and public media posts to help the reader recognize the miracles, meet the angels, and understand the messages.

I hope that this work will give you a chance to ponder those things greater than ourselves, however you may define that, and open your mind to what is all around us.

Sincerely and with deep love,

The author.

CHAPTER 1
CHAPTER 1 MIRACLES AND ANGELS

To properly begin, it seems necessary to explore the term miracle at least a little bit.

The Oxford Dictionary defines a miracle as a noun, "A surprising and welcome event that is not explicable by natural or scientific laws and is therefore considered to be the work of a divine agency." It is further defined as "A highly improbable or extraordinary event, development… that brings very welcome consequences."[1]

To have the term miracle applied to you in any form is quite a statement, to say the least.

> "Do miracles happen because we believe in them,
> or do we believe in them because miracles happen?"

For those reading this work who are Hallmark Channel fans, you will recognize the quote above as part of the commercial for the *Miracles of Christmas* series, which runs every October through the New Year. I know, I know. The plots are easily figured out and always have a happy ending. However, they are fun, uplifting

---

1. pp. 5, 6 The Oxford Dictionary

stories, and they are heart-warming. Yes, they do bring tears to my eyes. I'm a bit of a sap when it comes to family things. All that withstanding, the question is compelling. The response in the show is equally inarguable when the actor's character says, "I believe it's a little bit of both."

Your belief system will determine what your answer would be to the question. If you hold fast to the thought that humanity is alone and dependent only upon itself, the concept of miracles is most likely foreign to you or indisputable. Of course, you have the right to believe or not believe; however, I would bet you have used the term, in one sense or another, in your life. Perhaps you referred to the miracle of birth when your children were born or when something tragic or overwhelming happened that, against all odds, you survived. Maybe it wasn't something you experienced, but it was something someone close to you experienced. At the very least, I am sure you have heard it.

If, by chance, you are a person who believes in higher powers, you will most likely be more open to seeing miracles when some deem situations as "coincidences."

THE CONCEPT of angels can be looked at the same way, depending on your belief system and point of view. Are they winged creatures who float in the heavens and act as the minions of a greater God? Do they come to earth in times of trouble to meet the needs of people, societies, or individuals like Clarence does for George Bailey in the classic movie *It's a Wonderful Life?* In that inspirational and uplifting film, Clarence asks, "People believe in angels, don't they?"

"Yes," responds George.

Clarence then retorts, "Then why are they so surprised when they see one?"

Chapter 1 Miracles and Angels

The *Oxford Dictionary* defines an angel as "A spiritual being believed to act as an attendant, agent, or messenger of God, conventionally represented in human form with wings and a long robe; an attendant spirit, especially a benevolent one." For example, "There was an angel watching over me." Also defined as "A person of exemplary conduct or virtue."

Perhaps you view angels as people of the earth who come into our lives at the right time to save us from a particular situation. A good example was told to me many years ago.

A very close friend of mine, Rev. Jan Edmiston, related a story during one of her sermons while she was the pastor at Fairlington Presbyterian Church, just outside of Washington, DC. I was a member at the time and eventually was ordained a deacon. Jan and I had been friends for a long time when her first *call* (as it's known in the Presbyterian Church) was at my church in Schaghticoke, New York (a town you will hear more about a little later).

Jan says that one afternoon, she was driving in a very rural area when one of her tires had a blowout. By her own admission, tire-changing was not one of her fortes. As she pondered the situation, out of nowhere, a truck barreled up the road toward her. It pulled up behind her, and a man jumped out. She attempted to tell him what happened, and without a word, he went to work changing the tire. When he was finished, she tried to offer a few dollars for the aid, along with words of heartfelt thanks. He refused the money with a quick wave of his hand, without speaking a word, jumped back into his truck, and drove down the road. He was quickly out of sight.

What have we here? Was he just a very quiet man of goodwill? Could he have been someone a little bit more? She described him as an angel. He was the angel she required at that moment. "Pure coincidence," you might say. It could be… but perhaps it requires some deeper thought.

My belief system embraces everything I have mentioned. You will meet some of my angels in the pages of this book. I believe you will come to love them as I have. I continue to stay in touch with many of them. Some I expect to see again many years from now.

CHAPTER 2
THE BACK STORY

If you were put up against a wall and told you must describe yourself in ten words or fewer, "Or else!" what would you say? Pretty dramatic, I know. But the question under pressure allows you to think fast without putting too much pressure on finding the right words or creating a narrative that you believe others would find suitable. My answer was rather easy. I said, "I am an extraordinarily ordinary person."

That is an excellent oxymoron, but it's extremely accurate. I'm truly about as average as one can get. Okay, maybe I'm high average, but I am still in the average category. Permit me to elaborate.

I took a significant test many years ago, in seventh grade or thereabouts. It was a test of intelligence. I'm quite certain it was put together by very intelligent people to make themselves appear even more intelligent than they really were and make the rest of us feel, well, less than that. What was my level? My results were "high average." Now, if that isn't a backhanded compliment, I don't know what is. It's kind of like saying, "You're not as dumb as you look."

I wasn't the smartest member of my family. That honor belonged to my sister, Nancy. She was the valedictorian. I tried desperately not to think about it because there was no way I would ever match her achievement. She was two years ahead of me, and she was the legacy I had to follow in school. My teachers would say, "Here comes another Crooks!" Imagine their disappointment when I came with my "high-average" intelligence. Not quite the barnburner they were anticipating. I wasn't even the most creative or handy. Nope, all that talent is in my brother, Tim, who is nine years my junior. He can figure out how to build or fix anything. I could barely stop a nosebleed, much less a leaky faucet. I certainly wasn't the best looking in my family either. That title, and I believe my siblings would agree, went to our sister Sheila. The blonde-haired beauty was taken from us much too young. She was fourteen when we lost her in a tragic accident; I was twenty. She was fourteen.

From left to right, my brother Tim, my sister Nancy and me.

| My sister Sheila, circa late 1976. Aged fourteen years.

HOW ELSE CAN I illustrate my averageness? Well, let's see, I'm five feet ten and a half inches tall. Yes, that half-inch is vitally important. Why, you ask? Because the average height of males when I was young was five feet ten inches, thus that half-inch vaulted me into the high average category. I graduated twenty-fifth in my 1974 class of exactly 100 students from Hoosic Valley Central High School in Schaghticoke, New York.

Schaghticoke was a beautiful little town of approximately 500 people when I lived there. I have always enjoyed saying, "We lived in the suburbs of the town." I grew up in a large red brick house that had been built in 1816 on 250 acres of land. The home and property are still in my family, and if we have our way, it will stay in the family for generations to come. When I returned for my fortieth plus one high school reunion (that's fuzzy math), Schaghticoke was still a town of about 500 residents, and our home was still in the suburbs.

| The photo is of our family homestead.

Built in 1816, our home was known for years as the "Old Banker Mansion," which was the name of the family who built it and lived there until 1920. The Crooks family purchased it in 1958, when we moved from Cooperstown, New York, in November 1958.

I negotiated my way through a fine college education. I was a history major, a subject I love and still engage with to this day. It was never my source of income. Instead, I spent most of my career in the telecommunications industry, working in data, and I was a property manager for Walton Communities (an apartment community company). I also was a merchandiser for Lego Systems for about five years, and I had various odds and ends of employment, including a twelve-year run as a ghost tour guide in Roswell, Georgia, where I currently reside. I enjoy it when I am asked to portray the founding fathers of our city for special events. I held some lofty titles over time, including national director of sales and marketing training for a nationwide telecom company that no longer exists and CEO of my little consulting gig for three years advising Northern Telecom, a worldwide switch manufacturing company. My consulting work took me all the way to India in 2000, where I outlined the American Telecom model to a private company in Mumbai as the country was privatizing the telecommunications industry.

Though I now consider myself retired, I was most recently the chief of staff for State Senator John Albers of District 56 in Georgia, a man you will meet later in the story. I run my own little mobile notary business. I'm also part of a company called "Pets and Peeps," which takes care of dogs and cats (even chickens). It helps pay the bills and keeps me active as I do the other things in life that bring me joy.

Fifteen years ago, I was enrolled at Columbia Theological Seminary in Decatur, Georgia, where I studied to become a Presbyterian minister in their Master of Divinity program. One of the hardest days of my life was the day I left CTS to pursue other ventures I thought would take better care of my very young children at the time.

My greatest accomplishment to date is the legacy I leave in my three children, twins Vivian and Kristine, and my son Gary. Vivian came first and is exactly one minute older than Kristine. Kristine is taller, though, so they both have something to brag about. Gary came just shy of three years later. They all are my greatest joys.

Left to right: my niece Heidi, Vivian, me, Kristine, and Gary. Viv and Kristine's H.S. graduation day, so it's not extremely recent, but still one I like tremendously. Note my hair; it is mentioned later in the book.

On December 24, 2021, my senior pastor at Roswell Presbyterian Church, Rev. Jeff Meyers, delivered a wonderful meditation entitled "The Night Shift Shepherds." As I'm sure you have already put together, he discussed the angels who announced the birth of the Christ child doing so to the shepherds watching the flocks at nighttime. They were not the dregs of society, but they would be considered lower class. The point is, they were chosen to hear the words from that glorious choir of angels as opposed to those whom you might consider more worthy by their status in society.

Certainly, I don't consider myself as part of the dregs, but I certainly am not the person that you would point to and say, "Well, of course, *HE* would be saved. It's obvious!" I'm not a billionaire, a captain of industry, or any great leader to any great degree.

I tell you all these things so you understand I am merely an extraordinarily ordinary man. Like many in this world, I'm a fundamentally good person who is involved in many areas of community service, some church-related and some not. I am not unlike most of you reading this book. We are truly brothers and sisters on similar paths. I believe you will see yourself reflected in these pages, and hopefully, it will help you see your value and significance to be watched over and visited by *angels*.

CHAPTER 3
NAVIGATING THE TROUBLED WATERS

It seems like everyone remembers where they were when the COVID pandemic hit. It's akin to people remembering where they were when Kennedy was assassinated on November 22, 1963 (if you were alive and cognizant then). I was seven, living in upstate New York, and I had no idea where Dallas was. I was afraid whoever had shot the president could be lurking in our backwoods.

People remember where they were when Reagan was shot in Washington, DC, on March 30, 1981, at what became known as the "Hinckley Hilton." I was in Buffalo, New York, working as an admissions counselor for a small, upstate New York college. I had the same sick feeling when I heard about the assassination attempt as I had when Kennedy was killed. For those of you who were born after 1975, you most likely don't remember or know much about either event.

The most recent event that is an equally tragic milestone was September 11, 2001. I was sitting at home and just happened to turn on the TV when the event was unfolding. I couldn't believe what I was watching. It was once again a surreal moment that froze us all in time.

The point is that life changed in a significant way after every one of those events. It disrupted lives and took away a sense of serenity. In a lot of ways, the COVID pandemic rocked life, and maybe it rocked your hope for the future with the massive loss of life. It was January 20, 2020, when the World Health Organization (WHO) used the phrase "2019 Novel Coronavirus" or "2019-nCoV" to refer to the outbreak in Wuhan, China. It wasn't long before the debate "To be vaccinated or not to be" became the battle cry of many, and it continues to this very day.

To combat the disease and prevent further spread, governments implemented a "lockdown." The only time I left home during those early stages was one hour a day to run outdoors, which has always been considered the safest place you could be if outside the confines of your own home.

I worked for a multi-billion-dollar internet marketing consulting firm at the time, and I was making a healthy income in the low six figures. Life had been going along well by most people's standards. I lived in a nice two-bedroom condo ten minutes from work. I had room for my children to visit, one at a time, when they could do so. I was in good shape for a sixty-three-year-old at the time. I really couldn't complain, though we all find reasons to, even when they don't exist. *Humans, we're amazing, aren't we?*

Once in lockdown, everyone in my company was required to work from home. Most enjoyed it to a high degree, though we found we worked longer hours since all we had to do was roll out of bed into our fuzzy slippers and put on some nice tops, just in case we had to jump on a conference call, reminding me of high school graduation photos. You really didn't have to wear pants because they only took the photos from the chest up. I had one classmate, Michael Rosko, from Hoosic Valley Central High School, who didn't wear pants for his photo. My friends from HVCS know exactly who I'm speaking of, and I know you are all smiling. I'm sure he is, too! He is a great guy and was a good friend in high school. To be fair, lest you get an improper image, he was wearing cutoff jeans and sneakers. Don't worry too much, Mike, I'm quite certain everyone reading this had a friend in their school who did the very same thing, and they are a legend, as are you!

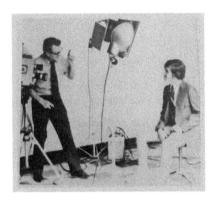

My friend from high school, Mike Rosko, having his senior class photo taken for the yearbook.

Everything moved along quite well until May 15, 2020. On that day at roughly noon, I jumped on a conference call with my then-boss to discuss some issue that I've long since forgotten. The HR representative was already on the line (a very nice lady whom I knew well). When I realized it was just the two of us on the call, I said to her, "I'm guessing this call is not going to end well for me." I knew there had already been several cuts by that time. We had lost a lot of business because of the lockdowns around the world. Up to that point, I had survived them all.

Losing my job was difficult. I was two years and eleven months away from retiring at age sixty-seven. But who was counting? I knew I was valued by many in the organization. I had reached the senior manager level and was aiming for director. I had several VPs and senior VPs who called that day to tell me how ticked they were that I was no longer there. "Who is going to handle the work like you?" they asked. I guess the stink of it was I knew I was valued; I just wasn't valued enough to be kept on longer, and no one seemed to have the power to stop it or take me back with them. I was given a little severance package that carried me to July 3, 2020. My health insurance stayed with me until then, as well.

Those of you who have been termed over time know that you are always offered COBRA coverage at some astronomical price that few can pay. So, what do you do? Pray and hope you don't get sick until you can find a new position. Well, some new opportunities did come my way.

Enter my dear friend, Senator John Albers. He called and said, "Jonathan, you don't have to do this, but I could really use you back on my staff to help with the upcoming campaign, and I'd like you to be chief of staff."

Although it did not pay huge dollars, the job certainly helped a tremendous amount from a psychological perspective. I was working with a very close friend doing something I loved. When that finished (on a positive note, by the way), I moved on to help in some other campaigns. All this work led to January 2021. I was still leading my Roswell Ghost Tours, which were always great fun, and many thanks to the owner, David Wood, for using me as much as he could. However, even with these "feeder streams," as I like to call them, I didn't have health insurance.

I had some decent dollars to help me along from the separation from my previous job, but I was going to have to start dipping into my 401K, which I didn't want to do; however, that's what it was there for, so dip into it I did. I searched for better employment but found there wasn't much call for a then sixty-four-year-old who was fast approaching sixty-five. The entirety of Social Security wasn't to kick in until sixty-six years and four months for those of us born in April 1956. I could opt for early retirement, but it was not a choice I wanted to take. I was able to secure COVID relief, as so many of us have. That certainly did help, though I'd have preferred not to need it or take it.

With COVID raging, I tried to be smart, but a year and a half into the pandemic, I was not going to stay home forever. There was concern over not having any health insurance, but I was in very good shape and was taking all my vitamins and working to keep up my immune system.

When you are finished having a good laugh over it, I'll tell you about the photo on this page. I had gone on an Isagenix[1] regimen about a year and a half earlier. For those not familiar with Isagenix, it's a product line to help with weight loss, building immune systems, and many more things. I had been faithfully using it and working out very hard to stay in as good a shape as I could. My friend Tray, who had sponsored me into the program, asked me for a photo to post in the limited distribution Isagenix family. I fought it tooth and nail. I really didn't want to do it. I'm just not into photos like this. She finally convinced me that it would be good for people my age to see it and to show that it was still possible to get into good shape. So, I acquiesced

In this photo, I'm 194 pounds and sixty-four years old.

and let her post it. Now I'm so glad I did. I have a record of what I looked like before Delta ravaged me. I have something to shoot for, and I promise you, I'm going to get back there!

Everything continued with the status quo until the end of July 2021. Then, my world changed.

AROUND JULY 10, I came down with a bit of a cough. At the time, it was more annoying than anything else, and it didn't appear to be much by way of sickness. But the cough became a bit heavier by the time of the photo below. It originated deeper in my lungs, but it still was not to the point of causing any great concern.

I'm on the left, and in order from left to right are Meghan Riley, David Wood, Alice Jankowski, Heather Nysewander, and Lauren Miller. Photo taken Monday, July 12, 2021.

In the above photo, I had been invited to a dinner with my friends from the Roswell Ghost Tour by the owner, David Wood, who is pictured here. We had a wonderful dinner on the evening of July 12, at the A-Street Cafe restaurant in Roswell, Ga. The cafe is no longer there.

BY FRIDAY, July 16, the cough had reached a point of concern, and I knew I was sustaining a low-grade fever. In addition, I started having problems with diarrhea. It still appeared to be manageable, but there was enough of a concern that I went to see a doctor. At that time, I was diagnosed with COVID-19. The symptoms were mild enough that I was sent home with some medication for the cough and instructed to take ibuprofen for the slight fever.

The notes from my exam from Wellstar's My Chart system that day were as follows:

Visit Vitals

- BP 118/69
- Pulse 74
- Temp 99 °F (37.2 °C) (Oral)
- Resp 16
- Ht 70" (1.778 m)
- Wt 88.9 kg (196 lb)
- SpO2 95%
- BMI 28.12 kg/m²

<u>Physical Exam</u>

Vitals reviewed.
<u>Constitutional</u>:
General: He is not in acute distress.
Appearance: He is well-developed.
<u>HENT</u>:
Head: Normocephalic and atraumatic.
Right Ear: Tympanic membrane and external ear normal.
Left Ear: Tympanic membrane and external ear normal.
Nose: Nose normal. No congestion or rhinorrhea.
Right Sinus: No maxillary sinus tenderness or frontal sinus tenderness.

Left Sinus: No maxillary sinus tenderness or frontal sinus tenderness.
Mouth/Throat:
Mouth: Mucous membranes are moist.
Pharynx: No oropharyngeal exudate or posterior oropharyngeal erythema.
Eyes:
General:
Right eye: No discharge.
Left eye: No discharge.
Conjunctiva/sclera: Conjunctiva normal.
Pupils: Pupils are equal, round, and reactive to light.
Cardiovascular:
Rate and Rhythm: Normal rate and regular rhythm.
Heart sounds: Normal heart sounds. No murmur heard.
No friction rub. No gallop.
Pulmonary:
Effort: Pulmonary effort is normal. No respiratory distress.
Breath sounds: Normal breath sounds. No stridor. No wheezing or rales.
Abdominal:
General: There is no distension.
Tenderness: There is no abdominal tenderness. There is no guarding.
Musculoskeletal:
General: No swelling or tenderness.
Cervical back: Neck supple.
Lymphadenopathy:
Cervical: No cervical adenopathy.
Skin:
General: Skin is warm.
Mental Status: He is alert.
X-ray Chest PA and Lateral (2 Views)

Result Date: 7/16/2021
EXAM: AVP XR CHEST PA AND LATERAL (2 VIEWS) CLINICAL INDICATION: R05 (Cough) . History of COVID 19. COMPARISON: No comparisons are available at this time. FINDINGS: The lungs are clear. The

cardiac silhouette, pulmonary vessels and mediastinal contours are unremarkable.

No radiographic abnormality identified. 7/16/2021 2:04 PM"

Author's note: As no abnormalities were found at that time, the positive diagnosis of COVID-19 didn't appear to be of great concern.

THE FINAL DIAGNOSIS at the time was as follows

"You have been diagnosed with COVID-19

You can try the following over the counter medications:

-start taking **vitamin D 4000 IU daily, Vitamin C 1000mg daily, and Zinc 50mg daily** to help boost the immune system

-Flonase (fluticasone) and Claritin (loratadine) or Zyrtec (cetirizine) for post nasal drip

-Tylenol 500mg (is the same as acetaminophen) or ibuprofen 600mg (is the same Motrin and Advil) for fever or aches (alternate Tylenol and ibuprofen every 3 hours)

-guaifenesin (Mucinex) for a wet cough

-dextromethorphan (Delsym) for a dry cough

-cough drops, Cloraseptic, tea with honey or lemon for a sore throat

BELOW ARE the current CDC guidelines for return to activities:

COVID POSITIVE: return 10 days from the start of symptoms PLUS fever free for 24 hours. If asymptomatic then return is 10 days from the date of the test.

> *The CDC does not recommend a retest to see if the virus has resolved since the test can remain positive for three to six months afterward.*

> *Please go to the ER immediately if you develop chest pain, severe trouble breathing, or oxygen level below 93% (if you have a pulse oximeter)"*

I HAD BEEN OFFERED the possibility of the monoclonal transfusion (mAb), which was being offered to patients with the omicron variant. The FDA granted emergency use of several monoclonal antibody therapies as COVID treatments. The FDA then granted the extended use of monoclonal antibody therapy as a preventative treatment for those at risk. However, at that time, my symptoms didn't raise alarm bells in my mind, so I declined. In hindsight, that may not have been the best choice.

I CONTINUED to take the medications I had been given and the vitamins I'd been advised to take. I remember being rather fatigued and sleeping a fair amount, but I didn't feel so poorly that I feared anything terrible was lurking around the corner. The most concerning symptom was the diarrhea I was experiencing. It just didn't seem to stop. As time went on, the stool became darker to the point of being a deep black. The only time I have seen anything resembling this was when I was directed to take iron tablets to strengthen the iron in my blood. Even then, it was a very dark green, not such a dark black.

Even with some lingering issues as outlined above, nothing

seemed too out of the ordinary for a fairly quick recovery.

I seemed to remain stable after the July 16th doctor's visit; however, by the 19th, I chose to have the monoclonal therapy treatment. I was administered the treatment on the 19th or the 20th; interestingly enough, I cannot find this in my medical records anywhere. It only took about thirty minutes from start to finish, and I was again sent home with the aforementioned medications. The cough and diarrhea continued, but I seemed stable as far as I could tell.

My daughter Vivian and her boyfriend Michael were both living with me, and they decided to take a short trip of just a couple of days. They left all my medications and vitamins on the kitchen counter so I could easily find and take them. When they returned, they said all the medications were still there, appearing untouched. I vaguely remember them being away or returning. I slept most of the time they were gone. I thought I felt fairly well and in control.

I was supposed to have led a Roswell Ghost Tour on Friday, July 23, but since I was diagnosed, I wasn't able to lead it. I was certainly beginning to feel worse, but I was still cognizant. I just felt very fatigued, and I had frequent visits to the bathroom. My weight dropped.

JULY 25, 2021

When Sunday July 25 arrived, things worsened. Michael was home due to testing positive for COVID, most likely catching it from me. Vivian, who was still fine, was at work. Around 4:00 pm, I moved from my bedroom to the living room couch. I vaguely remember being there. I wore a new tee shirt I had purchased at Lake Lanier Water Park.

Pictured is the outfit I was wearing as the EMT's came. Directly below the first photo is what my shirt looked like after they removed it once I was in the hospital. As you can easily see, they had to cut it off of me.

Michael said he heard me loudly coughing, and he came out of his self-quarantined room to check on me. He told me if I didn't start responding better, he was going to call for an ambulance.

In a foggy memory, I recall saying to him that it would be very expensive.

He later said he could tell I was going downhill but couldn't tell just how fast. He went back into his room and listened from there.

The coughing seemed to get worse, and it wasn't long before he came back out and asked me a few questions that I was incapable of answering. He asked something like, "What is your name?"

I was told I answered something along the lines of, "November."

Michael knew it wasn't good, and he took charge. He called 911, and the cavalry was on its way.

Michael then called Vivian and said she had better get there as soon as she could. She was twenty minutes away, and she got to her car as quickly as she could and headed home.

Almost immediately, the EMTs arrived and assessed the situation.

The oxygen in my blood had dropped to 57%.

It all seemed to happen so quickly, I had no idea what was happening to me. Much of this story was relayed to me later by those who were there.

I wasn't fighting the EMTs, but I certainly wasn't helping them much either. I was uncooperative at 190 pounds of (pardon the pun) dead weight. I was perilously close to death. The EMTs were agitated that I had been allowed to reach that point. I slipped down so fast, it's easy to understand why I had reached that point before they were summoned. They got me in the ambulance and left the community just as Vivian arrived. Much to Viv's dismay, she didn't see me before they took me away.

From this point on, I have no memory (except for four snapshot memories I will describe later) until roughly August 23, an entire month in the future. The accounts of my condition from this point forward, until August 23, come from the collective memories of my family, friends, and medical notes.

I ARRIVED at the Wellstar North Fulton Hospital, and the first notes on my condition were time stamped at 6:29 pm, July 25. As you read through those notes below, it will be apparent I was not in great shape. You will see they prepared to place me on a ventilator. Later documentation from July 27, 1:01 pm indicates that the "intubation," was at 5:30 pm on July 25.

The notes from July 27 regarding the intubation are as follows:
"Intubation method: Video assisted
Patient status: Paralyzed (RSI)
Consent: The Procedure was performed in an emergent situation [2]

Author's note: "Emergent situation" indicates that the situation was critical, and the doctors determined it needed to be done immediately. The (RSI) refers to a "rapid sequence intubation." It further means I was sedated and thus paralyzed so the procedure could be accomplished.

From the moment Michael realized I needed medical intervention through this critical time of intubation and stabilization was my first significant life-threatening situation.

First Notes from the Doctors

The following are the first notes from my doctors after I arrived. The date and time of the report are as follows:

July 25, 2021, 6:29 pm
"Pulmonary/Critical Care Admission Note
Cc: difficulty breathing
HPI:
Mr. Crooks is a 65 yo gentleman who presents to ed today with difficulty breathing.

We were called by the ED physician to come see him and on my arrival, the ED doctor was setting up to intubate pnt. He was on 100% nrb with low o2 sats and increased work of breathing. He was not answering any questions.

Review of records shows that he went to Wellstar Urgent Care on 7/16/21 with fever, cough, diarrhea, fatigue, and body aches for 5 days and was diagnosed as COVID positive. Non- vaccinated. Declined monoclonal abx transfusion. Was discharged home with symptomatic care and to monitor symptoms. CXR at that time was essentially normal.

Review of Systems: *Unable to obtain secondary to current clinical condition*
Objective:

Vital signs in last 24 hours:
Temp: [99.1 °F (37.3 °C)] 99.1 °F (37.3 °C)
Heart Rate: [92-103] 96
Resp: [37-44] 42

BP: (125-129)/(71-78) 129/78
(!) 77% on 100% nrb

Physical Exam:
General appearance: lying in bed, seen just prior to intubation. Non- verbal, ill appearing.
Head: Normocephalic, without obvious abnormality, atraumatic
Eyes: conjunctivae/corneas clear. PERRL, EOM's intact. Fundi benign.
Throat: lips, mucosa, and tongue normal; teeth and gums normal
Neck: no adenopathy, no carotid bruit, no JVD, supple, symmetrical, trachea midline and thyroid not enlarged, symmetric, no tenderness/mass/nodules
Lungs: very diminished bilaterally, increased work of breathing
Heart: regular rate and rhythm, S1, S2 normal, no murmur, click, rub or gallop
Abdomen: soft, non-tender; bowel sounds normal; no masses, no organomegaly
Extremities: extremities normal, atraumatic, no cyanosis or edema
Pulses: 2+ and symmetric
Capillary Refill: normal
Skin Color: normal, no cyanosis, jaundice, pallor or bruising
Skin Turgor: normal
Musculoskeletal: no joint tenderness, deformity or swelling
Neuro: lying in bed, eyes open, makes eye contact but not speaking, not answering questions.

Labs:
Labs pending

Radiology:
X-ray Chest PA and Lateral (2 Views)
CXR pending, not done yet.

Assessment:
- Acute hypoxemic respiratory failure
- COVID 19 pneumonia

Plan:
- CXR and labs pending, will follow up on results and will help guide treatment.
- Pnt being currently intubated by the ED physician. Will follow up on post intubation cxr, abg and will adjust vent settings. Send sputum culture.
- dexamethasone iv to be started in ED, discussed with the ED nurse.
- Call and discuss with ID, Dr. Castro. He will see pnt and consider to start actemra.
- Pnts daughter was not in ED when I arrived. Have attempted to call her to get more history but goes straight to voicemail. Will continue to try to contact her.

Sachin Lavania, MD
WMG Pulmonary & Critical Care Medicine"

It is worth pointing out that somewhere between 6:30 pm and 7:00 pm, I was placed on the ventilator as it is seen in Dr. Castro-Borobio's notes at 7:08 pm. He is the doctor from the IDS - Infectious Disease Services of Georgia.

The next set of notes is from July 25, 9:27 pm
July 25, 2021, 9:27 pm
Procedures by Christopher W Nickum, PA at 7/25/2021 9:27 PM

Procedure Orders
1. Central Line
2. Arterial Line

Central Line

Date/Time: *7/25/2021 9:28 PM*
Performed by: ***Christopher W Nickum, PA***

Author's Note: A central line, also known as a central venous catheter, is a tube placed in a large vein in the neck but can also be placed in the groin, chest, or arm to administer fluids, blood, or medications.

Arterial Line

Date/Time: *7/25/2021 9:28 PM*
Performed by: ***Christopher W Nickum, PA***

Author's Note: An arterial line is placed in an artery to check blood pressure more easily when it goes up and down frequently.

THE FOLLOWING ARE the medications I was immediately administered:
Look to Appendix A for Medication definitions.
Scheduled Meds:

•albuterol	2.5 mg	Nebulization	Q6H Resp.
•balanced salt irrigation	10 mL	Irrigation	Q12H
•balanced salt irrigation	10 mL	Irrigation	Q4H PRN
•chlorhexidin	15 mL	Mouth/Throat	BID
•[START ON 7/26/2021] Dexamethasone	6 mg	Intravenous	Daily
•dextrose 40%	1-2 Tube	Oral	Q15 Min PRN
•dextrose 50 % in water (D50W)	25-50 mL	Intravenous	Q15 Min PRN
•etomidate	20 mg	Intravenous	Once
•famotidine	20 mg	Intravenous	BID
Or			
•famotidine	20 mg	Oral	BID
•fentaNYL (PF)	25 mcg	Intravenous	Once
•fentaNYL (PF)	50 mcg	Intravenous	Daily PRN
•fentaNYL (SUBLIMAZE) infusion	0-200 mcg/hr	Intravenous	Continuous
And			
•fentaNYL	50 mcg	Intravenous	Q15 Min PRN
•glucagon	1 mg	Intramuscular	Once PRN
•insulin lispro	1-12 Units	Subcutaneous	6 times per day
•piperacillin-tazobactam	4.5 g	Intravenous	Q8H
•propofol (DIPRIVAN) infusion 10 mg/mL	0-50 mcg/kg/min	Intravenous	Continuous
And			
•propofol	10 mg	Intravenous	Q5 Min PRN
•rocuronium	80 mg	Intravenous	Once
•sodium chloride (NS) 0.9 % syringe			
•vancomycin	1,000 mg	Intravenous	Q12H

Continuous Infusions:	
• fentaNYL (SUBLIMAZE) infusion	50 mcg/hr (07/25/21 1902)
• propofol (DIPRIVAN) infusion 10 mg/mL	18 mcg/kg/min (07/25/21 1849)

| Chart 1

Author's Note: "The Old Man's Friend," that's what pneumonia has been referred to for ages. Pneumonia has even been thought of as a blessing to the aged because it tends to take a patient, particularly the elderly, very quickly. It is reasonably managed and recovered from by youth and those in excellent shape, but should you be older, meaning 65 to 70 years of age or older, the chances of survival decrease as the age increases. In addition, the chances of survival are greatly reduced if you have underlying conditions heaped on top of the disease itself.

THE VERSION of COVID-19 I contracted was the Delta Variant. It could sit in the same category and also qualify as an "Old Man's Friend." Delta (B.1.617.2) is a variant of the SARS-CoV-2 virus. It first was identified in India, and then it spread globally. What made Delta significant or special was that the mutations in a particular protein were tremendous. So, there were flu-like symptoms, but were exacerbated by pneumonia or double pneumonia.[3]

July 26, 2021

By 9:30 the next morning, July 26, 2021, my continuous infusions had jumped dramatically.

See below:

Continuous Infusions:	
• fentaNYL (SUBLIMAZE) infusion	250 mcg/hr (07/26/21 0546)
• heparin (porcine)	18 Units/kg/hr (07/26/21 0822)
• heparin (porcine)	
• midazolam (VERSED) infusion	2 mg/hr (07/26/21 0528)
• norepinephrine (LEVOPHED) infusion	9 mcg/min (07/26/21 0914)
• propofol (DIPRIVAN) infusion 10 mg/mL	50 mcg/kg/min (07/26/21 0718)
• sodium bicarbonate infusion	100 mL/hr (07/26/21 0538)
• sodium chloride 0.9%	3 mL/hr (07/25/21 2220)
• vasopressin	Stopped (07/26/21 0212)

| Chart 2

Medical notes indicated I had a fairly stable day. Nothing terribly worse nor better, just stable. Reading all the charts suggests that some tests were slightly better and some slightly worse.

July 27, 2021

For the first time, the notes communicated that I had taken the monoclonal antibodies; however, the earlier notes still stated that I had refused them earlier. It is interesting that there is no record of my having received them, but I can guarantee that I did receive them. As mentioned earlier, I fully recall going in for the infusion. It took approximately a half hour, though I could be slightly off on the timing. The notes for this day indicated that they had received the updated information from the family and entered the information into my records. My daughter Vivian remembered that I had taken the treatment and was able to correct the record. The doctors had been thinking of giving me the infusion when they thought I hadn't had it.

Further notes indicated that my shortness of breath was severe and that my mental state was "disoriented" which would suggest that I was at least partially conscious. They also marked my breathing sounds indicated "decreased air movement."

There was great concern regarding my kidneys; that concern

was ongoing during my time in the coma. A specific notation is made by the nephrologist, a doctor who specializes in kidney issues. Throughout my struggle, kidneys were a constant topic. At times the notes said my kidneys crashed, and some dialysis was necessary.

Nephrologist notes:
"Echogenic kidneys, suggesting medical renal disease.
Small indeterminate lesions in the left kidney, possibly complicated benign cysts but neoplasm cannot be excluded. These could be better evaluated by MRI abdomen without and with IV contrast."

> Author's Note: Additional notes from the same day indicated that imaging was conducted with mixed results in different areas of my body. Below are notes from Dr. Mirza who is scribing my "Critical Care Progress."

IMAGING: *Most recent images personally reviewed.*
No sonographic evidence of deep venous thrombosis from the groin to the knee of the right or left leg.
Nonocclusive thrombus within the left peroneal vein. Additional left occlusive thrombus demonstrated, which may represent a superficial calf vein."

> Sonography is defined as a sonogram or ultrasound exam. According to Google it is a "dynamic visual image of organs, tissues or blood flow inside the body."

The sonogram revealed I had a blood clot in my left calf, July 25th. This raised concerns for other potential clots. This concern continues to this day. I was placed on *Eliquis*, a medication specifically for blood thinning. Even with Medicare, it is not an inexpensive medication. At the time I write this, it runs $480 for the initial month and then $280 per month going forward. I was on this medication the entire time I was in the hospital and one additional month after release. Five months after my release from the hospital, following a cardiac stress test, I was placed back on Eliquis because of a heart flutter. I talk more about Atrial Fibrillation in the "The Good, The Bad and the Ugly" section of this book.

Below are some notes related specifically to my heart from July 27. I have highlighted the specific areas of concern at that time.

ECHO:
• *The left ventricular systolic function is normal with an ejection fraction of 56-60%.*
• *The left ventricular diastolic function is normal (based on LA volume index, TR velocity, medial and lateral e' velocities, and average E/e').*
• *The left ventricular cavity, indexed to body surface area and gender is normal.*
• *There is mild concentric left ventricular hypertrophy present.*
• *The right ventricular systolic function is normal.*
• *The right ventricular cavity size is normal.*
• *The inferior vena cava demonstrates a high central venous pressure, 15mmHg, (>2.1 cm and <50% decrease).*
• *There is trace tricuspid valve regurgitation.*

The "mild concentric left ventricular hypertrophy" refers to a "mild enlargement of the muscles of the sinistral cardiac ventricle, which includes an augmented cavity size and thickened walls," according to the Mayo Clinic. Again, according to the Mayo Clinic, a "trace tricuspid valve regurgitation" happens when "the valve between the two right heart chambers (right ventricle and right atrium) doesn't close properly. As a result, blood leaks backward into the upper right chamber."[4]

July 28, 2021

The 28th passed without any significant change; however, it turned out to be the calm before the storm of the next day.

July 29, 2021

After an extensive review of that day's notes, I determined the exact time of my apparent revolt when it came to intubation. At some point in the morning, I was awake enough to know I was on the ventilator and wasn't pleased about it. I was told that my "extubation of the vent" is not an uncommon event. I have learned that about 60% of patients extubate. Nevertheless, to have physically ripped the intubation tube out of my own throat could not have been pleasurable and certainly not the way it should have come out. I was off the vent for a short time during the day. I was reintubated at approximately 6:00 pm the same evening, and I was placed under stronger sedation, putting me back in a medical coma.

My infectious disease doctor noted in his report, "Self-extubated this am." Meaning I had ripped it out of my own throat. Seems a bit understated, but he does note the event.

July 30 to August 10

There was precious little change during this time, overall. I will note the interesting points made within this timeframe.

On Friday, July 30, Dr. Mirza, indicated for the first time that *Heparin* was to be withheld. He also stated, "Increase sedation. May need to be paralyzed and prone."

Heparin was withheld for several days. They have yet to discover that I am allergic to it, so it was restarted on August 2.

Heparin is used to decrease clotting of the blood.

The indication of "prone" meant I was to be turned over on my stomach for ventilation purposes. According to Wikipedia, *"Prone ventilation, sometimes called prone positioning or proning, refers to mechanical ventilation with the patient lying face-down (prone). It improves oxygenation in most patients with acute respiratory distress syndrome (ARDS) and reduces mortality."*[5]

My mental state was consistently identified as "Delirium with agitation." My temperature remained stable at 97.7 to 98.1 degrees.

During this time, I also was diagnosed with hyperkalemia. Hyperkalemia is a condition of having too much potassium in the bloodstream.[6] Although we need potassium, too much can be dangerous if above the 6.0 level. A normal reading is 3.6 to 5.2. My levels were running 3.9 to 5.3; not terrible, but it required monitoring.

On August 5, Dr. Bhutta noted that my respiratory status worsened. He also indicated I was unresponsive to stimuli. This symptom was prevalent from this doctor.

August 6, 2021

Dr. Bhutta once again noted that I was unresponsive to stimuli. This was crucial to what took place the very next day.

August 6th was a huge turning point in so many ways. I had been in the hospital and out of touch with everyone for almost two full weeks. People in my life were increasingly concerned.

Up to this point, my friends and family were unaware of what had happened to me or what was going on. I was not responding to any messages via text or email, and I hadn't shown up to any of my regular meetings. The buzz was getting louder. "Where is Jonathan? Has anyone heard from him?" Finally, a very close friend of mine from Roswell Rotary, Jim Savage, took the bull by the horns and found out what was going on. Jim lives just up the street from me, and he and I had joined Rotary the same day. We had become kind of blood brothers within Rotary. We usually sat together at meetings and, always kiddingly, gave each other the business, whenever possible.

The above photo, taken by Ian Mari, is Jim and I Photo Credit: PhotoMari-USA/BlufftonPhoto

He canvased my neighborhood, looking for me. He went door to door, asking for help. He was so persistent that one of my neighbors inquired what he was doing. He said, "I'm trying to find Jonathan!" He was directed next door, and he knocked. Vivian answered the door and Jim introduced himself saying he was a good friend. He then asked, "Where is your father?"

Vivian filled him in on what had happened to me and Jim was, of course, aghast!

This was significant in two very significant ways. First, the word was now out on the street, at least to all my Rotary friends, as Jim reported news of my condition. Second, my children recognized the need to let everyone else know what was happening. Kristine and Vivian decided that Facebook would be the best vehicle to get the word out quickly.

The following message is the first communication that went out over Facebook from my Facebook page:

"August 6, 2021

Hello all, unfortunately this is not Jonathan Crooks talking… This is Kristine and Vivian, his daughters. Our father has come down with a severe illness and is unable to communicate at all. He is currently in ICU with COVID Delta variant with other complications. Medical professionals have placed him in a medical coma to help the healing process.

At the moment, he is stable; however, [he] is in critical condition. Jonathan does have a living will that we are going to follow, and we plan on meeting with the medical staff to discuss a CARE Plan. I'm so sorry this is how many of you are finding out about our father, who is possibly your friend or family member.

We ask as a family if you have any major questions concerning the tasks my father was in the middle of, to contact myself first (Kristine Taylor) and then my sister Vivian Crooks. We will attempt to update his status as much as we can through multiple platforms (text, calling, Facebook). If there is anything that Jonathan has promised in the very close future that it will be either postponed or canceled indefinitely.

I know all of you love Jonathan with all your hearts and will do anything you can to help as he would do for you all. This family is hurting and in a lot of pain and are hoping for the best. Please keep him in your thoughts and prayers."

The response to this initial note was overwhelming and humbling. Each time I read the comments and shares and notes, I am brought to tears. One never knows how many lives he may touch. There were 139 emoji responses, 185 comments, and twelve shares. It exponentially grew from there. This note reached my Roswell Rotarian friends, my Roswell Lions friends, my Roswell Presbyterian friends, my Hoosic Valley High School friends along with my friends on Facebook. From there, shares went out and the word literally spread across the county (and even beyond, as friends told me later how my story had reached friends in England and other places). The prayer chains were massive.

Finally, my immediate family was not alone in this. There were so many people who called, texted, and sent messages to my family offering any assistance they could give. What that meant to my family and to me personally could never be put into words. All I can do is hug every person I encounter who outstretched their arms of love. From their lips to God's ears, prayers took effect immediately. I teetered between life and death during this time. I had a doctor who (I know was just doing his job) didn't seem to be in my corner. That may sound harsh, and I know it is, but when it's your life or your father's life that hangs in the balance, it becomes very personal. Emotions run high in these cases.

Notes such as the example below are a sampling of many notes of encouragement my family received. God bless you all!

High School Friends:

"Ann M Denio
My heart is breaking for you all please know I am praying for God to heal him, 🙏🙏🙏Lord hear our prayers!! Please know that a lot of people in Schaghticoke and surrounding areas are cheering him on!"

"Randy Herrington
Will do! Thank you so much for the update. Sending healing good thoughts 💚"

"Kimberly A. Loszynski
Vivian and Kristine. Your Dad is a very good friend of mine since high school. If any of you need anything, please call me. I will pray for him, he is a strong man."

FRIENDS IN ROSWELL FROM ROTARY, Lions, Roswell Presbyterian, and my Roswell world friends, where I now live:

> "Richard Hill
> I pass along some encouragement. I posted requests for prayers for your dad. My aunt has a friend who was placed in an induced coma for COVID a year ago. She did recover. Cling to hope. Prayers to you all"

> "Joy Miller Henson
> We are very fond of your amazing father and so heartbroken to hear this news. We will be praying and please let us know what we can do for him or for you girls. 💙🙏"

> "Claire Bartlett
> We have been praying daily for sweet Jonathan. He is well loved across all of Roswell. We'll keep up our request to God almighty to completely heal our friend, Jonathan, and for the hands of all who care for him. In Jesus name.
> Darrell & Claire Bartlett"

"Linda Morgan

Dearest Kristine and Vivian, I am praying earnestly for your wonderful father. As a former Sunday School leader of the FISH class, I grew to know your Dad as a loving son of The Lord, a generous man totally giving of his time in our mission projects, a loyal & regular attendee every Sunday and open in sharing both his opinions and deep knowledge of the Bible with us. He helped me in preparation for class many times. And your Dad kept us apprised every week on the updates of all three children. You are the light of his world and he just beamed with pride in mentioning your names. I look forward to seeing that smile again.

Many members of our former class are praying earnestly for him and your family. I am in a different class now and your Dad is on our prayers list.

Whatever you need, anything, please let me help you.

I will be contacting you soon as I am the gal from Prayers & Squares making a prayer quilt for your Dad.

I cannot imagine how difficult it was for you to write this post, but I thank you so much for the update. I'm sure you will hear this from many people. You can reach me through RPC. God bless ✝ ✝ "

"Dianna Avena

Many prayers are being sent up from the Avena household!! 🙏❤️ "

"Michael Sternberg

God bless him and give you two the strength to help him through this trial. 🙏 "

These were only a few of the numerous notes of encouragement we received, and I wish I could have included every one of them here. To all of you who were on your knees, may blessings always come your way throughout your life. This was an extremely critical time for me, and I needed every prayer that was sent on my behalf.

August 7, 2021

The note below is from my friend Leslie Bassett whom I met through the Roswell Rotary. I was told there were fifteen people gathered to pray for me this Saturday morning. I was later told by our current (2021- 2022) Rotary president, Terry Tayor, Leslie had arranged the "daylight vigil" at a Rotary gathering on February 26, 2022. When I later saw Leslie, all I could do was give her a tear-filled hug to thank her for organizing the gathering (pictured below). They didn't know how close to death I was.

> *"Leslie Bassett*
> *For anyone who is led to come, a group of us are gathering to pray for Jonathan Saturday morning at 9 am at 575 Riverside Road (splash pad). When two or more are gathered in His name…*
> *Do keep in mind, the vigil at the river is on Saturday, August 7, 2021."*

AUGUST 7, 2021, hospital note synopsis:

There was only one medical note in my records for Saturday August 7. It was quite surprising as there had always been multiple notes each day, generally from various physicians. The note documented the family CARE conference with Vivian and Kristine present. Gary was present via telephone.

A post was later made on Facebook after this meeting; things seemed to be going well. It was an upbeat note. The doctors had decided to move me off the ventilator and perform the tracheostomy.

Ventilators are generally used for several weeks only, if at all possible. The longer one is on a vent the worse the situation is. As you will recall, I had already pulled the ventilator out of my own throat back on July 29. I had to be kept on a high level of sedation so I wouldn't awaken enough to do the same thing again. Since my oxygen levels were improving, doctors decided to remove the vent. This was also part of the last treatments they planned for me. If the situation went south from here, my chances of survival would be close to nil.

It is not a coincidence in my perspective that Leslie organized the prayer vigil, and it was held the morning of the same day as the CARE conference. Fifteen or so friends were gathered in prayer that very morning, of all mornings. They had no idea what was happening at the very same time as their gathering.

I am sure they prayed for my protection. They prayed for the doctors and the nurses providing my care, that their hands would be led; they were certainly led that day. Coincidence? I ask you ponder deeper.

I confirm without hesitation, there was no coincidence here! I wasn't a seminarian for nothing, you know.

Leslie pictured with me. *Photo Credit: PhotoMari-USA/BlufftonPhoto*

August 8, 2021

On Sunday, August 8, Kristine and Vivian posted on Facebook. The note can be a little misleading as it pertains to timing. The tracheostomy (trach) discussion took place during the CARE Meeting. That discussion focused on the gradual transition from sedation and removal of the ventilator to the tracheostomy. The reference to "Monday or Tuesday" refers to the scheduled tracheostomy. In addition, so you understand the time sequence, the CARE meeting was on Saturday, August 7. Although there had been some improvement, I was still in terrible shape. They needed to stabilize me so I could survive the move off the ventilator to the trach. The trach placement required a surgical procedure. There was concern about conducting this kind of surgery in my condition.

My daughters didn't want to give all the details to the world at that point, so they attempted to post something that was not meant to mislead anyone, it sounds rather upbeat when in fact, but to help alleviate some worry. However, everything wasn't quite as rosy as it was presented. The information given was true and correct; however, it omitted details. This was a critical period; patients moving off the vent to the trach either got markedly better or quickly turned worse.

It didn't help that there was an incident with one of the doctors who updated my children during the CARE meeting. In the middle of the discussion, he repeatedly texted on his phone, upsetting my children. Kristine finally had enough and said, "Is that text more important than what we are talking about here?" Had the doctor said, "I'm so sorry, but I need to respond to this immediately," my children would have said something along the lines of, "We completely understand; we know dad isn't your only patient. But the way it was handled upset the children.

I hope you will understand the pride I feel for my daughter. I've great pride in all three of my children for staying strong during this time. As a former seminarian, we are taught not to have pride. I ask for special dispensation here for this one time.

You have heard me talk about angels in this book. I will talk more about those who come from above to protect you. You have read about some who appeared almost from nowhere at the right time.

I had one of those angels who appeared at the right time on

this day. She was a nurse who had been attending to me since the day I had ripped the ventilator out of my own throat July 29. At the time I write this, I have not yet met her while conscious; however, I have tracked down who she was and am working to reunite with her. This nurse was my guardian angel that day. She had been close enough during the conversations to know what was transpiring. She specifically stayed close so she could talk to my daughters. She commented the "texting doctor" didn't have the best bedside manner. Her words were a tremendous comfort to my children. "Your father **is** responding. It may be every third time, but he is responding and there is still life there. The doctors are just not seeing it when they try, but we [the nurses] see it. Do not end this."

I don't know how I will be able to hold my emotions back when I have the opportunity to meet this angel of mine. She knew she had to stay until she could get that message to my children. God bless the nurses - they do so much and get so little credit, or at least, far less than they should.

The following is the Facebook post on Sunday, August 8:

> "Hello all again, it's the Twins. Just giving a quick update. The CARE Plan went well. Monday or Tuesday the doctors have decided to move forward and prep Jonathan for the tracheostomy. This will allow for a more gradual transition off the sedative and allow for comfortable breathing. If the sedation is taken off while Jonathan is still on the ventilator, it will cause a lot of pain, discomfort, and he can possibly damage his own lungs trying to breathe. Trach's can be a temporary tool and the recovery process is easy.
>
> Since the last visit, Jonathan has slightly improved on his Oxygen intake to 35% (The goal is under 30%). However, he did have a slight fever (Never broke over 100*) and placed him back on antibiotics and changed all ports going into his body.
>
> Thank you all for the flood of prayers, it has been so helpful and beautiful. More updates to come."

Responses from more loved friends of mine from here in Georgia and back in my hometown in upstate New York:

"Mary Hunter Bivins
Kristine & Vivian, I am just now seeing this post! Your dad has been on my mind for the last three days! We spoke on my birthday in June. I just checked his Facebook profile to see what he's been up to before I called him. I had no idea! Please, please, please let me know where he is & what I can do to help him and you all, other than prayers which of course is a given! Keep the faith and my prayers are with you all & Gary!"

"Jeanie Gallagher
Thanks Kristine and Vivian for the update on your Dad, we all appreciate you so much for keeping us informed on his condition. May God bless your Dad with complete healing and quick recovery from his illness. Sending my love, thoughts and prayers to your Dad and all the family. Big comfort hugs!! 🤗 ❤️ 🙏🙏🙏🙏🙏"

"Gary Bruce
Prayers for your father, please keep us updated as his condition improves. He is a strong man and will beat this. Your love and him knowing the support he has will help him survive."

"Jim Lundstrom
Thank you, girls, for the update. Your Dad and you both are in my heart and prayers. May god watch over all 3 of you and give Jonathan the healing he needs to get better 🙏🙏🙏🙏🙏❤️❤️❤️❤️❤️."

Monday, August 9, 2021

This was the day I was moved off the ventilator and was placed on the trach. The photo below was taken just before the tracheostomy procedure.

"Primary Wound Type: Pressure Injury Wound Description (Comments): stage III pressure ulcer chin Location: Chin Wound Location Orientation: Anterior."

The following are the notes of the procedure:

Tracheostomy/PEG Tube Placement OP Note
Date of Operation: 8/9/2021
Attending: Dr. Gregory Coffman
Assist: Zachary Rader, PA-C
Procedure: Percutaneous tracheostomy placement

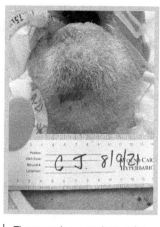

The wound you see just under my chin on the left side is described by Nurse Karen J as:

Pre-op Dx: Respiratory failure, COVID-19 Pneumonia
Post-op Dx: Respiratory failure
Anesthesia: Moderate sedation
Details of Operation: Informed consent was obtained after all risks, benefits, and alternatives to the procedure were discussed in depth. The patient was placed supine with a shoulder roll and the neck extended. The neck was prepped with chloraprep and draped in sterile fashion. All anesthesia meds were given. A timeout was performed in which the correct patient and procedure was identified. A skin incision was made in vertical orientation below the cricoid cartilage with a #15 blade scalpel. Hemostats were used to bluntly dissect down to the tracheal rings. The ET tube was retracted while palpating between the 2nd and 3rd tracheal rings until it was felt to be above this level. The finder needle was introduced into the trachea with bubbling noted within the saline filled syringe. The wire passed easily and the needle was withdrawn. The ventilator was turned off at this time to reduce risk of COVID-19 transmission. The Blue Rhino dilators were used to serially dilate the tracheotomy using Seldinger technique. An 8 Shiley cuffed tracheostomy was placed

over the wire. The wire was withdrawn and the ventilator was switched to the tracheostomy tube after inflating the cuff. The ventilator was turned back on and good tidal volumes were attained with no leak. The tracheostomy tube was sutured in place with 2-0 silk suture. The collar was placed around the patient's neck and the trach was secured in place. Good hemostasis was attained. The patient tolerated the procedure well. A stat chest x-ray was ordered.

EBL: Negligible
Complications: None
Plan of care: May remove stitches in tracheostomy after 7 days
Zachary Rader, PA-C
Trauma & General Surgery
August 9 and 10, 2021"

Except for the placement of the tracheostomy, two days passed without incident. That's a phrase I often use when it comes to flying. I will always ask whomever I am picking up at the airport if the "flight was without incident." If the answer is yes, which it generally is, we count it as a good flight. Most would agree. The same is true for me. If the day basically went by without incident, I am counting it as a good day, even if there wasn't a marked improvement. "Stable" may not be as good as improvement, but with all I had been through, not sliding backward was seen as a good day. August 9 and 10, can be counted as such. I was no longer on the ventilator, and if I remained stable on the trach, then it was a good thing.

August 11, 2021

Wednesday, August 11 brought in a new consult. I am noting it because it's the first and only visit from this doctor. Dr. Ghara M. Kunter arrived on the scene to consult on hematology and oncology. Dr. Kunter is associated with the Northwest Georgia Oncology Center. I point out this visit because of some of the notes and the fact I have not seen anyone from oncology before this visit during my stay at Wellstar North Fulton. The oncology duties fell to Dr. Nagender Mankan for the rest of my stay at North Fulton. Dr. Mankan came to see me every few days until I moved to Wellstar Windy Hill.

Hematology - Oncology is the study of two combined medical practices, according to the Regional Cancer Care Associates website. The website continues by defining hematology as the study of the blood's physiology and oncology as the study of cancer. The website defines these areas far better than I could paraphrase them, so I include their definitions here:

"Blood consists of four components – white blood cells, red blood cells, platelets, and plasma – that help oxygenate our organs and tissues, act as a defense against infections, and form clots to stop bleeding. But these components may also indicate the presence of abnormalities, which sometimes leads to blood cancers. That's where hematology-oncology comes into play."

All I can add to that is, "Well said!"
Below are the attending notes from the consultation.

"Attending note:
Patient was seen and examined
65-year-old male presented with altered mental status secondary to metabolic encephalopathy and COVID infection. He is currently on the vent due to acute respiratory failure and ARDS status post tracheostomy. His case was complicated by acute anemia secondary to blood loss from trach. He also has secondary bacterial pneumonia currently on IV antibiotics. Due to decline in his platelet counts, hit panel was ordered tested positive.
Recommend starting argatroban, hold heparin infusion or any flushes
We advised to monitor his blood counts and coags daily
Transfuse for hemoglobin below 7
Case discussed with ICU attending"

I have highlighted the salient points for your review. I've mentioned in other sections of this work that it was discovered I was allergic to Heparin and this is the second reference to withhold it from me.

According to the Mayo Clinic, Heparin *"is an anticoagulant. It is used to decrease the clotting ability of the blood and help prevent harmful clots from forming in blood vessels. This medicine is sometimes called a blood thinner, although it does not actually thin the blood. Heparin will not dissolve blood clots that have already formed, but it may prevent the clots from becoming larger and causing more serious problems.*

Heparin is used to prevent or treat certain blood vessels, heart, and lung conditions."[7] [Dr. Mankan noted for the first time in his report from August 13, 2021, that I was allergic to Heparin.]

On August 10, Kristine placed her next message on Facebook. The two dogs at the end of Kristine's note represent her two pups, Kit and Pan. As you can see from the note, there was finally a little more positive news to pass on, even if it wasn't the full information. As it came to pass, there were still some dark clouds to come, but these times gave continued hope.

The note that follows was placed on Facebook[8] on August 10, 2021, which was the day after the trach was placed:

"Good evening all, just a quick update for Jonathan. He had his trach placed on Monday, and all went well and has been going smoothly. They have already begun to lower the sedation, however, it will still be a while until he is actually awake. Since Monday Jonathan has received two blood transfusions due to his hemoglobin count being too low (Monday 6.8 and Tuesday 6.3 and the goal is 7). The hospital conducted a CT scan of his abdomen just to make sure there was no internal bleeding which there wasn't, which is making the hospital scratch their heads but are sure he is okay.

The hospital completely changed their procedures of visiting and under no circumstances is anyone to visit the hospital, even close family. The hospitals are experiencing another high outbreak and are prepping for the worst again. This will make it very challenging for Jonathan when he begins to fully wake up and he will be super confused.

I know he loves and misses you all. COVID has him in the ringer, but he is still fighting and kicking ass.

~Kristine 🐐🐐"

Again, the comments and shares were through the roof. I've included a few from family and friends, old and new. God bless you all...

"Brenda Garner Tootle
Charlie and I have been keeping up about Jonathan via Evan and his Mom, Kim (our daughter), and have been praying deeply for Him, Kristine, Vivian, and Gary. So, distressed that all this has happened. Continuing thoughts and prayers."

"Heather Wiggins McKinley
Continued prayers. I'm so sorry you can't visit your dad. Jonathan P Crooks we're all pulling and praying for you!"

"Elwyn Gaissert II
Prayers for continued improvement"

"Marilyn Lawton
Thanks for the update on his condition, Kristine. Everyone who knows Jonathan cares so much about his welfare & we hope the doctor will decide on what's best for him. Will continue to pray for his complete recovery."

"Patti Williams
Dan and I will continue to keep your dad in our prayers. Thank you for your continued updates."

"Maureen McDonald

Thank you for the update, so happy things are moving in a positive direction. 🩶 "

"Bob Hagan
Our continued prayers are with him 🙏."

"Kymberley Krasnow
We are sending all the love and good juju that can wrap around you JC!
Looks like your daughters are doing a hell of a job keeping us up-to-date and caring for you.
You and I have had many talks, my friend, about where we stand in the light... Know the light is wrapped all over you and God is with you my friend
All of your prayers are being answered as we speak healing is coming to your body and rushing to your side for rest
Namaste
Amen
Kymberley"

August 11, 2021

Although I had stable days August 9 and 10, the situation shifted and I took a downturn, and the doctors continued to make notes that I was not responding to their testing. The testing I am referring to involves responding to oral commands - things such as moving certain body parts and the like. This had become extremely critical in my evaluation - evaluation of improvement, evaluation for the continued fight for life on the part of all medical personnel. A telephone conversation took place on August 11.

It was during this conversation that my children were informed that they needed to prepare themselves for a likely decision to terminate my care. According to the doctor on the call, I was still not responding to stimuli. As you have read in the notes, that was what was being recorded. I had written in my "Living Will" the instructions that I did not want to be left on life support if there was no chance of recovery, or if I would be left in a greatly reduced state, should I survive. My wishes hung heavily on my children. My condition was reaching a point of decision. The tracheostomy tube was placed to help me breathe. I had been on the ventilator two full weeks on the ventilator and that the move to the trach was seen as somewhat of a last step. This was the critical time when patients either got better or turned worse rather quickly. In addition, my kidney function was still fluctuating. The kidneys seem to signal the first phase of a downward turn in these situations; as the kidneys go, so go the rest of the systems in the body.

Kristine, who was the chief contact for me, decided that they didn't particularly want the doctor who had been in the CARE meeting, who had been the lead doctor on my case as part of the team moving forward. There was a strained relationship between my family and that doctor. I saw him make only two more notes on my case while I was at Wellstar North Fulton Hospital. One note was the following morning, and the other was forty-eight hours before I was moved to my second hospital.

I always attempt to take an optimistic view of people and therefore I am looking for the best in this doctor. I'm sure he is a good physician. I simply don't believe he was the best one for me.

August 11 marked an extremely important twenty-four hours in Crooks family history. The day held great concern for me personally on many levels. Although my life hung in the balance, the day will be remembered with tumultuous joy for my family. It was on this day that my daughter Kristine received confirmation she was pregnant with her and Evan's first child, my first grandchild. I cannot possibly imagine the flood of emotions that ran through my daughter that day. Imagine the elation of knowing you are going to have your first child with your husband, coupled with hearing you may have to let your father go. She stood on a mountain top of euphoria while simultaneously staring into a great abyss of uncertainty and sadness. You know the outcome of my story by virtue of reading this book I have written, so it seems only right to include a photo of pre-Jonathan Henry Lockstedt. He was scheduled to arrive on March 31, 2022.

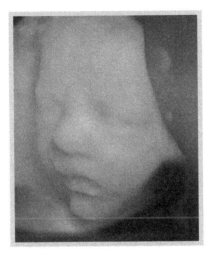

| Jonathan Henry Lockstedt! I'm pretty sure he has my nose.

On this joyous day, Kristine took a call from my doctors, informing her that the family may need to soon decide my fate; my condition had taken a turn for the worse.

August 12, 2021

Despite the day prior being uncertain in the wake of my condition, Thursday, August 12, was unremarkable. I will note the kidney concerns. Notes regarding my kidneys appeared throughout my crisis since its inception.

For some years, I had kidney issues. They have always worked, but I have been prone to suffer from kidney stones. I've never sustained one too large to pass on its own, which was a blessing. However, when a stone occurs, it is one of the most painful experiences I have had. Ask anyone who has had one. Female friends of mine have told me that it is the closest thing to childbirth a man will ever experience. I have been told by many women who have experienced both childbirth and kidney stones that, if given the choice, they preferred childbirth. That is saying something. I have been a witness to one childbirth, my son Gary's. From personal observation, I would have assumed kidney stones would be easier; however, I will take the word of the women who have dealt with both.

On August 12, the notes of PA Elizabeth P. Rambo and Dr. Nangender Mankan of Hematology-Oncology included the following often-cited statement:

"Kidneys: Nonobstructing bilateral renal stones are noted. Largest stone in the upper pole of the left kidney measures up to 6 mm. No overt hydronephrosis."

The remainder of the note indicates there was more than one stone. What it didn't note was how many stones were present at the time. It only was referenced as "the largest one."

Occasionally, it was noted that my kidneys crashed, which was an extremely bad sign. As previously noted, when bodily systems shut down, the dominoes begin falling with a push from the kidneys. This marks the beginning of the end and rapidly progresses.

August 13 to August 16

These three days didn't have much to report in terms of significant changes, though there are several items worth noting.

An ongoing concern of "acute ischemia" was mentioned in my medical records. According to Webster's Dictionary, ischemia is defined as a "deficient supply of blood to a body part due to the obstruction of the inflow of arterial blood."[9]

The following, concerning this possible condition, is noted in

Dr. Castro-Borobio's report of August 16.

"IMPRESSION:
No evidence of an acute intracranial abnormality.
If there is continued clinical concern for acute ischemia, consider MRI of the brain."

This could have been considered good news, particularly when considering my mental capacities if I survived the entire ordeal. The concern being if I had reduced mental abilities, my prolonged life would require assisted living and care. How would it affect the lives of my children? My living will stated that if I should fall into a medical condition that would result in a reduced mental capacity that would put a strain on my family mentally, emotionally, and financially, I did not wish those measures to be taken. That was my personal choice, and I certainly understand if others might have issues with that. From my perspective, I would have considered myself fortunate to have lived sixty-five years of a happy and fulfilled life. I would only want the best for my children and those who came after without the burden of caring for me in such a state.

On a positive note, I saw I had been taken off some of the previously administered medications since my arrival on July 25.

August 17, 2021

The prayer chain continued to extend across the country on Tuesday. Because of the prior touch-and-go week, my kids decided to wait for more concrete information on my condition one way or the other. They were in direct contact with those who reached out asking about my condition or their welfare, which must have been quite a task. It was wonderful of them to endure it as well as they did, to say the least. All those they were in contact with appreciated it so much. So many have told me how much they cherished the information shared and my children's willingness to provide it.

On Tuesday, August 17, the following message was posted to my Facebook[10] friends:

> "Hello all, I am so sorry it has taken this long to post about Jonathan, I had been out of town due to training and just kept up with the people who have directly texted me. There was a moment last week where [sic] Jonathan was in terrible shape to the point we almost had to let him go. However, he slowly seems to be stepping up the health ladder. I'm not sure if the doctor we had last week was getting to him at the wrong time of day because he was reporting to me that Jonathan was not passing any of his neurological tests (squeezing hands, opening his eyes, wiggling his toes), however, the nurses would tell me he was slowly making progress and was passing the tests. I did get confirmation from the new doctor that he is starting to pass more tests because he personally witnessed it. His lower body is weaker than the top half but is slowly getting stronger every day. Over the weekend he had [a] bad fever and his kidneys began to fail again but they have also gotten it under control. The goal this week was to get him into rehab either in the hospital or more likely the WellStar Rehab center on Windy Hill in Marietta. However, Jonathan needs to be more stable before he goes. Both the Rehab and the Hospital are on total lockdown and no visitation due to the spike in COVID.
>
> Please keep the prayers coming! I know he will be forever thankful!"

I seem to have turned the corner now and the notes in my medical chart indicated the same. The post also reiterates that lingering concern for my kidneys. It mentions the change in doctors; the new doctor had positive observations (which my angel nurses continued to confirm were true). Although we were not pleased with the attending doctor, we did not have him removed. We were grateful to have a different doctor who took over the duties. Providence once again raised its head.

My medical notes said I was cognitively more responsive to commands to do certain things, such as wiggling my toes and moving different body parts. I have vague memories of these things.

Once again, the response to my daughter's post was tremendous. There were 115 general responses along with 103 comments and seven shares to other groups. Some of the responses are below.

> "Ashley Curling
> Thank you for this long-awaited update!! You are angels for keeping everyone updated about his condition while processing and dealing with your own emotions and responses to the situation. I think I speak for many of us when I say we are very grateful and appreciative.
> Continuing to send up many prayers for his continued improvement and a complete recovery."

> "Richard Hill
> Thank you for the update. We keep you all in our prayers and know that God will give his body the rest and strength he needs to heal. Hang in there. Waiting and especially not being able to visit as in normal times can wear you out."

> "Sandi Rumsey-Flagler
> Your dad and I were in a high school play together. I heard about his hospitalization a couple of weeks ago. I've been praying every day since for his full recovery. May the Good Lord lay his healing hands upon your dad."

> "Mary Hunter Bivins
> My prayers continue for Jonathan! I check Facebook for an update at least a few times every hour! Jonathan is my only male best friend & one of my best friends for almost 20 years! He is my first choice for needed advice, a strong shoulder, fabulous conversation, laughter, dinner &

drinks! He is my rock! Jonathan will pull through this & he will be stronger than ever! I assume he has no idea how much he is loved! 🙏❤️ 🙏"

"Craig Sears
Thank you very much for the update. Still praying regularly for Jonathan. 🙏"

"Annamarie Mazza
Jonathan is a fighter I know he will make it through!!"

I've attempted to include different friends in the responses to each of the notes that were placed out by the kids. Some are friends of mine from high school so many years ago, some are friends of mine from here in Georgia, and some are friends of my children who also hung on every note. I've always told my children's friends that if you are friends of my children, then I have adopted you as my own children, too. For if you are kind to them, you are kind to me.

August 18, 2021

August 18, there was a positive report from Dr. Castro-Borobio of the Infectious Disease Services of Georgia with regards to my brain.

" CT Head Without Contrast
Narrative
EXAM: CT HEAD WITHOUT IV CONTRAST
CLINICAL INDICATION: *Altered mental status, COVID-19 positive.*
TECHNIQUE: *CT scan of the head with multiplanar reformatted images generated from the data set without IV contrast. Dose reduction techniques were utilized.*

COMPARISON: *None available.*

FINDINGS: **The brain is normal in appearance. Mild diffuse volume loss is present without definite lobar predilection, commensurate with the patient's age. No acute intracranial hemorrhage, abnormal mass, or mass effect is demonstrated. No hydrocephalus or abnormal extra-axial fluid collections are present"**

August 19, 2021

I received a percutaneous endoscopic gastrostomy (PEG tube) for feeding on August 19. The procedure requires placing a flexible feeding tube through the abdominal wall and into the stomach.[11]

The PEG tube stayed with me until just before I was discharged from the hospital. Initially, it was to remain with me for six weeks and would have gone home with me. The tube really wasn't a big deal, but it was a bit obtrusive when I would turn over in bed. It never pulled out or hurt much when it occasionally was tugged. The reason it was removed earlier than expected... well, you'll have to wait to hear about it. It was pretty funny, though!

August 19-21, 2021

Apart from the PEG Tube placement, August 19-21 was pretty calm. According to the notes, I was more awake and responded to commands despite my weakened state. The notes indicate I had lost more strength in the lower part of my body (which made perfect sense) and correlated to rehabilitation later in the journey to work on balance and walking.

A post was made on Facebook on August 21, but it was not sent out by the kids. This one went out in response to a conversation they had with Barbara Gifford, a friend from my hometown of Schaghticoke, New York, whom I have known for decades! We went back to the ages of my youth.

> "Barbara Gifford
> Schaghticoke Church
> August 21, 2021
> Here is the latest news on Jonathan P Crooks.
> So happy to announce the great news on Jonathan!!
> From his daughter…
> Daddy is doing very well, and he is starting to return to his normal self. They are officially starting his discharge paperwork for the rehab."

There are "Great News" responses on my Facebook page, but I can only imagine that the news shown above found its way to others through shares from other friends' pages.

August 22, 2021

I was more awake, and they had begun working with me on swallowing test trials as evidenced by the notes below.

"Patient was seen for bedside swallowing evaluation given placement of Passy Muir speaking valve. Patient accepted trials of ice chips (x5), thin liquids (~3 oz via cup and straw), ~1 oz puree, and ~1 oz soft chewables. Patient was unable to demo self feeding given UE weakness. With water-delayed cough. With soft chewables - oral residuals/ prolonged mastication. Recommend instrumental swallowing exam (FEES) for objective swallowing assessment and to determine dysphagia POC. Oral care completed following trials. Recommend ice chips sparingly for comfort."

The note was written by Kara A Jones, speech language pathologist (SLP) after she had evaluated me.

According to Speech Pathology Graduate Programs.org, the definition of "SLP" is as follows:

> "Speech-Language Pathology is the scientific study of speech, fluency, feeding and swallowing, and all the mechanisms of speech and language, along with the therapeutic application of corrective and augmentative measures to help people with speech disorders speak and communicate better. It falls under the communication sciences and disorders discipline, which also include the closely aligned—but separate—study of audiology.

Speech-language pathology is focused on a range of human communication and swallowing disorders affecting people of all ages."[12]

I saw several SLPs during my stay at the different WellStar locations. They would evaluate my ability or lack thereof, to swallow different foods and liquids. Those evaluations would determine what I could eat or drink at any given time. In the evaluation above, they were looking specifically at the ability of my epiglottis to close off my breathing tube so as to take liquids into my stomach and not my lungs.

The epiglottitis is defined by Harvard Health Publishing as follows:

> "The epiglottis is the flap of tissue located just above the windpipe (trachea) that directs the flow of air and food in the throat. When we breathe, the epiglottis moves to allow air into the lungs. When we eat, the epiglottis covers the top of the windpipe so that food goes into the swallowing tube (esophagus) and not into the lungs."[13]

Most have experienced a little bit of fluid, "going down the wrong pipe." In extreme cases, a piece of food can get stuck in the throat, requiring the Heimlich maneuver to extract it. When on prolonged life support and/or having a tracheostomy weakens the epiglottis and esophagus, requiring rehabilitation. I had been in a coma and neglected using my throat for nearly a month. I had a tube inserted in my throat most of that time and my body had to "relearn" swallowing, as well as many other things.

I was weak and coughed, or better said, choked on water and other "thin liquids." The epiglottis was not correctly closing resulting in the fluids going down the "wrong tube." This ended up being a bit of a problem for me during most of my stay at the three hospital locations I ended up in. I required my liquids to be thickened for most of my stay.

Another result of waking and being somewhat cognizant I was tested on speaking and cognitive responses. The SLP was responsible for helping me with the swallowing and speaking. The notes on this first evaluation are quite interesting. I recall having a difficult time speaking and communicating in general. I remember being frightened about my state and wondering if I would ever be able to speak again.

"Subjective:
Patient agreeable to evaluation. Nodding and shaking head in response to questions. Cleared for Passy Muir Valve by Dr. Lavania. RT Harold transitioned patient to trach collar prior to session and cleared patient for PMV trials."

A quick definition of the "PMV" trials should be helpful. According to Hopkins Medicine, a tracheostomy with a Passy-Muir Valve (PMV) is defined as follows:

> *"The Passy-Muir speaking valve is commonly used to help patients speak more normally. This one-way valve attaches to the outside opening of the tracheostomy tube and allows air to pass into the tracheostomy, but not out through it. The valve opens when the patient breathes in. When the patient breathes out, the valve closes and air*

flows around the tracheostomy tube, up through the vocal cords, allowing sounds to be made. The patient breathes out through the mouth and nose instead of the tracheostomy.

Some patients may immediately adjust to breathing with the valve in place. Others may need to gradually increase the time the valve is worn. Breathing out with the valve (around the tracheostomy tube) is harder work than breathing out through the tracheostomy tube. Patients may need to build up the strength and ability to use the valve, but most children will be able to use the speaking valve all day after a period of adjustment." [14]

I adjusted to the PMV well; however, I do recall I often applied pressure to the area so the air would flow properly through my vocal cords. I also recall having to strain to be heard at all. I couldn't maintain it for long, and the SLPs who worked with me were concerned I was potentially damaging my vocal cords. The long-term effect was their greatest concern. For several days, I was unable to speak at all. My daughter Kristine had brought me a small whiteboard to write on, but I was so weak I was unable to write. This led to frustration on my part as I was virtually unable to communicate for those several days. My dear nurses, with great effort, desperately tried to understand what I was communicating to them, and often we never got close to an understanding. Though it was frustrating, I worked diligently to never get angry over it. I knew they were trying to understand me. Additionally, being afraid I might never speak again, I didn't want to strain to communicate. I recall telling myself that if that were the case, I still could see, hear, write, and learn sign language. I've always believed my greatest asset was verbal communication, and losing it would be devastating. I felt it was akin to a pianist who lost the use of their hands.

SOME OF THE more specific assessments were as follows: (For clarification, WFL stands for "within functional limits")

"Baseline Assessment:
Behavior/Cognition - Alert; Cooperative; Confused; Requires cueing; Distractible.

Auditory Comprehension:
Yes/No Questions - Basic WFL; Complex Impaired.
Basic Questions - Impaired
One Step Commands - WFL (with cues/models)
Two Step Commands - Impaired
Multi-Step Commands - Impaired
Conversation - Impaired
Auditory Comprehension Comments - Patient benefited from simplified syntax, repetitions and models for basic comprehension. Cognition is barrier.

Verbal Expression:
Open Ended Questions - Impaired
Conversation - Impaired
Verbal Expression Comments - Limited/incomprehensible verbalizations with PMV placement.

Cognition:
Arousal/Alertness - WFL
Orientation Level - Oriented to person; Disoriented to place; Disoriented to time; Disoriented to situation.
Routine Problem Solving - Impaired

Processing Speed - Delayed"

I have highlighted the section on cognition because no one had yet told me I had been in a coma for four weeks. Therefore, the fact I was disoriented about time, place, and situation makes perfect sense in hindsight.

August 23-24, 2021

When considering major progress or setbacks, the 23rd and 24th are unremarkable. I progressed slowly each day, but I had lost a tremendous amount of strength. I saw both the occupational therapist (OT) and physical therapist (PT) each day, and evaluations were made every twenty-four hours.

It's an understood insider's hospital joke that medical staff wakes you up to give you a sleeping pill. It's funny and I'm quite certain that it is often true. In this case, I can confirm that my day started quite early. There is no sleeping in as somewhere around five o'clock in the morning someone is coming in to see you. My PA arrived at 6:04 a.m. on the 23rd and 4:56 a.m. on the 24th.

At this time, I had moved from "sleepy and not very responsive" on the 23rd at 6:04 a.m. to "sleepy this AM but responsive" at 4:56 a.m. on the 24th. That was a step forward.

I sustained a bedside procedure, a bronchoscopy, on the 24th. According to the Mayo Clinic website, bronchoscopy is defined as follows:

"Bronchoscopy is a procedure that lets doctors look at your lungs and air passages. It's usually performed by a doctor who specializes in lung disorders (a pulmonologist). During bronchoscopy, a thin tube (bronchoscope) is passed through your nose or mouth, down your throat, and into your lungs.

Bronchoscopy is most commonly performed using a flexible

bronchoscope. However, in certain situations, such as if there's a lot of bleeding in your lungs or a large object is stuck in your airway, a rigid bronchoscope may be needed.

Common reasons for needing bronchoscopy are a persistent cough, infection, or something unusual seen on a chest X-ray or other test.

Bronchoscopy can also be used to obtain samples of mucus or tissue, to remove foreign bodies or other blockages from the airways or lungs, or to provide treatment for lung problems." [15]

Clinical notes say that I was given mild sedation for the bronchoscopy. I don't recall anything about this procedure.

Behind the Scenes - August 22-24

Awake from my medically induced coma and making some progress, the medical staff's attention turned to where I would go next and how quickly they could get me there. Although extremely weak and struggling with speech, the hospital needed the bed for other patients.

You will recall I was being called "patient zero" for the Delta Variant of COVID-19. Technically, that means I was the first one through the hospital's door infected with the B.1.617.2 variant. The doctors had yet to see it at North Fulton until I arrived. Conversations with those who had worked with me revealed that the floodgates opened with patients who were infected after my arrival. At this time, I had been at Wellstar North Fulton for a month, and many more patients flooded in, understandably requiring me to move facilities sooner rather than later if at all possible.

Several landing options were available to me, but the decision was to be based on which location had the first bed available. The first suggested location was unacceptable to my family. Kristine was familiar with the location, and she was totally against my staying there. The family requested I be moved to Wellstar Windy Hill. Everyone worked fast to have me sent to the preferred facility. Fortunately, I had wonderful friends who chomped at the bit to help! The children approached my dear friend, State Senator John Albers, for aid. He immediately contacted our friend in Roswell Rotary, Jon-Paul Croom (who was President of Wellstar North Fulton), to see what could be done to get me to Wellstar Windy Hill. A few phone calls were made, availability was checked, and I was ordered to transfer to the first available bed at Wellstar Windy Hill. I don't know what Jon-Paul had to do to get me there, but he made it happen. I shall be forever grateful to him and Senator Albers for their efforts. They are both extremely good men and good friends, and my children and I cherish them.

August 26, 2021

My PA saw me at 5:39 a.m., and I was again awake and responsive. He noted I could bend my legs and raise my arms, which certainly was progress.

This is a big day for me!

At 2:09 p.m., my primary doctor signed my discharge papers, and I was transported to Wellstar Windy Hill. Praise be!

I had moved to the next stage of recovery!

CHAPTER 4
THE DAWNING OF A NEW DAY

I was at WellStar Windy Hill for the next two weeks in room 311.

It had been a long, hard road, and although I had made great strides, I had a long way to go. Much further than I could have imagined when I arrived at checkpoint Bravo. Little did I know what challenges lay ahead of me. At the time of my admittance, I was equally unaware of the incredible people I would meet, the friendships I would make, and how hard I would have to work. In hindsight, I was imbued with joy, hope, and fun under the understanding and encouraging care of those professionals.

I was alert enough to make connections with doctors and nursing staff who fought this disease alongside me. Anyone who knows me knows I'm a people person. I enjoy getting to know people, and I'd like to think most enjoy getting to know me.

The next two weeks were filled with new firsts, excitement, and overcoming some of the greatest fears I have ever faced. I had to relearn how to do just about everything. But before we delve into all the new adventures, I will share the Facebook post from August 27 by my children.

August 27, 2021

"Hello all, this is Kristine. As of yesterday afternoon, with the help of some very close friends and teamwork, Jonathan has officially been transferred to Wellstar Ltac Rehab on Windy Hill in Marietta! Jonathan is finally in a stable enough position to begin working off the Ventilator and Trach, along with starting physical therapy. Very late last night I was able to drop off some of his personal items, his beautiful prayer quilt that is in the picture below, a little stuffed animal, and his cell phone. The nurses are going to charge his phone; however, I don't know how fast he will be able to use it. It will probably be a little longer before he is going to start to respond to his phone due to his physical limitations. I asked his nurse if it is okay to send things to his room, such as cards, balloons, toys, flowers, and they said it is fine just to send it to the hospital directly with his name and room number which will be provided down below. At the moment, the hospital still does not have visitation at this time. However, we are attempting to see if they can make an accommodation since he just got in and let Vivian and I go see him just to make the adjustment easier and less stressful. If we are able to get this opportunity, I will make sure I share all of your love to him and pass the messages on.

Thank you so much for all the prayers, thoughtful gifts, and teamwork. Daddy is going to get it done and kick more ass than he ever did before!"

Every time I read these notes and see the responses, I can't hold back the tears. I still can't believe I was in the shape I landed in. In a million years, I would never have thought I would be in that condition. I cannot express what all the love, care, and prayers meant and continue to mean to me. As I have already done with the other updates sent out, I want to share some of the responses this note generated. There were 172 general, meaning emoji, responses along with 112 comments and six shares that I know of.

I know the shares extended further than just the initial shares, as I would hear from people from all over.

"Bob Tobey

Lord, we praise You and we thank You for Your presence. Thank You for watching over Jonathan and being with him during his battle with COVID. Our hearts are overwhelmingly grateful for Your grace and mercy. Give strength to Jonathan as he continues his journey to full recovery. This we pray in Jesus' name, Amen."

"Katie Morlock-Troline

Thank God he is stable and on his way toward recovery!! Continued prayers for your precious daddy for strength and healing!! Thank you so much for the updates. God bless you and your family!!! ♥🙏🙏♥"

"Bill Via

Jonathan - we are with you buddy! We are confident you will come through this in great shape. We will continue to pray for you."

"George Snow

Thank the Lord and the medical staff. This news has been a blessing to me, as he truly is a great friend and a great person. May God continue to bless your family."

"Colette Gissendaner Davis

Thanks for the great news. Grateful that God is giving your Dad to push through this devastating virus. He is so blessed to have his daughters with him. Prayers for the next phase of the journey… but knowing Jonathan… his strong will and faith in God… he will triumph."

"Claudette Harrell Gallman

Keep fighting Jonathan and we are continuing to pray for your recovery. Thank you to your faithful daughters."

"David Lyle

Thank you for the update. Just hate for you (referring to my children) and Jonathan. However, I am very happy for the progress and news that he is on the mend. Love my friend and prayers for a full and speedy recovery. 🙏🙏🙏🙏"

Kristine mentioned the beautiful quilt in her note. This quilt came to me from my church, Roswell Presbyterian Church in Roswell, Georgia. It was made by our church's "Prayers and Squares" group. It is a wonderful ministry. It is also a very special quilt as it is one of a kind. Each quilt is designed for the specific person to receive it and reflects something they love. For me, it was my love of turtles that is represented. The quilt, once put together, is placed in our Narthex for members of the congregation to view who it is for. There is a note with each quilt informing the reader of the situation the receiver is struggling through. If you look closely, you can see the blue ribbons throughout the quilt. What you can't see is the knots in those ribbons. Each knot is tied by someone in our congregation who said a prayer for me over the quilt. I have tied many knots on quilts made for others. It is an emotional, heartfelt prayer that each person lifts. It is one of the most meaningful gifts you can imagine. This came to me while at Windy Hill, and I used it when I sat in my chair. It now rests on my favorite chair in my living room. When I first came home, I would place it over my legs to keep me warm, and I still use it today. It continually reminds me of all the wonderful people from my church, the people who watched over me from afar, those who watched over me in the hospitals, and those who give me warm hugs every time I see them. I love this quilt, and I love everyone who gifted it to me. Those of you reading this story are also officially part of this family. You have been admitted into a worldwide family of incredible people united in faith and love. May God continue to bless you all the days of your life.

This is a horse I received from Vivian and Kristine. They know of my great love of horses, having grown up with them. All three of us had gone for a trail ride not long before I fell ill. It was the first time I had been on a horse in years, and I was pleased I took right to it as a duck to water. The little fella pictured here has not been named yet, but he watches over me as I work on writing this story at home.

The Dawning of a New Day

THE PHOTO on this page you have seen before in the opening of the book. As you will recall, it is a photo of Vivian and Kristine's high school graduation day. Viv is on the left, and Kristine is on the right. My son Gary (I'm guessing you could figure it out without aid) is to the right of Kristine. It bears repeating because it shows who we are to each other. The genuine smiles of a fun, happy day. This is the kind of day I cherish, and it is burned in my memory. We are like any family; there are times when everyone doesn't completely see eye to eye with someone or another and gets a little peeved at another member of the family. But in the end, we are family. The misunderstanding never lasts. These smiles are who we really are to each other. It's what I would have missed most had I not made it through the ordeal. The thought there would be pain or sorrow on any of their faces is almost beyond comprehension for me.

Kristine mentioned in the Facebook post that cards, balloons, and flowers could reach me at Windy Hill. It was so wonderful when I received those things. I gazed at them during my time there. They brightened my day more than you know.

I was only at the Windy Hill location for two weeks, from August 26 to September 8, and I was on the mend. Therefore, the notes on My Chart were far less voluminous. However, I was not free from issues.

I vaguely remember arriving at Windy Hill. I was transferred by ambulance, and I recall it being a very quiet ride. Kristine's note indicated she and Viv attempted to get permission to visit me.

They knew it would help me to see them after such a life-threatening ordeal, and of course, they wanted and—I'm quite certain they needed—to see me, as well. They were concerned for my mental well-being. They wished to inform me what I had been through; I still didn't know that I had lost an entire month.

I arrived at approximately 4:15 p.m. on the 26th of August, and there wasn't much to be done that day except to get me situated and comfortable. A general exam was administered to get my initial assessment in their charts. Below are the notes from that first day.

"Physical Exam
HENT:
Head: Normocephalic.
Mouth/Throat:
Mouth: Mucous membranes are moist.
Pharynx: Oropharynx is clear.
Eyes:
Pupils: Pupils are equal, round, and reactive to light.
Neck:
Trachea: Tracheostomy present.

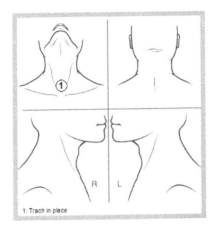

1: Trach in place

Cardiovascular:
Rate and Rhythm: Normal rate and regular rhythm.
Heart sounds: Normal heart sounds.

Pulmonary:
Effort: Pulmonary effort is normal.
Breath sounds: Normal breath sounds.

Abdominal:
General: Abdomen is flat. Bowel sounds are normal.
Palpitations: Abdomen is soft.

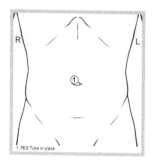

Musculoskeletal:
Cervical back: Neck supple.
Skin:
General: Skin is warm.
Neurological:
General: No focal deficit present.
Mental Status: He is alert.
Psychiatric:
Mood and Affect: Mood normal."

Author's note: The main features displayed above in the two sketch drawings refer to the tracheostomy to help with breathing and the PEG tube location for feeding purposes.

THE MORNING AFTER MY ARRIVAL, August 27, I was given the first examination I could remember since the onset of COVID-19 at home. The following photos are from that exam.

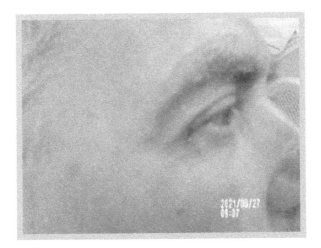

The image above is of my right eye. I have no idea where this cut came from. There were creams applied to it the entire time I was in the hospital at Windy Hill and while I was at WellStar Cobb Hospital, which was my final location before heading home. It had healed by the time of my departure home on September 22.

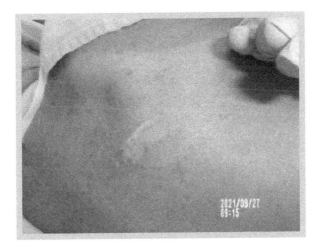

The image above is labeled "resurfaced ulcer to mid back." It doesn't appear bad to me upon inspection. I don't recall any wound there myself or any discussion about it. It could have been from the extended time I spent on my back during the coma.

The Dawning of a New Day

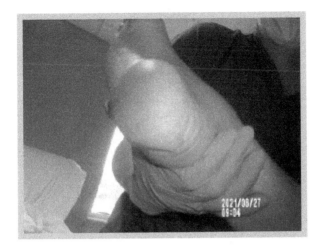

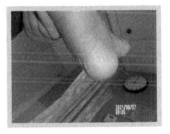

THE TWO IMAGES shown are of my left and right foot. What is most noticeable to me is how swollen my lower legs are from the ankles up. I was required to wear compression socks for several months after I was released from the hospital. Both my legs have now returned to their normal size; however, it truly took months to achieve it.

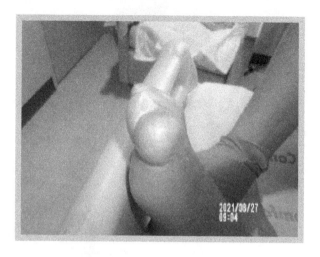

This final image is of my right big toe, what I refer to as my "angry toe." It is the result of my first gout attack when I was about forty. It was very painful at the time, and I've had many gout attacks since. The attacks usually occur at different locations in my body. I now take a medication called *Allopurinol* twice per day to keep my uric acid down.

When Kristine first came to see me in the hospital at Wellstar North Fulton, though she knew what room in the Intensive Care Unit (ICU) I was in, she said she didn't recognize me. The only way she was sure it was me was because she recognized my "angry toe." It sure looks angry!

AUGUST 27TH WAS the first full day at my new location, and there were quite a few visits to my room to assess where I was medically, physically, and mentally. I will attempt to provide a summation of these visits to provide an overview without oversharing.

I was visited by my speech-language pathologist directly after the nurse who took the photos above of my wounds. There are several items of interest to me in terms of firsts. She notes I was sitting in the chair to conduct the thirty-nine-minute interview. That is quite a milestone as I had not been upright in some time. She noted that the communication between us was impaired and that I mouthed the words. The main hurdle was my lack of voice. Most of the evaluations administered by my pathologist, Jill H. Cochran SLP, that day were within functional limits (WFL). I interpreted that as responding as best I could, but it probably wasn't outstanding. However, one of the most promising and pleasant responses to an assessment regarding my behavior and cognition was recorded, "Alert, cooperative, and pleasant mood." That one does make me feel good, and that's what I always strive to be.

Sitting up in the chair was such an accomplishment that I need to expound on that. If ever I felt like a cow, this was the time. I was completely unable to stand at this point. So, the ability to move from the bed to the chair alone was totally out of the question. So, how was it accomplished? Enter the "feel like a cow" statement. If you have ever seen a cow lifted into the air, you will have a pretty good image of what they did for me most of my time at Windy Hill. There is a contraption of straps placed around you as you sit in bed. You are then "airlifted" by the straps and moved above the chair. You are then lowered into the chair and *voila*, you are sitting in the chair! Sounds like fun? It was once you got used to it and knew that you wouldn't be dropped. The illustration below is as close as I have found so far to show you what I am attempting to describe. In my case, I was lifted from the ceiling and moved along a track in the ceiling over the chair and then lowered.

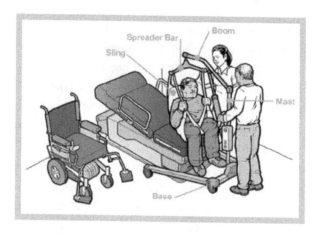

My first physical therapy assessment by Alex Seton, PT, on the 27th was as follows:

> "Assessment: The pt demonstrated good initiation of mobility and maintenance of SpO2 > 95% during mobility while on t-piece. The pt demonstrated deficits in mobility independence, sitting balance, activity tolerance, safety awareness, overall strength/ROM and coordination. The pt would benefit from skilled PT services to address the above stated deficits to maximize his mobility independence while vent weaning."

There were several deficits in this first evaluation. Although I was extremely weak, I didn't understand how concerning it was. The greatest fear among the staff is a patient falling. I could tell when a patient fell. There would be a flurry of activity in the hall, followed by silence, and an exaggerated length of time that I would be seen. Eventually, one of my nurses would come in, and I'd ask if someone had fallen. The answer was always yes. If you were going to be scolded at any point in time, it was always connected with you having done something that might have ended with a fall. The nurses would tell you that if you did fall it most likely would lead to an extension of your stay and certainly be a backward slide in your progress. The point was always well made and even better received and accepted. It was the last thing you wanted to do. I was on the receiving end of a couple of those lectures during my stay. Boss Lady, my nurse's nickname, would push her tongue hard against her cheek when she had to admonish me, and it was deserved, but she always fought back a smile.

I dished out nicknames to several of my nurses. There was Boss Lady, who was technically Nurse Karen. She was extremely nice, even though she was always the one who had to scold me. After my lectures, I responded by saying, "Yes, Boss Lady, I promise not to do it again." She always laughed. I'll never forget a time when she came in with one of the other nurses and she turned to the other nurse with her hands on her hips and the biggest smile you can imagine, and said, "Do you know what he calls me? He calls me Boss Lady!" I will NEVER forget her. I hope she never forgets me.

For an incredibly long time, I had to be catheterized at both ends. When I finally was released from that, one side seemed to work fairly well. That happened to be the backside. The front side, well, not so much. One evening, I really had to go to the bathroom for a back-door excursion. The date was September 1, my PT, Alex, recorded it in her notes. I had not walked yet, and certainly I wasn't going to try, but I felt I could crawl to the bathroom on my hands and knees. The siderails of the bed were up, so the only way to accomplish the mission would be to climb up and over the bed railing. I had been calling the nurses to aid me in this endeavor, but they were otherwise engaged with other patients. Occasionally, it just couldn't be helped that they took a bit longer than you would like. I've always been extremely regular with these functions and when I have to go...I HAVE to go! I held out as long as I could, and I decided it would be best if I could get myself to the potty. I know! It was not the smartest thing to do. I never said I was the brightest bulb in the box. I moved myself to the side of the bed and I got one foot over the top of the rail, and suddenly Boss Lady entered the room.

In her best authoritative-caring voice she said, "Where are you going? What are you doing?"

I still had a voice deficit which was much more hoarse than anything. I answered in a booming whisper as I pointed to the bathroom, "I'm trying to go to the bathroom!"

My first scolding began, "Don't you ever do that again!"

I never again attempted the feat. I knew she was correct, and it was silly of me to even have tried. Remember, I'm Mr. High Average, smart enough to know I shouldn't try, but willing to try anyway. The result was a mess, but I was intact and that was the important thing. Fortunately I was wearing the adult *Depends* product.

The second and last time I was scolded by Boss Lady happened a week later. Once again, I had to go to the bathroom. I had not yet visited the bathroom while at Windy Hill on my own and that was a personal goal I had set.

This time, I had again called the nurse's station for some help. I was no longer wearing the adult *Depends*, so this was a more critical situation than the last time. I had scooched myself to the end of my bed, a deft move of which I was immensely proud. I let my legs dangle off the side with a huge smile on my face at having accomplished that. In came Boss Lady, and she gave me that look. I knew I wasn't going get a pleasant greeting like, "Top of the Mornin' to ya!" No. I knew I was in trouble again.

"And what do you think you are doing?" she asked.

"I was just getting positioned to go to the bathroom," I said in the sweetest voice I could muster. "I just wanted to make it easy for you." *Nice try, Jonathan, but no dice.*

"I appreciate that," said Boss Lady. "But you haven't much strength and what if you had lost your balance and fallen off the bed? If you do, you're going to be with us an awful lot longer!"

I'd been bad again! With my best sheepish downward gaze, I said, "I'm sorry."

Boss Lady smiled and said, "Move back and I'll get you the bedpan."

Curses! Foiled again! I thought. At least that was the last time any of my nurses had to scold me.

Another nurse I bestowed a nickname to was Princess Dianna. Nurse Dianna was the head of the nursing staff at night. She was a pretty lady who always had a smile on her face. I just loved her. She was always so nice to me, and I'd like to flatter myself that she enjoyed me as well. My daughters had brought my cell phone, and I would watch YouTube music videos on it. I played all kinds of music. Some of the nurses smiled and danced past my door when I would play songs by Earth, Wind and Fire and the like. I felt like I was bringing them a little joy. Giving back, if you will, the care they had been bringing to me.

Some of the patients could be a handful. There was one lady across the hall from me who used to constantly yell, "Hey...HEY!" She was increasingly persistent if the nurses didn't come as quickly as she desired. They often came in my room after hers, and I'd just smile and they would roll their eyes and say, "She's lonely." I felt for the poor woman, but she was challenging for the nurses and my heart went out to them too.

Princess Dianna would set up outside my door to get all the evening medications ready for all the patients on the floor. I would play music for her, and I was pleased to watch her sway and smile to the music. It made me feel useful again and not just someone who always needed help.

I told my nurses, "You all have so much to deal with for us, but nobody said we couldn't have some fun at the same time."

Their smiles were glimpses into heaven. They were angels.

We did have fun!

August 27 - 29, 2021

I was fascinated with my occupational therapist's notes. I was very weak when working on the activities I was asked to do. I was surprised by my supposed inability to understand that she wrote about in her notes.

> *Clinical Impression - Pt presents with decrease balance, strength, activity tolerance, standing tolerance, safety awareness, and cognitive deficits which impacts independence and safety*
> *Problem Solving - Assistance required to identify errors made; Assistance required to generate solutions; Assistance required to implement solutions*
> *Awareness of deficits - Decreased awareness of deficits*

I can say with certainty that I was acutely aware of my balance. Even months later, as I write this, there are moments where balance is an issue with me. I am also aware that I was very weak in my hands. I was appalled upon returning home to see how old I looked in the mirror. It did take me to tears.

A NOTATION in my chart by Dr. Gilbert on August 29, indicated Kristine had been updated at my bedside the day before. Dr. Gilbert was the chief physician for my case at Windy Hill. Kristine had brought some personal items to me, including my cell phone and the stuffed horse. The horse carried a note from her and Vivian.

Dr. Gilbert's note stated I was still being fed via my feeding tube. I had not yet moved to real food. It's interesting to me that I never felt hungry, but the feeding tube also helped with the ease of ridding wastes from my body.

During Kristine's visit, she told me something I desperately wished to respond to, but I was unable to verbalize it at the time. I was still floating in and out, and I remember trying to respond and I just couldn't. Later that day, I could start talking to people via my cell. I enjoyed looking at the call history. I missed a call from my sister Nancy, who had attempted to reach me on July 24th and 25th; and two very close friends Amy Andrews on the 28th and Jeff Block on the 29th tried to reach me unsuccessfully. I'm guessing the cell lost power after that. The next call didn't get through until 7:42 p.m. on August 28. I spoke to Nancy for 4:24 minutes. I then called Kristine at 7:56 p.m. for seventeen minutes and one second. During that call she asked me, "Do you remember what I said to you when I saw you?"

"Yes," I said with my very weak voice. "You said I was going to be a grandfather!" It was a wonderful moment for me as it's my first grandchild.

After completing the call with Kristine, I immediately called Vivian at 8:16 p.m. for twelve minutes and four seconds, and we chatted about how all was going where I was. I then dialed Gary at 8:36 p.m. We chatted for six minutes and forty-five seconds. My voice was so weak I had to hold the trach area so the breath could go through my vocal cords. It wasn't easy, but I did it. I needed to hear their voices. In all those conversations, no one had yet told me I had been in a coma. I thought I had spoken to Gary four or five days earlier, but it had been five weeks!

I gazed at the huge whiteboard that hung on the wall across from me. It told me who my nurses are for the evening, who my doctors were, and various other bits of information such as what I could eat, if anything, medications I was taking and so on. Way up in the left corner, I could see the current date. They changed it every day when they updated the board.

There was a distinct moment when I saw 28, 2021. I thought to myself, "Well, I remember July 25th so that probably is correct." I had only been at Windy Hill for two days when I watched a nurse update the board and she rewrote the full date.

I'm thinking it was July 28th. When she left the room, I absently stared at the whiteboard and all the updates. Suddenly, I realized what it said. It didn't say "July 28th," it said "August 28"!

I frantically looked for the nurse call button and pressed it like there was a three-alarm fire in my room. When the nurse came in, I whisper-yelled something along the lines of, "What the heck!" as I pointed at the offending date. That is when I heard the news for the first time. She told me I had been in a coma for four weeks. Had I been more cognizant, it probably would have struck me even harder than it did. However, what she had said didn't really sink in other than a big WOW moment. After she left, I didn't think much more of it at the time, however after returning home it had a rather profound effect upon me.

After coming home, I got hooked on the Netflix show *Manifest*. The premise of the show involves a flight with 191 passengers leaving Jamaica for New York City. The passengers experience an hour and a half flight. However, when the plane lands, it is surrounded by emergency vehicles and the passengers deplane and are shocked to find out they at have been gone for five and half years.

I feel like I experienced something similar. I woke one morning without feeling the time had passed; however, my family and friends suffered through four solid weeks of uncertainty—blood, sweat, and tears—fearing the next phone call or message would be that I didn't make it. I never knew a thing. All I have are memory snapshots when I awakened. The pain, the hope, the prayers, the pleading—I didn't have to endure any of it. I had to fight, come back, and get better, but I had no concept of the extent of my condition until into recovery. The fears I faced in rehab, loss of strength, weight loss, and frustration were **nothing** in comparison to what my loved ones and friends endured. It makes my heart ache to think about it now. All I can hope is that my return to health was worth the pain you suffered. I want you all to have joy and peace.

CHAPTER 5
WHERE DO WE GO FROM HERE?

As I approached the end of August, I received daily visits from occupational therapists and physical therapists.

On August 30, I was back on some semblance of an actual diet. I ate a banana. However, I had been relegated to drinking thick liquids still. Thick liquids were the worst! I was thankful to eat eggs and yogurt. I hadn't eaten anything solid in over a month, so I had to relearn how to eat. That was nothing compared to finding strength and learning to walk again.

It was around this time I was told I had drop foot which meant I couldn't raise or lower my foot or feet. I will discuss this more in the section of the book on side effects of COVID. I was unable to move my right foot in an upward motion toward my knee, and I couldn't push it downward toward the floor. The result? I could not walk with any semblance of normalcy. I had to walk on the heel of my foot and drag it with me. I felt a bit like Igor from the Mel Brooks and Gene Wilder movie *Young Frankenstein*. "Walk this way," says Igor, portrayed by Marty Feldmen. The bottom line is, I was completely unable to walk heel to toe. There was no movement or strength.

I was told to exercise in bed to work on this problem. I was given an instruction sheet (pictured) that told me to do ankle pumps. Seems simple enough, one would think, but initially, they were nearly impossible for me to do. I hadn't any muscle strength to support that motion. It was as if the message to move wasn't transmitting from my brain to the muscles and feet, via the ankle. The top of my right foot was numb, indicating some level of nerve damage. I already had problems with my right leg because of a years-old herniated disc in my back. Not having use of my right calf was now even more of a problem. I was petrified I might not walk again.

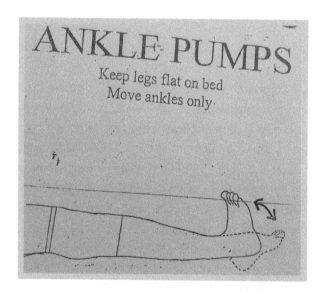

With a fear-driven determination, I moved my feet downward as I pressed on the footboard of my bed. I couldn't wait to show my physical therapist or anyone who would listen, that I was gaining some motion. With each passing day, I pushed harder, but I was still unable to pull my foot upward. The other part of the exercise was to turn the ankle in a rotating motion. Any motion was better than no motion.

As the days progressed, I became more active. Emily, who was a PT student, and Alex, head physical therapist worked with me daily for forty-five minutes. They helped me with movements in bed along with transferring to the chair for other activities. While in the hospital, I was in one of two places, either in bed or in the chair next to the bed.

While in bed, the movements were to move up and down in the bed and to roll from side to side. Sounds easy, but in practice it wasn't. I had so little strength to work with. I had been lying on my back for so long, except when the treatment required me to be on my stomach. I hadn't moved myself in over four weeks.

My speech was slurred as I neared the end of August. I required the bedrails be raised while in bed, and the only time I had any desire to go anywhere else was when I had to use the bathroom. However, those functions were accomplished with a catheter left in place, or a bedpan. As we moved further into the week, I set the goal to go into the bathroom, which I wasn't able to accomplish before I left Windy Hill. I never got to see what the bathroom looked like, except from my bed.

My occupational therapist, Jameelah, also worked with me on everyday tasks related to grooming. We concentrated on brushing my hair, shaving, washing and drying my face, and washing hands. I was rather slow. I had little energy to accomplish all that was requested. I knew what to do and even how to do it, but I was weak. I exercised and practiced these tasks while sitting in my chair, and if I had to move the therapist used a gait belt, which is a wide, adjustable strap used to help patients with mobility issues.

On August 31, Dr. Gilbert reported that my recurring gout issue had returned. It was attacking my right wrist and inflamed my *angry* right toe. I was in pain. Gout is painfully recognizable since I've dealt with it for so long.

With the arrival of September 1, there was increased concern about pressure ulcers (or bed sores).

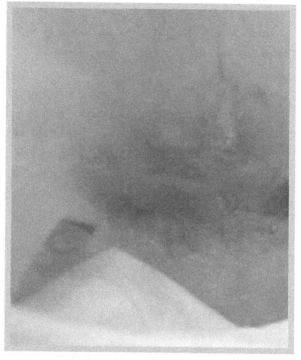

My lower back, just above my buttocks.

Certainly not a pretty picture, and just one more thing I had to deal with. These sores came from being on my back in bed for so long. Moving around seemed to irritate the sores, but moving around is the only way to stop them from reoccurring.

Fortunately, the laceration and infection in my eye was improving with the cream that was being applied daily.

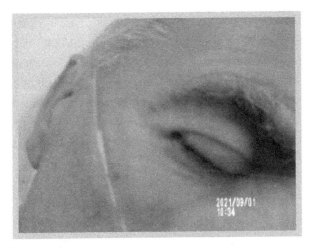

The picture shows the improvement from the photo you saw while I was still at North Fulton. My eyelid appears swollen, but I can't detect the cut anymore.

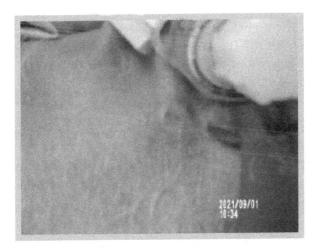

Pictured is the trach ulcer just to the left of the blue ribbon. I don't recall the device connected to the trach. I remember when there was simply a covering over it that I had to hold to more easily speak. On September 1 they removed the trach you see pictured above.

IN PHYSICAL THERAPY, I continued to improve with sitting and moving to a standing position. I would stand and then sit three to four times. It was extremely scary for me to stand. I felt as if I had to lean so far forward to stand up. I was afraid of falling over, which they never would have let happen. I was amazed at how strong my two therapists were. They were so incredibly supportive. They even told me I was their favorite patient. It wouldn't even have bothered me if they said that to all their patients, they were so nice.

As of September 2nd, six days from leaving Windy Hill, I began to eat better. I have to admit I was not the favorite patient of my speech language pathologist. I hated thick nectar liquids I was required to drink. They really were awful! In hindsight, she was correct in using these to retrain my swallowing reflex. In good conscience, I need to say that in her defense. I snicker about it now, but at the time, she avoided me when I asked for her to reevaluate my abilities. I became the "hey... HEY!" lady. I could hear her on the floor, but she stopped coming to my room. I like to think I am pretty easy to get along with, but I learned not everyone is going to like me. The SLP came in one last time on September 6, a day and a half before I left.

On September 2, my doctor noted I was moving to the rehab hospital *"as soon as a bed was available."*

My favorite doctor, Dr. Pashant Mishra was wonderful! He had such an engaging personality. My daughters had been trying to see me and wanted to visit me together. Because of all the COVID restrictions in place at the time, they were unable to, until we discovered Dr. Mishra could grant the request. During one of his routine visits, I asked if my daughters could come in to see me at the same time, and he said, "Absolutely and I'm the one who authorizes it, so you're all set."

I'm certain Dr. Mishra saved me for last as he made his rounds. He would sit at the end of my bed and chat for a good half hour. He told me about the Labor Day party he and his wife were throwing, all about her favorite barbeque chicken wings—how they are prepared—and all the details they planned for the party. It was the first time in a long time I felt like a normal human being again. I'd love to see him again.

Each day I improved but my chart did note I was "fearful." My greatest fear was that I would fall over. Regardless of that fear, I stood four times per session, followed by sitting right back down. The therapists called the movement "get up and go." I complained about shortness of breath (SOB) but I would still take two steps (with help) to my chair, to the side of the bed, and then sit.

On the positive side, my heart rate rose quickly as I went through my standing routines and moved two steps to the chair, but my recovery was extremely fast. I had a secret desire that it wouldn't come down quite as fast, so I could rest a bit longer, but that wish was never granted. When Alex and Emily (my therapists) said I was good to go, I would do just that. I knew the more I did now, the faster I would get better. I had an overwhelming desire to please them. To hear I was doing remarkably well spurred me forward. I was gaining cognitive understanding with each day as well.

When Jameelah (my OT) visited, I knew I was in for a rigorous workout. Today, those same tasks would be child's play; however, at the time, it took all the strength I had. On September 2, I was taken through an exercise of placing clothes pins, fifteen as I recall, up the side of a pole. So I clipped them from the top of the pole down, all with one hand, one after the other. Then I removed them with the same hand, repeating the exercise with the other hand. The goal was to accomplish the task without stopping. I got better as time went on.

Interestingly, I am right-handed, thus my right hand is, by nature, my stronger hand. However, as I recuperated, my left hand was stronger in every exercise. I always started with my right hand, and I knew if I could get through the exercise with it, the left hand would be much easier. Not at all what one would expect.

The following is the note discussing the clothespins.

"Balance Comment - Pt participated in therapeutic activity standing frame for 25 minutes to increase standing tolerance, BLE Strength, activity tolerance, and safety with ADL task. Pt performed therapeutic activities during tsk ROM ARC, ballon tap, and clothespins to increase BUE strength, AROM BUE, grip strength, and activity tolerance and safety."

Standing for any length of time was very taxing.

Notes from my PT related to my standing and sitting, with steps forward and backward, are below:

"Transfers Comment - pt performed 5 trials of Sit <> stands /c weight shifting and stepping forward and back for 3 trials, pt required mod vc to initiate sit > stand including cuing for hand placements for the first 2 trials as well as cues to lean forward and extend hips while in standing, pt required vc to sequence the stand to sit, pt also required tactile cues for hip extension in standing. Pt required sitting rest breaks between each trial."

pt - Patient
vc - Voice Command

I WAS GIVEN a walker to lean on as I stood. It provided stability and confidence. My PTs were always right next to me and helped me as needed to rise and sit more slowly. The gait belt you see pictured below was always placed on me during my PT work, so they would have something to grab me with should I fall.

Saturday September 4 was a wonderful day. Vivian and Kristine came in to visit that morning. Viv was able to stay for about an hour and half, and Kristine stayed about three hours. It allowed us to catch up for the first time, in person, in over a month and a half. Just seeing their smiling faces gave me strength I hadn't before had. I'm sure they had a hard time seeing me in that condition, but we were there together and that's all that mattered. I was able to pass along instructions on certain *housekeeping* items such as access to passwords and non-automatic payment for bills. I could have just looked at them for hours and not said a word and been eternally content. It still brings tears to my eyes to remember that moment.

My PT reported on Monday, September 6, some interesting points.

"Treatment Vitals Comment - HR elevated up to 150 bpm with transfers but recovered back to the low 100s with seated rest breaks."

My PTs often said they were surprised how quickly my heart rate would go back to a resting rate and that it was a testimony to the shape I was in before illness. My body remembered. I had always had a heart rate in the low to mid-sixties. That's where it had returned.

The other note I find of particular interest is:

"Subjective - "I have been getting better every day."

That is what I still say even today when asked how I'm doing. More specifically, I'll say, "A little better every day!"

"Patient Goals – ambulation."

I was so afraid I wouldn't walk again; I was so weak. But I was also determined I would.

As mentioned earlier, September 6 was the last time I saw the SLP while at Windy Hill. Her evaluation of me seems the most negative of any written. However, as I have already stated, I was always pushing her for a more normal diet and particularly the move to thin liquids. Very soon she would be rid of me, and I have a feeling that was a pleasant thought for her. However, I do say it with a smile now.

Dr. Mishra, my favorite doctor, had ordered an evaluation for "Physical Medical Rehab" on September 6. The evaluation was as follows:

"Requires, can tolerate, and can be expected to actively participate in a minimum of 3 hours of therapy daily for at least 5 days per week."

The three hour per day formula was strictly adhered to as I left Windy Hill and proceeded to WellStar Cobb Hospital two days hence. As you will see, I would have 1 ½ hours per day in

Occupational Therapy and 1 ½ hours per day in Physical Therapy.

The last evaluation with regards to PT and OT functions at Windy Hill is below:

"Current Functional Status
<u>PT</u>
Bed Mobility
Rolling Right: Mod assist, Manual Pelvic Assist, Manual Shoulder Assist, With Bed Rail, Min Verbal Cues
Rolling Left: Mod Assist, Manual Pelvic Assist, Manual Shoulder Assist, With Bed Rail, Min Verbal Cues
Scooting in supine: With draw sheet, Toward HOB (Head of Bed)
Scooting in sitting: Forward, To right, To left, Max assist, With draw sheet, With bed rail
Supine to Sit: HOB up, With bed rail, Mod assist, Min verbal cues, Tactile cues, Manual shoulder assist
Sit to Supine: With bed rail, Max assist, Min verbal cues, Tactile cues, Assist left leg, Assist right leg
Bed Mobility Comment: sitting up in a chair

Transfers
Sit/Stand - Devices: Gait Belt, RW
Sit to Stand Assist: Mod assist, Mod Verbal Cues, Mod Tactile Cues
Stand to Sit Assist: Max Assist, Mod Verbal Cues, Mod Tactile Cues
Transfer 1 Type: Bed to chair, Chair to bed
Transfer 1 Devices : Oxygen, Gait Belt
Transfer 1 Assist: Mod assist (squat pivot transfers)
Transfers Comment: Pt performed sit to stand and stand to sit x 3 at MOD

A secondary to pt requires assist with coming to stand but requires verbal and tactile cues to reach back when sitting

Gait
Gait Comments: unable at this time

OT
Functional cognition
Orientation Level: Oriented X4
Overall Cognitive Status: Intact
Follows commands: Intact
Sequencing: Independent sequencing
Processing speed: Intact
Psychological features: Fearful
Motor Planning: Appears intact
Praxis: Appears intact
Level of alertness: Alert
Problem Solving: Assistance required to identify errors made, Assistance required to generate solutions
Awareness of deficits: Decreased awareness of deficits
Initiation: Cues to initiate tasks
Perseveration: Perseverates during conversation
Cognitive fatigue: Not present
Attention Span: Attends with cues to redirect
Safety Judgment: Decreased deficit awareness"

There was one more wound care exam before moving to the rehab hospital. I will spare you the photographic inclusion. I'll leave it to the statement from the record of Nurse Denise on September 7.

"Sacral wounds resolved. New lesions noted to peri rectal skin."

My PT records indicated that I was able to move six feet on

September 7th. To this point, the extent of my walking motion was two steps to move, with a walker and the gait belt, in a circular motion to sit in my chair or stand and move back to the side of my bed. My PT, Alex, indicated my heart rate would rise to the 150s but still moved back down to the low 100s upon rest as you recall from earlier.

I remember I was able to walk from the side of my bed to the door of my room. It was the furthest I had moved in two months. With the walker, I felt safe but still was concerned about the possibility of falling. I still hoped to reach the bathroom before I left Windy Hill. Ultimately, I never accomplished the task there.

I had been able to perform the sitting and standing task quite well. I was getting quite consistent with good form and confidence. My final PT at Windy Hill took place on Wednesday morning, September 8 and it lasted forty-eight minutes. While I finished it, Dr. Gilbert prepared my discharge papers and instructions.

I had used a wheelchair to move around a little bit. It was just nice to get out of the room and "stroll." It was different scenery, no matter what it was, it was refreshing!

My PT made the following final observations:

"The pt is very motivated to participate in PT treatment sessions and progress his mobility independence."
"The pt continues to have deficits in balance, activity tolerance, safety awareness and mobility independence."

My final OT report included the following:

"Pt participated in therapeutic activity with 1 lb wrist weights standing reaching for resistance clothespins to increase BUE strength and activity tolerance for ADL tasks and transfers. Pt requires 4 rest breaks during tasks due to increased HR. Pt performed 8 sit to stand picking up cones for lower surface to increase strength in BLE. Pt

participated well but required a prolonged rest break twice during the task."

Before I knew it, the EMTs arrived to whisk me away to my next big adventure. I was off to WellStar Cobb Hospital. It was to be my last stop before heading home. My PTs at Windy Hill stated they expected I'd only be at Cobb for ten to fourteen days. They were very pleased with how I had progressed. I was ecstatic to hear their prognoses; I really wanted to go home and return to real life again.

I remember my transport to WellStar Cobb Hospital, unlike the previous trips. The EMT who sat in the back of the ambulance with me was as verbose as I was. We had a wonderful journey full of conversation. He couldn't have been nicer nor more attentive. We spoke at length about my medical "adventure." I was almost sorry when the trip was over. Nevertheless, I arrived at my new *home* at Cobb. I received a robust welcome from the nurses on the floor, welcoming me and giving me basic instructions on ordering my meals and the agenda for my days ahead. My chief nurse explained that I would receive a daily schedule of my daily three hour OT and PT exercises. I was ready to get started, and they were ready to help.

CHAPTER 6
ONE MORE STOP UNTIL HOMEWARD BOUND

September 9 was a brand-new day with brand-new challenges. I had been made aware that Cobb was my last stop before heading home. I was still quite weak, but I knew the only way to get better was to do whatever they wanted me to do, whenever they wanted me to do it.

There were many challenges ahead. The things I had taken for granted had to be relearned, and I had to build up stamina to do them. The OT folks worked with me on daily living activities (ADL) such as brushing teeth, combing hair, shaving, taking a shower, washing hair, doing laundry, making dinner, putting dishes away, and practicing general hygiene.

In addition, we had to work on exercises that mimicked getting out pots and pans, putting on clothing, folding clothes and putting them away. Then there was going to the bathroom. Little did I know that going to the bathroom normally would be one of the next big challenges.

The PT folks were concerned with my relearning to walk, stand, sit, walk forward, walk backward, take stairs, get in and out of the car, step up on a curb, sit at a table and eat dinner. They also wanted me to increase my back strength.

Therapy started on day one at Cobb Hospital. My OTs and PTs

from Windy Hill prepared me well. "Let's do this," I thought. I was raring to go right until the moment I realized I couldn't stand up. My knees suddenly hurt so badly that I was unable to do anything. I said aloud to my first therapist, "You must be thinking, 'Those OTs and PTs from Windy Hill are full of it, telling us he is standing up very well and even took a few steps. Now he can't even rise from the bed!'"

I was mortified! How can this be? The pain was excruciating. It was in both knees. I've had gout attacks before, and they can be disabling. However, they were always localized. I'd have one knee go and then the other went right after I got the first one back in operation. But never had it happened like this. I was amazed when a portable x-ray machine arrived in my room, and they x-rayed both knees while I was in bed. Within an hour, the staff had reviewed the x-rays and declared I had arthritis in both knees.

"Wonderful," I said. "What do we do now?"

They had the solution. An over-the-counter cream called *Voltaren* was applied to both knees. Within a half hour, I was back on my feet, and it was full steam ahead. My goal was exactly as noted by my therapists: "Go home without any equipment." I didn't want any part of wheelchairs, walkers, or canes. I was determined. My goal was to walk on my own and get back to who I was before this adventure began. I was determined to do it. It wouldn't be easy, and I knew that. I didn't really understand how much work it would take or how long it would be. I just knew I was going to do it.

So where to begin? A sponge bath sounded as good as anything. I accomplished this while sitting in bed. Lovely! Still, it was a start. The next task was getting dressed. I moved to a wheelchair to accomplish that. I was determined to do it without help, if possible. It wasn't completely possible, but at least I accomplished it with "minimal assist." Next: the bathroom.

Toilet Transfers:
Toilet Transfer From: Wheelchair
Toilet Transfer to Raised toilet seat without rails
Toilet Transfer Technique: Stand pivot; To left
Toilet Transfers: Moderate assistance

MY DAY SOUNDED EXTREMELY MUNDANE. I assure you; it was anything but. When you have lost your strength to 6% of what it had been, sitting up took effort. Making these movements and motions took a tremendous amount of energy and I tired very quickly, but it was wonderful to use the bathroom again. It was a blessing to sit on a toilet and not have to use a bedpan.

Anyone who has been in a hospital will tell you, you must check your humility and dignity at the door. Every move is a success, no matter how small it seems in retrospect.

Communication/Cognition:
Understanding Verbal Content (QI): 4 - Understands: Clear complex comprehension without cues or repetitions
Expression of Ideas and Wants (QI): 4 - Express complex messages without difficulty and with speech that is clear and easy to understand
Social Interaction QI: Interacts Appropriately at All Times (cooperative, participates)
Problem Solving QI: Solves Complex Problems w/Only Mild Difficulty/Self Corrects/Extra Time
Memory QI: No Memory Impairment

I was so pleased they stated I was cooperative and participated clearly, otherwise I'd have had to answer to my children, who would have admonished me.

I wanted to go home. I knew I wasn't ready to go home, but I was eager to reach that point as quickly as possible.

I was evaluated on cognitive recall and scored very well on day one at Cobb.

I was administered a *Brief Interview for Mental Status or BIMS. The BIMS is used to screen a patient's cognitive impairment.*

"The 15-point BIMS can be administered in an average of 3.2±2.0 min, resulting in low user and administrator burden,[1] and categorizes test takers as severely impaired (0-7 points), moderately impaired (8-12 points), or cognitively intact (13-15 points)." The higher the score, the lower the impairment to the cognitive response.[2]

I scored fifteen on day one! This is a big deal when you consider where I was when I entered WellStar North Fulton with dangerously low oxygen level. The concern was that the lack of oxygen had affected my brain, and if it affects my ability to think clearly. Fortunately, that concern could be put to rest.

To test my strength level (or lack thereof), a prehension test was administered to both hands. According to the *Merriam-Webster Dictionary,* prehension is defined as *"The act of taking hold, seizing or grasping."*[3]

---

1. National Library of Medicine: MDS 3.0 brief interview for mental status. https://pubmed.ncbi.nlm.nih.gov/22796362/
2. Marks TS, Giles GM, Al-Heizan MO, Edwards DF. How Well Does the Brief Interview for Mental Status Identify Risk for Cognition Mediated Functional Impairment in a Community Sample? Arch Rehabil Res Clin Transl. 2021 Jan 13;3(1):100102. doi: 10.1016/j.arrct.2021.100102. PMID: 33778475; PMCID: PMC7984985.
3. "Prehension." Merriam-Webster.com Dictionary, Merriam-Webster, https://www.merriam-webster.com/dictionary/prehension. Accessed 14 Jun. 2024.

I WAS TOLD that the norms for someone sixty-five years old should be a mean of ninety-one for the dominant hand and seventy-six for the non-dominant hand. My scores on September 9, were sixteen for my right hand and twenty-nine for my left. Though both hands were testing very low in strength, my left hand was stronger at this point. Everything with me seemed to be just the opposite of what I would have expected. These numbers explain why I was unable to write on the whiteboard Kristine had brought to me when I couldn't speak. Based on this test, I was concerned I may have sustained a stroke, and I asked my therapists that very question. They all assured me I had not; my lack of strength was a result of the extended time in the coma.

To aid me in this part of my recovery, I asked Kristine to bring me a hand press. Pictured below is that press.

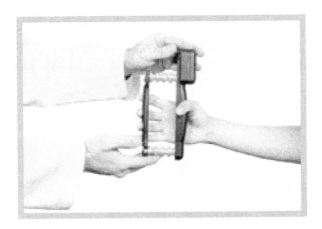

THIS ONE IS QUITE COMMON, and you may very well have one at home. When I worked with it in the hospital to strengthen my hands, I was able to press it a few times with my left hand. However, I was unable to press it, even once, with my right hand without the help of my left hand to get it started. In April 2022, I pulled it out again just for fun. I rapid-fire squeezed without any difficulty with both hands.

Walking was the next big challenge. I had "drop foot" in my right foot. I couldn't lift my foot in an upward direction from the floor. This made normal walking rather impossible. I dragged my foot and had to be very intentional about lifting my foot up and away from my left foot so I wouldn't trip. I tried to walk with a walker. My physical therapists listed the obstacles as follows in my chart:

PT Goals
Barriers
Decreased activity tolerance;Decreased standing tolerance;Decreased coordination;Decreased balance;Decreased strength
PT Interventions
Strengthening;Bed mobility/transfer training;Gait training;Wheelchair mobility training;Balance activities;Therapeutic exercises;Therapeutic activities;Stair training;Curb training;Modalities;Patient/family education;Self-Care/Home Management Training

I was unable to stand for very long when I attempted to gargle, brush my teeth, shave, and brush my hair at the sink in the bathroom. I was only able to stand for approximately a minute and a half at a time. I would have the wheelchair locked behind me so I could sit when needed. Because I was having such a hard time standing, I planned what I would do when I returned home. I decided to place a chair behind me at my sink so that I could sit, if necessary, until my strength returned.

I would go into the bathroom before the OT arrived so I could get through the process by sitting in the wheelchair rather than standing. That went against my self-mandated directive of moving ahead at the best possible speed. What it did allow me to do was accomplish the tasks on my own, which made me feel at least a bit better about myself.

The wounds I had on my backside continued to plague me. They were rather painful and made it difficult to sit or lie on them for long periods of time.

Diet and swallowing were still a bit of an issue. I moved to solid foods when I was able to easily swallow them. The delicious "thick liquids" I detested were still required. I secured Amour drinks from my children, which tasted much better, but they weren't my favorites either. However, they were light years ahead of the thick nectar drinks that could gag a maggot. Finally, on September 10, I was administered a barium swallow test.

Johns Hopkins Medical defines the barium swallow test:

"A barium swallow test is a special type of imaging test that uses barium and X-rays to create images of your upper gastrointestinal (GI) tract. Your upper GI tract includes the back of your mouth and throat (pharynx) and your esophagus.

> Barium is used during a swallowing test to make certain areas of the body show up more clearly on an X-ray. The radiologist will be able to see the size and shape of the pharynx and esophagus. He or she will also be able to see how you swallow. These details might not be seen on a standard X-ray."[4]

I was so pleased to take this test, as it would determine once and for all if I could remain on a regular food diet and finally be able to have regular drinks. It was a fascinating test. If you've never seen your skeleton chew and swallow in real-time, you are missing out on quite a show. They had me chew and swallow some different items such as yogurt, a cracker without liquid, a cracker with liquid, and then water. Each time I ate a cracker and swallowed, it looked like a mouse was running down my throat! I watched in boy-like wonder as a two-inch solid dark mass moved down my throat. I laughed while watching it.

The diagnosis? I could finally drink thin liquids again. I could hardly contain my delight as I returned to my room and ordered my meal for the evening. I ordered a hamburger and Sprite to drink! Waiting in gleeful anticipation for their arrival was almost more than I could stand. Dinner was served! The hamburger was like eating over-cooked shoe leather, and the Sprite tasted like a liquified bucket of bolts. Needless to say, the meal was a bit of a letdown. Now to be fair about the food, almost everything I had was quite outstanding. I honestly didn't eat much I didn't like, with the exception of that hamburger. The Sprite disappointment was a case of losing my taste and smell due to COVID.

By the time many of you read this, you may know what this is like. For me, it was as if I was tasting only certain ingredients from

---

4. "Barium Swallow." *John Hopkins Medicine*, 2019, www.hopkinsmedicine.org/health/treatment-tests-and-therapies/barium-swallow.

the drink. The next evening, I decided to try a Coke instead. It tasted slightly better, but I was only tasting certain ingredients and that was a no-go as well. On night three, I tried the last resort of sodas. If it didn't work, I was going to be relegated to drinking juices, which wouldn't have been a bad alternative; however, I was craving a soda. I knew the juice drinks were fine. I had already been drinking them for breakfast, so all would not be lost. The final soda possibility was ginger ale. I've never been a huge ginger ale fan, but any port in a storm (the other sodas had sunk). As it turned out, the third one was the charm. The ginger ale tasted the way ginger ale is supposed to, and it became my go-to dinner drink until I went home a week and a half later.

Around September 10th, an MRI was ordered because I had a problem related to the nerves running down my legs. I had never had an MRI before and as I've gotten a bit older, I've become a bit claustrophobic. MRIs are taken in an enclosed space, and I was concerned how I might react to it. However, I told myself I would be just fine and to relax. Ray was the technician who wheeled me on a gurney to the imaging center. He was extremely nice and warned me it would be rather cold, and he said I could have a blanket if I'd like one. I assured him I would be okay and thanked him. The tech who administered the MRI was also extremely nice. She explained everything to me and said it would take about twenty-five minutes. I was given a hand-held button to push in case I had any problems during the test.

Into the MRI machine I went, and though I was a bit uncomfortable entering the tube, I went through far enough that I could see out the back of it. If I raised my head backward slightly, I could look out and away from the tube. That was comforting. The machine was extremely loud but not unmanageable. As the testing proceeded began, I felt a consistent burning sensation on my left side in two distinct points. As the test continued, the burning would ebb and flow. I got so I knew roughly how long it would last, but as the test continued, it became hotter, finally reaching a point of becoming unbearable. I still had very little voice; it was very weak and soft. I started pushing the button and was a little frantic that the tech was not responding.

I pushed the button very hard and still, there was no response.

I was trapped as my arms were pinned down. I couldn't move them, nor could I move my legs and it was all I could do not to panic. I knew I had to be close to the end of the test. I attempted to time the test based on the number of songs they played to distract the patient from the procedure.

I called out as best I could muster. I cried out, "Help, help me!" No response! Finally, the machine stopped. The tech finally heard me.

She was mortified. " I couldn't hear you. I couldn't hear you, I'm so sorry!" she said. "What was wrong?" she asked.

I told her about the burning sensation in my side, and she checked me over but was unable to find any marks. She also said she had never seen anyone come out anywhere near as hot as I was.

I might have been angry, except she was horrified and felt so badly.

The emergency button had not worked properly so that was why she wasn't alerted.

I tried to put on a cheerful face and said, " Please get the button fixed before the next person comes in." We never discovered why I felt that burning sensation.

When the results of the MRI came in, my doctor pointed at it and said, "See all this? That's all the damage that had been done to your back twenty years ago. The good news is, there isn't any new damage." That was that.

On September 11, I became fully engaged in my experience as I commented to Dr. Jordan, my rehab doctor, about my approach to my rehab. She documented our conversation in her notes of the day:

"*Subjective/Events over the last 24hrs: No overnight events. Complains that his treatment team is not consistent. Discussed that on the weekends or when someone takes vacation, we will have another therapist fill in but try to keep a consistent team during the week. Continue to require intermittent cath. Last BM 9/10."*

I'm sure the strength of her statement made is just the shorthand of the write-up. I wasn't really complaining, as I liked every therapist I had been working with and had made a point to convey that. I was just commenting to Dr. Jordan that I was having to explain to each new person who came to work with me my overall situation, or at least felt I needed to. Perhaps that wasn't true, but I wanted to ensure they knew the full situation with my drop foot and what I could or couldn't do at the time. Dr. Jordan was tremendous, and I trusted and relied on her.

The reference to the "BM 9/10," if you haven't guessed, referred to my last bowel movement. Lovely I know, but you might as well take the whole journey with me.

As each day passed, we moved closer to regular movement. I used a wheelchair in the morning to take care of bathroom needs. We started walking with the walker more, which was both tiring and exhilarating at the same time. I wanted to walk; I just couldn't go far quickly. I would try to, though, as is evidenced in my PT Marie's notes below:

Comments
Demonstrated good foot clearance with R ace wrap. Pt ambulated with good gait speed. Needs VC to pace himself.

The "VC" refers to "vital capacity." My heart rate would rise rather quickly, though it did recover quickly as noted before. The "R ace wrap" referred to above is referencing the bandage they placed on top of my foot and up my leg to hold my right foot up and in place. It allowed me to walk much more easily and normally. Without the bandage, my right foot would drag and curl inward toward my left foot, thus drastically slowing my gait and making me unstable while walking. As I was using my walker; I had a habit of looking downward and thus hunching over. My PTs constantly reminded me to stand up straight. I got in the habit of telling myself, out loud of course, "Straighten up, Jonathan. Straighten up!"

One of the tasks I had to perform was walking up steps. By September 11, I could negotiate four steps on the stairs. Just two days earlier, I had managed to only step up ONE step of the stairs then turn around and step down. It was all I could manage to do, and I was wondering, "How will I ever do this?" I remember being pleased I didn't have to try it the next day. By the 11th, when we went to the "playground" (as we patients called the weights and exercise room), I was determined to try the stairs again and was able to handle the four steps. "Maybe I can, by God, maybe I can," I thought!

The photo below is of PT stairs in one of the WellStar North Fulton Hospital Medical buildings. They are like what I was working with at WellStar Cobb Hospital, though not as large.

THE WELLSTAR COBB HOSPITAL, stairs being so high, added to the initial fear of climbing but multiplied exponentially the reward when I was successful.

To give you an idea of what I looked like while in rehab, the photo below is from September 10, the day before my ascent of the stairs.

One More Stop Until Homeward Bound

Though not particularly very handsome, I'm at least clean shaven and sporting a smile. I was on the mend, and there were many reasons to smile even though there was a long way yet to go.

While at Cobb, I worked with Nurse Valary Anderson Dreyer. She was on loan to Cobb from her home and family in South Carolina. She was only at Cobb for two weeks, the two weeks I was there! "What a lovely coincidence," you say. I've learned over the course of my life there are no coincidences.

She came to see me every day. I looked forward to seeing her as she was the nicest, most encouraging of all the nurses. Though she always had to wear a mask (they all did), I could imagine the brightest and warmest smile underneath it. When I finally saw it unmasked the day I left the hospital to return home, my imagination was realized. She was every bit as lovely as I thought she was. She talked with me whenever she could. She was my confidante for all things secret. Okay, maybe not secret, but if I

wanted to know what was going on, she was the one to ask. To all my new friends, this is Valary. Valary, it's my pleasure to introduce you to all my new friends reading this book!

Valary, your friendship during those two weeks was invaluable to me. How wonderful it has been to stay in touch with you since then and to watch with great joy the triumphs of your family and share the new births and triumphs of my family with you. You shall always be special to me and hold a special place in my heart.

Four real goals needed to be attained at this point in my recovery (in no order as they were all necessary to getting back to some semblance of normalcy). The first was standing for longer periods of time. The second was walking. The third was getting my balance back. The fourth was getting my strength back. All other goals were subsets of these four. According to my OT Ashunti's notes, I was only standing at the sink for a minute at a time. A minute and half if I pushed it. Ashunti needed to try a different approach. She said we were going to the "playground" to play a game, *Connect Four*. Familiar with it? The object of the game is to place four of your chips in a row, column or diagonally before your opponent does and block them from doing so in the process. I stood at the table and played two games with Ashunti. I won both of them, I might add!

When we were finished, she slyly said, "You realize you've been standing here for eight and a half minutes without any problem at all."

All I could do was say, "Pretty smart, Ashunti. Pretty smart!"

She had told me I could do it, I just needed TO do it. I had no problem standing at the sink anymore. Good job kiddo! Scratch one!

Strength was a different story. I was so weak from my ordeal. I didn't realize just how weak I was until I asked my daughter Kristine to bring me a hand weight. This she did along with the hand press pictured earlier. She asked me what size weight I wanted. I thought for a moment and guessed I could probably handle a five-pound weight just fine. I thought about it some more and decided maybe a three-pound weight would be better. When all was said and done, I decided on a two-pound weight after chatting with my PT staff. As it turned out, a two-pound weight was not only sufficient to get me started, it was also all I could handle.

Pictured below is the two-pound weight she brought me. I was lucky to raise it five times per hand over my head as I lay in bed. We didn't spend a lot of time on weight work while I was in the hospital. All of that was really to come after I left the hospital. However, I rode a bike in the playground area. It was for endurance, and it was hard to get through the sets they had me do. I did them though, every one of them. I refused to give up during any session, but I sure did appreciate it when they would have me rest a little bit.

Below is an example of the type of bikes we had to work on. You would move your arms and legs at the same time, and I would ride for a good thirty minutes with a minute break every ten minutes.

WE STARTED DOING some weight work each day as well. I used a four-pound medicine ball and five-pound weights. We would do sessions of ten curls, ten lifts to the side, and ten overhead lifts. They were brutal, or so they seemed. For one who was used to working out every day with weights of ninety-plus pounds on the curling machine and seventy-pound free-weight curling bars to now be relegated to using five-pound weights (and struggling with them) let me know in no uncertain terms just how far I had fallen. Still, I was doing it and that was enough to keep me going. I knew I needed strength, and I needed to walk!

Walking... now that was going to take more time, more effort, and more aid. I was taking steps by using a walker with a wheelchair right behind me as I walked. The ace bandage tape holding my foot in place helped keep my foot where it needed to be so I could walk and get my legs moving to strengthen them. Eventually, I used a cane and the wall to aid with balance. We spent the most amount of time on these activities in the playground to get me going.

The playground truly was fun! I got to chat with other patients when I was there, and we all encouraged each other as we were put through our paces. The PTs and OTs encouraged banter among us. They were aware of the therapeutic aid we were giving each other. When you would see someone who had been there longer than you and saw that the person was more advanced, it gave you an incentive to push harder so you could get there as well. As it came closer to my time to leave, I did my best to encourage those who came behind me. We all would just smile and say, "Keep pushing, you're going to get there, I promise!" And we meant every word of it. We looked for each other every day.

I remember the first day I walked out of my room with the walker and the wheelchair right behind me. The third floor I was on was in a square, meaning there were offices in the middle and the hall moved in a square around them. I managed to walk eighty feet with the walker, and it seemed I had sprinted an entire football field. I had to sit for a bit and then got back up and moved a bit further. The next time I tried to do the same walk, the next day, I moved 150 feet and you'd have thought I just won Olympic gold in the 100-meter sprint. I was so elated as I had gone one and a half times around the square that day. The nurses, PTs, and OTs watched me pass their open office doors and would encourage me with the biggest smiles and a thumbs up. They truly knew how far I had come.

There were two other devices used to help me move forward faster. By this time, I knew I wasn't going to be at Cobb much longer. On September 12, the plan was for me to head home

Friday, September 17th. That was only five days away! I knew I still had a long way to go. The best way to work on walking was to do it. As much as possible I would spend time in the playground.

Enter Parallel Bar Lane. Pictured is the modified version at WellStar North Fulton, but you get the idea. The one I was using at Cobb was a good three times longer, at least.

The purpose of walking the bars was to walk without any aid. The bars allowed you to hold something for support and balance while you walked. They also built confidence. I started by holding onto both sides and tried to walk with a good stride. As I kept working with them, the PT said to drop one hand and walk. Almost instantly, I said, "Oh the heck with this!" I dropped both hands and walked the best I could. I knew very well I had my PT right outside the bars, and I knew I could grab them myself if I was concerned. I had to walk again.

The other piece of equipment that came to aid the process was my foot brace. I was fitted with a standard right foot brace that would give me stability without the ace bandaging.

The only problem I had with the brace was I had a very difficult time getting it to fit in my shoe. I had only one pair of shoes with me, my running sneakers. I was unable to open them up wide enough to fit the brace. Once again, I had to ask my children to bring something. I asked for a different pair of shoes.

Below is the standard foot brace I used.

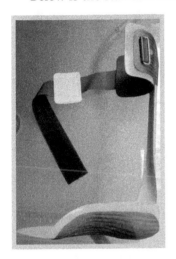

I normally wear size nine and a half shoes. The brace was nearly impossible to get into my shoe, but with help, I managed. What an amazing difference it made walking! The back piece was at a perfect right angle under my foot and up my leg. This completely negated the drop foot problem, at least with walking. My balance was so much better with it on, and that helped build my confidence.

Pictured is my normal nine-and-a-half regular-size shoe and the eleven-and-a-half wide shoe I had to wear with the non-custom brace. I received a custom brace after I left the hospital. Vivian brought me a different pair of shoes that I was able to get the brace into it. When I returned home, I purchased the larger shoe you see below. I went with black shoes to match anything I might wear well enough so as not to draw attention to the brace.

When the doctor fitted me for the custom brace, he made a molded cast of my foot. It was like a plaster of Paris casting; however, this substance dried in about a minute and then was opened off my foot. I was told my custom brace would be ready in a couple of weeks and would make walking much easier. I was also told that I may have to use a walking brace for as long as a year to a year and a half. This depended on how well my drop foot healed, if at all. I tried not to think about that prospect and focused on walking normally and healing my foot.

Simultaneously I worked on strength, balance, walking, speech, and cognitive skills therapy. How well could I communicate? Could I negotiate simple and complex sentences? Could I remember phrases the speech therapist wanted me to repeat or remember? The following are the notes of my speech therapist (ST) from September 12.

SLP Assessment

SLP Assessment
SLUMS administered with a score of 28/30 indicating normal cognitive function. Patient did misunderstand question number 5 on SLUMS initially but corrected his answer independently. Patient had intermittent sips of thin liquid during the treatment session with x1 cough with multiple sips.

The SLUMS test as defined by the *Verywellhealth.com* website:

"The Saint Louis University Mental Status Examination (SLUMS) is a method of screening for Alzheimer's disease and other kinds of dementia. It was designed as an alternative screening test to the widely used Mini-Mental State Examination (MMSE).

The idea was that the MMSE is not as effective at identifying people with very early Alzheimer's symptoms. Sometimes referred to as mild cognitive impairment (MCI) or mild neurocognitive disorder

(MNCD), these symptoms occur as people progress from normal aging to early Alzheimer's disease."[5]

Also, from the *Verywellhealth.com* website comes the scoring table:

"Scoring of the SLUMS Test

The SLUMS consist of 11 items, and measures aspects of cognition that include orientation, short-term memory, calculations, the naming of animals, the clock drawing test, and recognition of geometric figures. It takes approximately seven minutes to administer. Scores range from 0 to 30.

SLUMS scores:

Scores of 27 to 30 are considered normal in a person with a high school education.

Scores between 21 and 26 suggest a mild neurocognitive disorder.

Scores between 0 and 20 indicate dementia."[6]

According to the table, I had scored a 28/30 which placed me nicely in the "normal person" range. I do remember missing one question and did correct myself when I realized what they were asking. I simply had gone too quickly as opposed to not understanding the question. Otherwise, I would have received a higher score.

Christina, my SLP, went on to write:

---

5. https://www.verywellhealth.com/
6. "How Well Does the SLUMS Test Screen for Dementia?" *Verywell Health*, www.verywellhealth.com/the-saint-louis-university-mental-status-examination-98618.

Expression of Ideas and Wants (QI)
4 - Express complex messages without difficulty and with speech that is clear and easy to understand
Understanding Verbal Content (QI)
4 - Understands: Clear complex comprehension without cues or repetitions

Monday September 13th was a very big day for me. For the first time since July 25, I took a shower! It had been over a month and a half since I had done so. I said, "Oh this feels great, I could sit here all day!" I took a shower on what is called a shower bench. Pictured below is my shower bench that was given to me on my return home by my dear friend, Senator John Albers. You use it by placing two feet of the bench in the bathtub and two feet out of it. You then sit on the end and scoot over after swinging your legs in the tub. Then you can sit and comfortably wash. Just washing my hair was such a treat. It's these little things we all take for granted that take on such new wonderful meanings. As you see from the photo, you can raise and lower the seat accordingly. It is extremely sturdy and provides great confidence until you can stand in the shower again.

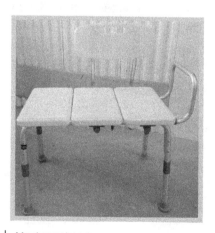

| My shower bench

Tuesday September 14th: I walked 350 feet. I'm increasing each walk and that drove me forward. I continued my work climbing stairs and was getting better at it, but it was certainly challenging.

The next photo is of my neck where my trach was performed. Slowly the wound healed, but it was still open as you can see. There were two levels of healing, as it healed from the inside outward. By this time the inner portion had closed, however, the outer portion had not yet completely closed over. By the time I left the hospital, the wound had completely closed and even the doctors were amazed at how well it had healed. Today it is not easy to see unless I point it out to people.

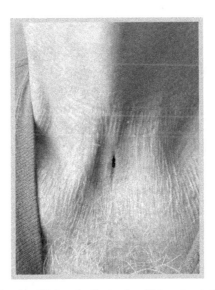

Photo taken Wednesday September 15, two days before I was to leave for home.

I walked every day. The difference was I walked with just a cane now or balanced using the wall if necessary. Significantly, I felt my strength returning to walk again, however I did tire rather quickly, but I did recover quite quickly.

This same day was extremely momentous for a very different

reason. It was the first day since July 25, except for my two ambulance rides, that I went outside. It was a beautiful day. Though I was in a wheelchair, I was outside. The sun shone, and it felt nice and warm. We went to the garden which was where a volunteer tended to all kinds of plants, from tomatoes to flowers. I sat on the side of the raised beds and did a little tending myself. Even now, seven months later, emotions well as I reflect on that day. I felt like a human being again, sitting outside, chatting with the attendant, and asking all kinds of questions about the different plants. I really didn't want to go back inside. I was allowed to take a few plants with me to my room. Sometimes, the littlest things bring the greatest joy.

As it is September 15, it is probably important to point out that I was just two days away from my discharge from the hospital. Part of discharge eligibility comes down to bowel movement and bladder relieving. I was doing just fine on the first, but not so much on the other as I mentioned earlier. I still required some catheterization daily. I could move a small stream on my own, but I was unable to completely empty my bladder. I did require catheterization first thing in the morning and then again about six at night. I increased my daily intake of *Flomax* to two tablets per day in hopes it would alleviate the problem. However, as of the 15th, it was still a "no go." Pardon the pun!

Thursday, September 16, I was able to demonstrate another normal home task. I could do my own laundry, fold it, and put it away. Sounds simple enough, but for me it was a major step forward. Just accomplishing something normal felt so good!

Finally, Friday, September 17 arrived, and I was going home!

"Not so fast!" My doctor said, "Well, we've decided you're not going home today. We think it is best you remain a few days more. You'll head home Wednesday the 22nd."

I can't say I was devastated, but I certainly was disappointed. I just wanted to go home, and now I wasn't going to go for five more days. They basically do not discharge patients over the weekend and not on Mondays because of staffing levels. So Wednesday the 22nd was the new appointed day.

We continued to work on skills such as hand/eye exercises which included hitting a beach ball back and forth, another was to pick up cones off the floor, which required bending over and keeping my balance. I was getting better, and I was able to accomplish both tasks. One of the other exercises I had to do was to reach low and high and touch a pad on the hand of my OT. The purpose of the exercise was to simulate reaching for items such as plates from a cupboard or for pots and pans for cooking. I didn't fully appreciate the exercise until I had returned home and was using those skills to cook dinner for my son Gary, who had come up to stay with me those first five days home. I laughed out loud as I performed the functions and said, "Great job, gang! You really got me ready!"

Another task I was required to performed on the 17th, was getting in and out of a mock car. This was one of the coolest contraptions they have in rehab. The mock car can be raised or lowered depending on what type of vehicle you will most often be using. So, if you have an SUV, for instance, the techs can raise the mock car up. If you have a Ferrari that is low to the ground, they can lower it down and see if you can get in and out. I passed that test easily and it was fun. In addition, I had walked 500 feet to and from the car area, so I moved better and further! Very exciting!

I visited the chapel that day. It was something I had wanted to do since arriving. It was beautiful, and I felt right at home there. It truly was peaceful. For me, being a former seminarian, this was extremely meaningful.

Friday the 17th had come and now gone and even though I didn't go home, I accomplished several good things. Little did I know, Saturday would be a whole different story.

Saturday the 18th arrived without much fanfare, but that changed in a hurry. I had a difficult night on the 17th. I had been trying to urinate using the urine catch bottle, with little success.

Flomax was attempting to work, but it just wasn't happening yet, and it became very painful to try. The urge to go was excruciating.

Having not slept very well, I asked my OT Andrew if I could take a shower, and he readily agreed. That always made me feel better, and I was getting much better at it. Since I was using the same type of shower bench I would have at home, I felt comfortable. Upon returning to my room, I got dressed and sat in my chair, awaiting the PT morning session, which was to begin at 11:30.

It was ten thirty when suddenly, I began to shiver. Not badly at first, but something didn't seem quite right. I'd had little fits of shivering in the past when I would sit in my chair next to the window, so I assumed it was a little cooler over there. I wasn't supposed to get out of the chair and move around the room by myself, but my bed was right next to my chair, and the sweatshirt I wanted was only on the other side of the bed on a chair. I decided I would retrieve it myself, rather than call for a nurse. The sweatshirt was easily reachable from the bed, so I took one step to the bed and then reached for and grabbed the sweatshirt, placing it on myself. I then took one step carefully back to my chair. I then began to shake much harder. After a moment or two, a nurse happened to stick her head in the room and, upon seeing me, turned abruptly on her heels and raced out the door. The next thing I knew, my medical doctor was there, my rehab doctor was there, and I was surrounded by four or five nurses. They all stayed very calm, but something was wrong.

They took my blood pressure, and it was 206/93. My heart rate was at 151 BPM. Those numbers weren't good. They quickly realized that they needed to empty my bladder. As they started the catheterization, my blood pressure quickly went down, and I remember hearing someone say, "Okay, we've got him! Now we need to see what's going on."

They ran all kinds of blood tests on me. I had a urinary tract infection (UTI). UTIs are very common in women, but rather uncommon in men. The UTI was not the only thing going on. I had some sort of bacterial infection, that fortunately, had not yet reached the bloodstream. I was placed on all kinds of antibiotics. They gave me the most powerful and broad reaching they could give me until they figured out what it was that I had. I was once again tied to a drip bag. Because of the incident, I was excused from both my PT and OT sessions for the rest of the day. I was given a sedative to help me relax, and I went to sleep for a while. By the next morning, they had figured out what bacterial infection I had. It turned out it was common enough that it could be treated with oral antibiotics. I wouldn't have to stay longer in the hospital; I would be able to return home on my new appointed date of Wednesday, September 22. That was certainly good news—much better news was that they figured out the problem. Thank goodness I was still in the hospital when it was discovered!

Sunday, September 19, passed quietly but with a new twist. I walked outside for ten minutes. What a wonderful day it was. The sun was out, the birds were singing. It couldn't have been better. Just a few more days, and I'd see my son, who was coming from Florida to be with me, along with my daughter Kristine, who was to drive me home.

Monday, September 20, brought another interesting phenomenon. If you will recall, I had been placed on a PEG tube for feeding while I was in the coma. Though I hadn't used it for several weeks, the tube was still in my stomach. It wasn't particularly a problem, but it was about seven inches long, and I was in favor of it being removed sooner rather than later. It was not scheduled to be removed until September 29th, which was a week after I went home.

On September 20, I heard a strange sound. It was like a gurgle, gurgle, POP; gurgle, gurgle POP! After a minute or two, I realized it was coming from my stomach. I lifted my shirt and watched as the PEG moved, ever so slightly, out of my stomach. I immediately called the nurse's station and asked for someone to drop in as soon as they could. When the nurse came in, I explained what was happening and I said, "I believe the PEG is extracting itself out of me."

A call was then made to another department, and it wasn't long before another nurse came to see me. I explained the situation. She confirmed that was exactly what was happening, and she asked, "Would you like me to remove it now?"

To which I replied, "That would be lovely!"

I looked away, and pop! It was out. She asked if it hurt. I told her not at all. I was so pleased to have one less thing to take home with me, and one less follow-up appointment to make.

I had begun dressing myself without aid, except to place my braced foot in my shoe. The arrangements were being made for me to head home the next day and I was elated. There was one more adventure to deal with though.

Tuesday, September 21, the day before I left, and I had one more test to pass. Even though I had done the mock car already, I had to demonstrate to the lead PT that I could handle getting in and out of a car once more. I walked down the hall toward the elevators. I walked with only my foot brace on, no wheelchair. It had felt like ages since I had last used it. I wasn't using a walker; I hadn't used that or a cane either. I remember being a little wobbly, meaning not as clear-headed as I had been. I chalked it up to the different medications I was on because of the bacterial infection. I reached the elevator and pushed the button to go up.

When the door opened, I instinctively stepped backward one step and then stepped forward toward the elevator door. I hadn't taken a step backward in any of the therapy, and it completely threw me off balance. I started to fall forward.

As I fell, I felt the last two months in the hospital flash before my eyes. I hadn't come close to falling once. I was chastising myself that on my last day before going home I was falling down.

There wasn't anything to grab onto, and I fell forward through the elevator doors. I tried to find anything that would slow me down, but I just kept going down. I threw my hands in front of me to stop myself from slamming into the floor. I barely kissed the floor with the top left side of my forehead. I immediately sat up, which made me feel better right away. The old commercial with the woman who fell rang in my ears, "I've fallen, and I can't get up!"

I needed help to get to my feet, but I stood. I looked at my PT in horror. She instantly and correctly interpreted its meaning.

"It's okay, Jonathan," she said. "You're going to be able to go home tomorrow."

We continued up to the next floor, and I was able to demonstrate the ability to get in and out of the car without help or incident. Later, I was told by my therapists that I fell in slow motion.

When we returned to my room, Dr. Jordan had already ordered a CAT scan to ensure my head was all right. Since I was on an anticoagulation med, they wanted to be sure all was okay. It was, and I was relieved. Once I returned to my room, it was time for another PT session and I said, "Let's practice walking backwards."

Back we went to "Parallel Bar Lane" to practice backward motion. I was determined to get those steps down. We did! Success! I'd spin and turn and step back and then step forward just to prove to myself I could do it.

FINALLY, Wednesday, September 22 arrived. I was going home!

Kristine, Gary, and my son-in-law Evan came to pick me up and sat through the instructions with my doctors, nurses, PT, and OT leads. I had a good breakfast that morning and it was a bitterly sweet day of goodbyes and thank-yous. I promised I'd come back just to bother them all, but under my own steam!

I was given the "Congratulations" document you see below, signed by so many of my therapists, nurses and doctors. You see the notes from so many of these incredible people who helped me recover and never gave up on me!

I was wheeled in a wheelchair for the last time—the only way to leave a hospital—and took photos with my Nurse Valary and Nurse M'balu, who was the head nurse on shift at the time. Below is the photo by Kristine's car with the three of us. I haven't been that weight since high school, and I can guarantee you I wore it much better in those days than I did that day. It didn't matter - I was going home!

CHAPTER 7
THE GOOD, THE BAD, AND THE UGLY
COVID-19 RECOVERY MANUAL

There are so many ways COVID has affected people, and the recovery in all areas can take a while. For some things it could be years for a full recovery, if at all. I will take you through where I am today and tell you what my approach has been since day one of leaving the hospital. I should also point out that not everything is a direct result of COVID. There are areas of health concerns that are best considered COVID-related, but they were a consequence of being very ill. Some of the related effects might also be the result of medications I was prescribed. In addition, there are possible side effects that may or may not be COVID-related, but no one is sure either way. I am not a medical professional, and I am relying on the opinions of those who are, as well as some of my own research in certain areas. I'll attempt to call those out as I go along.

For reference purposes, I am writing these sections early January through May 2022, so it has been three months from my actual hospital release date of September 22, 2021. I'll attempt to outline the time frame for references.

To set the bar regarding my approach, any challenge I faced post-COVID I adopted the attitude "Failure is NOT an option, and NO is not an acceptable answer!"

I'm reminded of the movie *Apollo 13*, starring Tom Hanks. Ed Harris, who portrays Flight Director Gene Kranz, states, "Failure is not an option!" when they worked to bring the Apollo 13 astronauts safely back to Earth.

"No is not an acceptable answer," is all mine. That is what I told my physical therapists, my occupational therapists, and anyone else who even thought about saying "No" to me. I suggest you adopt the same attitude in your own recovery, whether it be from COVID-19 or any other challenging recovery. Keep in mind the "No is not an acceptable answer", related to what I said to myself versus to my attendants. They never said "No" to me, though they might have attempted to set realistic goals. I appreciated their attempt to do so; however, as Spock states to newly anointed Captain Kirk in the newest rendition of the movie *Star Trek*, "I would cite regulation, however I know, you will simply ignore it!" That is precisely what I did. In other words, they gave me timeframes, and I ignored them and pushed to beat those, by a lot.

I said the same thing to my lungs, my drop foot, my balance, and my ability to ever enjoy fun things like dancing again! See it, believe it, pray for it, make it happen, and keep going until it does.

I'm going to provide to you, in the most realistic way I can, the challenges I have faced and still face. When I provide updates on Facebook to all who have followed me, and when anyone asks me how I am doing, as I had mentioned earlier, I will generally say, "Outstanding", or "A little better each day." I will always put the best face on that I can because that is what everyone wants to hear. It isn't that they want it sugarcoated, but they want you to be okay, and they have prayed so hard on your behalf, that they need to hear that it is working.

Well let me tell you - it **is** working! It just might not be as quickly as we want it to be. You are still here for a purpose. You are here to deliver a message, and because of that knowledge, you will succeed. I flat out guarantee it. It may not be exactly as you want it to be, but you will succeed.

So, what have I faced? Let's take one area at a time.

Lungs

One of the areas that COVID targets most is your lungs. It's certainly one of the most dangerous as it affects your ability to breathe, and we need to breathe to live. Welcome back the "Old Man's Friend." Pneumonia, double or not, wreaks havoc on your lungs. It encumbers your ability to take in and deliver oxygen to all areas of your body. When I first came out of the coma, attempting to pull a deep breath was difficult. During rehab, it was rather scary because I wondered if I would ever have any real lung capacity for breathing again. Just being able to stand for a few minutes, or trying to walk with a walker around the square hallway on my floor was a real strain. You'll recall, I first started walking with a walker, and a nurse followed behind me with a wheelchair that I could collapse into, as I tired so easily. It was frightening. My first time out, I was able to walk a whopping eighty feet before I had to sit down and catch my breath. Think about that for a moment. That's not even thirty yards on a football field. Before COVID, I would have sprinted that full-tilt in literally a couple of seconds, even at sixty-five years old. I don't know how long it took me to walk eighty feet with the walker. I was winded, and I was really pushing it to impress my PT. I needed positive reinforcement.

My PTs and OTs were all so wonderful. I have to often dry my eyes when I think of them. They were always so encouraging to me. No matter what I did, they would say, "You are doing so well! Don't be discouraged. I'm so proud of you." They told me I was their best patient. I truly believe they meant it, too. They weren't just saying it. They said they always looked forward to working with me because I would push myself to do better and be faster than expected. I refused to say no. I wanted to impress them and wanted them to want to work with me. They told me that some of their other patients just wouldn't put in the effort, and that bothered them because they wanted the patients to get better. Okay, okay. It didn't hurt that all the female PTs and OTs were young and lovely. I used to kid them that they all looked the same, and behind the masks, I couldn't tell who was who. They were all about five feet seven inches, long and lean, and all had long dark brown hair. They would laugh and say, "I can see why it's difficult." Beyond the kidding part, they were all incredible, knew precisely what they were working to accomplish, and were tremendous professionals. I loved them all. There were a couple guys I got to work with as well, and they were just as outstanding. They all had a wonderful sense of humor and that was important for me and my recovery. I loved that I could make them all laugh. You'll recall from my describing my time at Windy Hill, I told my nurses, "We may be doing a lot of tough work here, but no one said we couldn't have fun while we do it!" I was determined to have fun while I relearned to do all these things that for sixty-five years had been second nature.

Now back to my lungs and my lung-expanding equipment. There are a few devices that can be used to help increase your lung capacity. The photo below is of one of those devices. I call it "The Duck Call" because that's what it looks like to me.

For those who might not be duck hunters, the duck call is just what it sounds like. It is used to pull ducks down to your pond. I've never personally used one, but I certainly have seen them in use. I used to go duck hunting many years ago when I was young. I never took one down. I was a much better shot than I ever let on. I could hit clay pigeons out of the air with ease, but I really didn't want to hit the real ducks. So, I'd shoot, but I hit "mostly tail feathers." As an aside, a book entitled *Mostly Tail Feathers* was published by a company called the Taylor-Powell Press, which had been named for my older sister and me when we were very young. The names Taylor and Powell are family last names and are used as our middle names.

The duck call lung device was designed to increase lung capacity by pulling in as much air as possible and blowing it out through the device. I was instructed to do this ten times in a row, one after the other, and I felt my lungs expanding. I found, early in my rehab, that the times I would use these devices before I had my OT and PT sessions helped my therapy tremendously.

The second device pictured is designed to accomplish the same thing as the duck call, but it does the reverse action. By pulling the air in instead of blowing out, I was supposed to keep the little yellow tube (on the right in the photo) in the middle of the two lines. It was tougher than you might think. That, of course, is the point. Getting the tube to stay in between the lines works the lungs.

There can be a fair amount of lung damage with COVID-19, leading to long-term negative effects. I have been quite fortunate. I was told my lung damage would be permanent; however, my lungs seemed to have healed well. I did find myself having shortness of breath very quickly in my recovery although I bounced back quickly. That was a testimony to the very good shape I was in prior to COVID. It was hard, but I always wanted to move forward and do as much as I could in the half-hour or hour session I had with each therapist. We would add something new each day, both in the Windy Hill rehab and the Cobb Hospital rehab. I thought about my baseline and judged myself against it. Often, I would say, "I couldn't have done that two days ago." The therapist would quickly agree, which confirmed that I was moving forward.

As stated, I was fortunate with my lungs. If you have not been quite as fortunate with your COVID recovery, or whatever challenge you may be facing now, keep pushing, you'll get there. Don't accept that you can't do it. Discouragement is the greatest enemy of progress. Just when you think you can't do something, you will, because you refused not to try.

I've had a few X-rays of my lungs. The first was when I first was admitted to the hospital, The last one was a few days before I left the hospital. My doctor said my lungs were improving, and that was great news. I had been told the lung damage with Covid was irreversible, or at least that was the prevailing thought at the time. As of mid-December, I was back to my 3.3 miles outside at a walk and then finally jogging a bit. Every time I do it, my lungs are stronger, and I can go a little faster each time. Eventually, I will time myself to see how I am doing. I used to keep track of the runs I did daily outside when I was in my twenties. I won't get close to those old times, but I will get faster each day.

Early in my time out of the hospital, I went to the Atlanta Botanical Gardens with a good friend of mine, Gia Nichols. She was determined to get me out and show me I could do things. God bless her determination and energy. Gia is a beautiful girl with long, gorgeous reddish-blonde hair and a smile as big as the great outdoors. She has the energy of ten people combined. I found that trip was very hard for me to do. I had a small energy reserve, and I tired much faster than I would have wanted, but we got out there, nonetheless.

On the evening of January 1, 2022, my son Gary, his girlfriend Jess, my daughter Vivian, her boyfriend Michael, and I went back to the gardens to celebrate the New Year. We had a blast, and I was able to walk all the gardens without any trouble at all! It was so fulfilling! The s'mores we cooked over an open fire were some of the best I'd ever had. I knew I was getting better, and that trip proved it.

Drop Foot

Drop foot is an interesting phenomenon. I was told it is a common side effect of COVID. Drop Foot means the foot will not move in a certain direction or multiple directions. The foot moves in four directions normally. Test the movement with your foot. The foot naturally pushes down as if you were stepping on the gas pedal in your car. It pulls up as you release the gas pedal. Your foot also moves inward and pushes outward. The inward motion is tied to your pushing downward and the outward motion is tied to lifting your foot upward. It makes sense when you move your foot around and notice what muscles are used for each motion. Thinking about it is something we don't tend to do, as it is all so instinctive and natural.

One of my doctors told me drop foot was common because we tend to sit cross-legged. I didn't find that to be the case with me because I never cross my legs. My leg muscles were of such a size (being rather strong) that I never crossed one knee and had it sat upon the other knee. More recently, after an MRI of my back, the spine doctor suggested the herniated discs in my lower back caused the drop foot.

It was interesting the way drop foot affected my right foot. I was able to move the foot inward and outward with little effort, engaging all the base muscles that are tied to both upward and downward motion. I was unable to push downward or lift upward. I was able to move my toes in a gripping fashion. That gave me a bit of hope. There was at least some movement.

I asked when the full motion would return, and the answer was the same one I received twenty-five years earlier when I herniated a disc in my back. The doctor told me the feeling would come back in my leg in days, weeks, months, years, or never. Well, it's been twenty-five years, so I'm going with the "never" prognosis. As it turns out, the same estimate was given to me for the recovery from drop foot. The additional problem, or adding insult to injury, was the drop foot problem was on the same leg and foot that was affected by the disc problem, my right foot. That greatly concerned me. As I lay in bed in my second hospital location at Windy Hill, I continually worked to pull my foot up and push it down. Quite quickly, I was able to push it against the end of the bed. This helped me with my initial rehab work when trying to stand and take a step.

While at Windy Hill, we did some basic rehab work. It was geared toward strengthening so I could stand and eventually walk again. Yes, I said eventually walk again. One of the things you find when you've been in a coma is that for every week you are under, you lose 50% of your strength. Therefore, after week one, I was down to 50% strength. After week two in the coma, I was at 25% of my strength, week three took me down to 12.5% of strength and by the end of week four, I was at 6% of my prior strength. It was all I could do to stand up and not fall over, much less walk. My rehab physical therapists had to pull me up to stand. Due to my weakened condition, my drop foot greatly inhibited my progress. However, being able to push down, even a little bit, helped the recovery process.

Where am I currently with Drop Foot? Over time I worked with two different braces which eventually led to my ability to walk without the braces. However, I still walk a bit like a duck with my right foot. I tend to slap my foot down when I walk because I'm still building the strength for upward motion. I must be careful to be sure I lift my foot. The other effect has been I still bring my right foot inward a little bit if I am a little tired. Therefore, I must be careful not to clip my right foot on my left foot and trip myself. When I first walked without my custom-made foot brace, I would drag my right foot a little bit on the ground, particularly if the ground was slightly raised on the right side. This could also trip me up.

When I'm out and about by myself, I watch what I do and always know my bailout points. I will always be sure there is a grassy area right next to where I am, as best one can, so if I do go down, I will angle myself for it to have the softest landing I can. The last thing I want is to find myself back in the hospital.

At the request of my children, I carry my cell phone with me, just in case I ever do go down and need some help. So, in the end, I'm not allowing my drop foot to hold me back as I continue to build back my foot strength.

PICTURED ABOVE, you see my right foot appears as if it is wrapped. I have a compression sock on along with the brace I was given in rehab at WellStar Cobb Hospital. Amazingly, I could wear one of my regular shoes over the brace. The brace runs up the back of my leg and then under my foot to hold it in place. There is a Velcro strap at the top of the brace, just above the calf, which you can't see in this photo, to hold the brace in place. You can see the strap by referring to the photo earlier in the book.

On Tuesday, February 1, 2022, I had a follow-up visit with my spine doctors to review my MRI taken approximately a month before. It revealed I have four herniated discs in my lower back and three in the neck area. The discs in my neck now seem to contribute to some numbness and restricted movement in the middle finger of both my right and left hands. It is worse in the left hand. It is mostly on the tips of the fingers. I can move my fingers fairly well, but it bears watching.

The concerns of the lower back are central to my balance. Fortunately, most of the numbness in my legs is isolated to the tops of my feet. It would be of greater concern had they affected the bottoms of my feet as that would have more directly affected my balance. Before COVID, the problems had been located only on my right foot and leg. Now it's a concern in both legs. Again, fortunately, the left leg is only minorly affected. However, according to my doctor, a narrowing around my spinal cord, seen in my MRI in the affected areas, may very well have caused the drop foot issue to begin with.

Taste and Smell

This has been a bit frustrating. I enjoy eating, and I enjoy taste as much as anyone. To not be able to completely taste is disappointing. As we all generally know, our ability to taste is tied to our ability to smell. If you have a common cold that has blocked your sinuses, you usually don't taste food as well. With the common cold, eventually breathing will normalize, and taste and smell returns.

It's strange how COVID affected me because taste seems to come and go. I can almost tell when I get up in the morning if I can taste that day. The taste in my mouth is just plain different. Very sweet drinks are not as sweet anymore. Drinks I would have avoided in the past, I now drink so that I can taste something. At times, I can only taste certain ingredients, thus changing the entire taste of the drink. I can taste more on average now, which has been very encouraging. The conventional thought is that my taste and smell should return in six to nine months. I certainly hope that is the case.

I am now a few more months down the road since I originally wrote the above section. As of May 2022, my taste has entirely returned. It was a welcomed occurrence.

Sweating

This may seem very strange. This is one of those areas where it isn't so much a COVID aftermath symptom, as I believe it is more related to the depth of my own illness. I suppose it might be tied to certain medications I've been on as well, but I have been unable to make that connection for certain.

I have been an athlete all my life. I participated in high school soccer all four years. I was a center fullback, as we called the position in those days. Today, it would be more of a sweeper position. I played baseball for two years and was a pitcher. I was good enough to make the team and play. I also played basketball for one year for my high school team. After my high school years, I had just started to play some semi-professional soccer but contracted mononucleosis, and that ended that. I was also, post-college, an assistant varsity coach for a college-level soccer program. So, relatively speaking, I was a very good athlete. I have always been one who worked out quite hard, so I sweat a lot.

A strange side effect I found with COVID was that for the first three months after I left the hospital, I didn't sweat at all when I would work out. I thought that, perhaps, I just wasn't working out hard enough. Certainly, I wasn't doing the workouts to the level I had been before COVID struck. However, I was hiking and running outside, and when in the gym, I was riding the stationary bike for twenty minutes at a good level (roughly eighty-five rpm). I wasn't quite back to the pre-illness, but I was close. I wouldn't sweat at all. Suddenly, three months after being out of the hospital, I started sweating again. When I returned from my outdoor work, my workout shirt and sweaters/sweatshirts were very wet. Any return to normalcy is nice, even sweating. Sweat has always made me feel I had accomplished something good in my workout.

Nails

My fingernails have a line that runs through them in the same position as the nail. This phenomenon is a result of a serious illness. Some others who had a similar illness have told me they had the same symptoms. As my nails grew out, the line moves and is eventually clipped off. The nail above the line was slightly lower than the new nail growth. There were no other problems associated with this symptom, it is merely noticeable.

Of all the medical issues I dealt with, the nails were the least of my worries, but they were worth mentioning. It is just a reminder that my body went through a serious illness.

Hair

I'm always amazed at the things that cause worry versus things that don't. I'm reminded of the old joke about the night Abraham

Lincoln was assassinated at Ford's Theater in Washington, DC. As the joke is told, some reporter asks Mrs. Lincoln, "Besides the assassination, how was the play Mrs. Lincoln?"

I feel like the reporter asking about the play here, but it still bears noting. Hair growth is something I noticed. Normally, I get my haircut every four to five weeks. I had my hair cut about two weeks before COVID hit me. I entered the hospital and was promptly placed in a coma for four weeks, making it six weeks since my last haircut. I then spent four and a half weeks in the rehab hospitals, bringing the total to a solid eleven weeks since my haircut. I had to wait almost another week before my dear friend Brenda Woodhead (on her day off) cut my hair. By the time I got a haircut, I felt like I belonged with the Beatles, the Early Years. I was about ready to start braiding it! Okay, so that's a slight exaggeration, but that's the way it felt and looked to me. I wasn't exaggerating by much.

Although my hair had grown relatively long, it didn't have the fullness it used to have. It reminds me of what my friends who are bald will say, "God made a few perfect heads, the rest he covered with hair." My head is, without question, not one of the perfect ones, so the hair is not only needed, but I could argue it is required. Besides, I like my hair. It may be somewhat strange for a man to admit, but I'm saying it anyway. It has turned a nice silver white as I've approached sixty-six years of age. They tell me it's supposed to be that way.

My friend Brenda said she had a much milder case of COVID herself. It did land her in the hospital for about a week, and she too had lost a good bit of hair. She informed me that many of her female clients who had COVID lost hair in large clumps. Brenda, fortunately, has a lot of beautiful brunette hair, so she was able to lose some and still have stunningly beautiful hair.

In my research, I learned it isn't just on your head one experiences hair loss. It was a whole-body occurrence. I noticed other areas of my body had stopped growing hair, including the back of my neck, which I normally would have to groom between haircuts and some wisps on my back. Pardon the graphic content, but hair growth under my arms seemed to stop completely. For my American female audience, that would be a welcomed occurrence, though I still wouldn't recommend my path to achieving it. For the men, it can be a bit different. For those of us who work out a good bit and prefer it not be there, or bodybuilders who also remove it, this might be a welcomed side effect. Again, it wasn't a good method to achieve the result.

Upset by the loss of hair on my head, I did some research on the subject. As we all know, "If it's on the internet, it must be true," said with tongue in cheek. What I was able to find out (a bit comforting at the time) was that having a high temperature for any period, or a deep illness, causes your body to go through a "shedding" process. I'm quite certain that COVID, to the degree I had it, and being in a coma for four weeks qualified me for membership in the deep illness category. Now, we all lose a bit of hair all the time. Just look at the drain in your bathtub after your next shower. With COVID, some lose it at a much faster rate. I was quite certain that all was for lost. I mean, if I am going to lament something, I won't hold back. I can go all the way to the ridiculous!

As you recall, I'm a former seminarian. I'm supposed to be better at this. My studies indicated to me that we are all made in God's image. I'm quite certain I have heard and read that. I'm guessing you have, too. That means that God must have a sense of humor and all I can say is, "Thank God for God."

I am quite certain, God is sitting up in heaven with head in hands saying, "Jonathan. I love you, son, but really? I saved you from death at least four times and the thing you have chosen to be upset about, with ALL the things you could have chosen from is your HAIR?" Let me just state, I do apologize. "God, thank you for all you have done for me. My only defense is I'm human, I'm stubborn, I'm male and I'm stupid. You get to pick the order."

The good news on all this... my hair is growing back in all the areas I mentioned. So, there is hope. The research I found indicated that the shedding process lasts six to nine months, and then it should reverse and go back to normal. The hair on my head is slowly growing. Now I'm just hopeful it will come back with the great volume it always had, and I know every woman who had to endure this phenomenon hopes for the same.

I wrote the above section back in January or February 2022. I can update it as of May 2022. You will be happy to know my hair has returned and is even thicker than pre-COVID. How nice something is better than before.

Eyes

As a young man, I always had excellent eyesight. I was 20/20 in my right eye and 20/15 in my left. It means I could see very well. This remained with me well into my forties to almost fifty. Generally, eyes do weaken over the years, and this affects most people. So, to reach fifty years and not need any aid was a wonderful thing. Suddenly, I developed what I called "elongus armus" disease. (Spellcheck is having a field day with that one!) The definition of this term I made up is my arms were no longer long enough to hold a book out far enough to be able to read the words. It also signaled I needed reading glasses, at least to a minor degree. Over the years, as I have aged fifty to sixty-six years, I have had to increase the strength from 1.25 to 2.0 magnification. That's not too bad. I never needed glasses to drive or for general walking around activities, only for reading.

Since COVID, this has all changed. I have been told, and I tend to agree, that this is not a direct result of COVID, but rather could be a by-product of it, possibly associated with different medications I was given or am still taking. However, I feel the result has been rather dramatic. I can no longer drive without some aid for my eyes. I have to wear my old 2.0 reading glasses to see clearly during the day while driving. Though I can still see passably well enough to walk around without glasses, I find I do see better if I wear the 2.0 glasses even for that. As I watch TV from my chair at home, I do have to wear my reading glasses - I didn't before COVID. Therefore, as many of my friends do and probably many of you do as well, I have glasses strategically placed all around my home (I get rather frustrated if I need a pair and they aren't where I am quite certain I left them). An interesting side note is I find I see quite well without the glasses when driving at night, though this may be changing, too.

When I am reading, I now must use 3.0 reading glasses. I have yet to see the eye doctor about what is truly affecting my eyes and what, if anything, can be done about it. There are so many types of corrective laser surgeries that might be able to help. My close friend, Russ Fawcett, is now ninety-seven years old. A couple of years ago, he had some work done on his eyes and now he doesn't need any aid for seeing, even at ninety-seven! Quite amazing!

Voice and Tracheotomy

As I talked about in the section of my hospital coma period and during my rehab, my voice was an issue on many levels. I was originally put on a ventilator; then, when I was briefly brought out of the medically induced coma, you recall, I proceeded to rip the vent out of my own throat. I'm sure that day I was far from their favorite patient. I don't recall any of that, and I'm certainly glad I don't! I can imagine I was quite frightened by it. Having a tube running down your throat is not a pleasant thought, no matter what the reason. I'm also quite certain I was having an extremely difficult time breathing with any sense of normalcy.

One of the last resorts to assist breathing was to perform a tracheotomy. According to Johns Hopkins Medicine, a *"Tracheotomy or tracheostomy is an opening surgically created through the neck into the trachea (windpipe) to allow direct access to the breathing tube and is commonly done in an operating room under general anesthesia."*[1] I spoke at length about the ventilator and tracheostomy in early sections, so I won't repeat that here. Go back and take a second look at that discussion if you need to.

The chief concern after I came off the trach was the thought that I might be forcing too hard to speak. The doctors were afraid I might damage my throat and vocal cords. Although my ability to speak seems fine, there is an area that has been affected regarding my voice: my ability to sing (or rather, my now- somewhat-limited ability to sing). I know this may seem a rather minor thing, and compared to not having survived it is a small thing. Just noting it as an area that has been affected.

When I was in high school, I was elected to the area's All-State Chorus. It was something I was very proud of. I gave my first solo performance in fifth grade, if memory serves. "The Christmas Song" written by Robert Wells and Mel Torme in 1945, a classic Christmas song. "Chestnuts roasting on an open fire" is the opening line if you are struggling to place the song. I also performed in high school dramatics and singing was included in the musicals we performed. I sang in the chorus throughout high school, and I was president of the Senior Chorus during my senior year of high school. I sang with our church choir as well. One of

---

1. https://www.hopkinsmedicine.org
   Others
   Find any Answer
   https://findanyanswer.com
   Merriam Webster Dictionary
   https://www.merriam-webster.com/
   Harvard Health Publishing
   https://www.health.harvard.edu/category/common-conditions
   The Oxford English Dictionary
   https://www.oed.com/?tl=true

my favorite memories was singing with my stepmother in our church choir. She was always a tremendous singer possessing an extremely beautiful voice, although she would disagree. She would be incorrect on that. Mom is now ninety-nine years old and still loves her opera. Music and singing have always been something I loved. I was a natural tenor/baritone and could go to bass if pressed hard enough.

I still love to sing in church and that is where I have felt I can hear my best voice. Since COVID and the trach experience, my voice is no longer what it was. I can still sing a bit, but I have found, at least so far, it is not as easy as it always had been, and I certainly cannot hit the notes I could always hit before. This saddens me.

With all that said, I am pleased and blessed that I can still speak. It could have been hurt far worse. Being a public speaker for many years, the inability to speak well would have been devastating and would have adversely affected my livelihood. Having a tracheotomy will have various effects on the patient, I believe I was blessed.

Finding Words or "COVID Brain Fog"

You may find this section title a little puzzling. It isn't uncommon that when we get longer in the tooth, our ability to recall is sometimes compromised. COVID also seems to be a contributor to what some have deemed "COVID brain."

According to Yale Medicine, COVID-19 or Long COVID has left people with an inability to clearly think, they are forgetful, they can't focus, and/or they have trouble finding the right words in a conversation. For most, studies are finding the symptoms go away with time, but in a few people, there are lasting effects. In March 2024, an estimated 7% of adults in the US (about seventeen million people) reported having Long COVID, and almost half of those people reported having memory issues.[2]

When I say, "I'm having trouble finding words," what I mean is, I can't readily find words in conversation that normally would have been on the tip of my tongue. This may seem like a little thing, but it's significant when most of your livelihood is based on your ability to speak extemporaneously.

As I have had conversations with others who have dealt with COVID at all different levels, the term that is often used is, "fog" or "brain fog" and now "COVID fog." This tends to make me think that it is more of a COVID aftermath than it is an interesting coincidental occurrence. Let me give you an example. My friend Brenda told me that she has the same problem. Her example will amplify the concern. It's not specifically larger compound words that one has trouble with. Brenda related to me that she couldn't find the word "bread" just a day or two before in a conversation she was having. I'm finding this is occurring more and more myself. I'll be speaking and a very simple word just isn't there, and the person I'm speaking with will have to supply the word to me. This is extremely maddening and unnerving. It really is quite different from the feeling you have when you are in the shower and wonder if you have washed your hair or not yet. We laugh at ourselves at this type of occurrence, as we all do this and know that the only reason is we were so lost in thought on some other topic that we "browned out" on the shampoo part. Losing words is completely different, and honestly, it's a bit scary. No one wants to appear the fool, and that is exactly what you feel like when this happens to you.

I had the honor of laying wreaths at the foot of war veteran graves on December 18, 2021, as part of a program called Wreaths

---

2. "Long COVID Brain Fog: What It Is and How to Manage It." *Yale Medicine*, www.yalemedicine.org/news/how-to-manage-long-covid-brain-fog. Accessed 15 June 2024.

Across America. This year we served in the pouring rain and still had fifty to sixty volunteers there to take part in this great honor. When we finished, a few of us went to a wonderful eating establishment called *Lucky's* in Roswell, Georgia. *Lucky's* is named for one of the dogs of the owner, Diane Geyer, who has been a friend of mine for twenty years now. They have the best burgers!

I was seated with three gents, Tony Lay, Ron Cowan, and Jim Davis who are members of one of the local VFW posts. All three are exemplary individuals for whom I have great affection and respect. As the four of us sat enjoying our burgers, we got to talking about our COVID experiences. All three of these gentlemen are approximately ten years my senior. Aware of my struggle with COVID, they related their own experiences, and there was a common thread in their stories. They all felt that post-COVID they had problems with their short-term memory. They each stated it had become obvious to them since COVID. It will be interesting to follow as time passes to see if this is something that clears itself or remains long-term. As you can well imagine, I'm hopeful it will wane over time.

Heart and Blood Pressure

One of the other main areas of concern with COVID involves heart and blood pressure-related problems. I have not had a major problem with my heart per se.

My children were informed that I may have had a very mild heart attack while I was in the coma. My heart appears to have stayed strong, evidenced by the fact I can go out and continually shorten my time in my 3.3-mile outdoor workouts and my ability to raise the bar on my bike workouts at the gym. I did take a small dose of aspirin each morning, 81 mg, for months after my release.

My blood pressure is a little different story. I have been on a rather low dosage of blood pressure meds for several years. My blood pressure would always be in a good range. When I was in the hospital, I used to have some fun guessing what my blood pressure would register as. My nurses and I always said that if I ever hit the numbers exactly, we would play the numbers on the lottery. I was always VERY close as it became very predictable. I would generally run 125/82 or thereabout. I remember one time registering at 116/74. I felt rather good about that. As I recall, I wasn't on any medications at that point.

Since I have come out of the hospital, my blood pressure has been running 155/90. We then doubled my medication to find it only dropping to 144/88. Neither of these numbers is terrible, but it is certainly not where I had been or would prefer to be. I've never felt faint or anything close to something I would be concerned about. I'm just hopeful it remains such.

Blood Clots

One of the biggest areas of concern related to COVID has been blood clots. They can cause all kinds of problems from strokes to death. They are nothing to be toyed with. When I was first brought into the hospital on July 25, 2021, it was found that I had a blood clot in my lower left calf. I was immediately placed on Eliquis for three months. The final month was the first month I was out of the hospital. I have not had a problem since the initial discovery of the clot; however, I have been placed on a very low (81 mg.) dosage of aspirin, which I take daily in the morning.

I have several pairs of compression socks I often wear to ensure clots are not a problem in the future. There are so many different types of compression sock levels. They even have some rather colorful options you can choose from.

As of this updated writing to the above, no longer am I required to wear compression socks, nor do I take aspirin. Any time I have been able to cut back on any medication is a cause for celebration for me.

Nerve Damage

COVID has been known to attack your nervous system. I was not spared in this area. As I have mentioned in earlier sections, my prior underlying problem was the loss of feeling in my right leg due to a herniated disc in my lower back. Even though I had disc surgery, the feeling never came back, nor the full use. Before COVID, because of the disc problem, I only had the use of ¾ of my right leg. I don't have a right calf anymore and haven't for twenty-five years. It just simply isn't there. So, what does that mean? It means I eventually had to give up playing basketball and golf as I have little push-off on that leg.

I have been down the nervous system road before, and I know what it feels like when it happens. Many of you reading this now may have had sciatica issues in your past as well and you know when it hits because it hurts, and it hurts bad! Pain shoots down your leg. As I lay in my bed at Cobb Hospital, a week before my stay there was through, I started getting shooting pains down my left leg. This was particularly concerning as I knew exactly what was happening, and I knew it wasn't good. I would try to move myself in the bed to relieve the pain and it would subside for a while. The concern was I knew how it had already affected my right leg and now I might have to face the same in my left. I was already having a difficult time standing and walking as it was. What if I now lose ability in both legs? Will I have to use a cane, a walker, or possibly, a wheelchair to get around the rest of my life? These are the thoughts that flooded my consciousness. They keep pushing their way in.

So, what was happening with my left leg? The latest MRI revealed four herniated discs in my lumbar area and three more in my neck area. Where did all of this come from? Is it the result of being thrown from horses when I was much younger? Are they from improper form when lifting weights for so many years? Is it somehow the result of COVID? The jury is still out. There is a line the width of a finger down my left leg that is numb. Also, the top of my left foot is numb. Fortunately, it doesn't bother me, and I don't even feel it generally unless I specifically run my hand over the area.

Unfortunately, the neck herniated discs are now affecting my hands. This started after I left the hospital and came home. It started to be far more prevalent in my right hand in general, however over time, it has moved more to my left hand. I can easily move all my fingers; the feeling is not completely normal. The largest effect is when I sleep. When I wake up in the middle of the night, I must drop my arms down to my sides for a minute to get all the feeling back in both hands. It doesn't affect my arms at all, only my hands, or my fingers. It seems to directly correlate to the angle of my neck in bed.

I am being evaluated periodically now to see what the best course of action is for treatment. What I hope to avoid is any type of surgery.

Balance and Strength

January 24, 2022, was a red-letter day for balance! I fell twice! Aside from the one time I had fallen in the hospital the day before I was finally to go home, I had not fallen at all. In four months of being home, I hadn't had a problem. Oh, I had a couple of "catch myself moments," meaning I had to make a quick step to keep my balance and then pat myself on the back for having done so. In truth, those "catch myself moments" were a couple of "whew" moments that I had not taken a fall. It reinforced my thought that I was doing fairly well with my balance.

January 24 was different. I was out to have lunch with my dear friend Russ Fawcett. He'd invited me out to catch up. We had been going to brunch every Sunday after church since I came out of the hospital. It began during the time I thought I wasn't supposed to drive. Once I found out I could drive again, we decided to ignore that fact, and he came and got me every Sunday and then returned me home after a wonderful brunch somewhere. Our church outing ended just before Christmas time for a very good reason. I'll come back to the January 24th story in just a moment.

During the 2021 holidays, I was first asked to, and then just continued to, drive another church member to church. My dear friend Andi Hussing didn't have a vehicle and needed a little aid to reach the church. Another church member, who preferred to remain anonymous, was paying someone else to get Andi to church and then return her at its conclusion. However, this individual, for some reason decided not to show. Another dear friend Becky Stout, also from Roswell Presbyterian, recommended that I pick up the duty (honor) of getting Andi there. It was helpful for me to pick up a few dollars and I knew Andi well, so it was fun to catch up with her. Once the benefactor finished what they wanted to do, I just continued to take care of it on my own. I can't think of a better way to spend a little time than taking someone to services, and to take Andi is truly an honor. We chatter back and forth like a couple of church mice. She's a doll!

On January 24, Russ picked me up, and off we tootled to downtown Roswell. We found a parking space for handicapped parking on the side street from the entrance to the restaurant. At 97, Russ had secured a permanent handicapped parking permit. I was given a temporary one. We began the short trek up the side street to the entrance. Unfortunately, there was no walk-up ramp to reach the sidewalk. The walk-up ramp was at the corner up the street. So, rather than walk up the street, we decide to step over the curb onto the sidewalk. Russ was a little unstable that day, so I offered a hand, which he gladly accepted. Unfortunately, I wasn't in the perfect angle to aid him, and he bulled ahead before I could get into position. Sadly, he tripped on the curb and went down. I was able to grab him, and he fell in slow motion as I, in essence, lay him down. However, I also went down and fortunately caught myself just in time before I hit the side of the road. As it was happening, I had a flashback to when I had fallen in the hospital. I could see the pavement coming toward me, almost in slow motion, as I had seen the floor of the elevator coming at me in the hospital. The difference this time was, I was able to stop myself before I hit the payment with my face or head. It was amazing the things that ran through my mind as I fell. I feared would I break something, a hand, or wrist, would I knock myself out or cut my head open? Had Russ been hurt in any way? All these horror thoughts went through my conscience as I was falling. Fortunately, both Russ and I were fine. He was lying on the sidewalk and I on the pavement on the street. We were just far enough from the corner that no one saw us go down, or at least that's the story I'm sticking with. Either way, no one came to our rescue. I was able to get up and then help Russ get up. After the obligatory queries of, "Are you all right, anything broken or cut?" to each other, we determined we were both fine and there was no way we were going to let a good fall get in the way of a great lunch. So off we went!

Above are Russ and I at an Atlanta Hawks game. Russ had been a special guest invitee for the Hawks salute to Veterans Night. Russ was ninety-six at the time and was representing the WWII veterans. I was honored to take him.

My second encounter happened later that day after I had returned to my daughter Kristine's home in Canton. I had been staying up there while she and Evan were off on a final vacation before becoming parents. I was assigned to take care of the dogs, Kit and Pan. Kit, now six years old, is half Shiba Inu and half Pomeranian. Pan, approximately a year old, is a full Shiba Inu. They aren't big dogs by any means; however, they are very strong dogs and very active. I took them out to the yard and run them as much as possible for exercise. They loved to play catch with their tennis balls of all colors. Though I would much prefer to walk them on long walks as I used to do with Kit, I had to be careful not to be pulled down. They are on forty-foot lines that give them lots of room to run and play. As sometimes happens, the ball I threw landed just out of their reach and then GrandPaw, as I'm referred to, had to fetch the ball himself. Though I attempted to be as careful as possible not to get tangled up in the lines, I got tangled up in the lines and down I went. This time I went down on soft grass and not pavement; and to further aid my fall, I fell a bit uphill, shortening the fall.

Above are Pan on the left and Kit on the right. I'm their "GrandPaw".

I managed to survive both falls, or all three if we include the one in the hospital, without harm. The first fall taught me I wasn't fully prepared to make all moves. The second two taught me though I'm stronger, I'm not fully recovered strength-wise or balance-wise yet. I still have a good way to go.

COVID will affect everyone differently in the areas of strength and balance. It depends on how deeply or seriously you had it. Being in a coma for four weeks deeply affected me. I have already outlined the loss of strength figures each week in the coma, so I won't go through that again. Suffice it to say, I had very little strength to work with at the start. As I have indicated earlier in the book, I had lost fifty lbs. Much of this weight loss was in muscle and fat. My skin was hanging off me. When I looked in the mirror, I no longer was a sixty-five-year-old male who looked more like the early fifties to most. I was a sixty-five-year-old male who looked ninety-five years old. It was all I could do not to cry when I saw what I had become. I had put in so much time and effort to be healthy.

I was informed that I had lost more strength in my lower body versus my upper body. Balance is the key. So many little muscles through your lower legs and feet along with the bulky muscles of the thighs and buttocks are used in so many ways. I had no idea any of this was happening until I was forced to concentrate on every little muscle to make it all work. Your Feet sends so many messages to the brain regarding what is beneath you. Not having all the little muscles in my feet to work with and then closing my eyes, for instance, in the shower while washing and rinsing my hair, I realized all the information with regard to balance that was coming from my feet alone. I didn't understand how much until I was relying on those messages to stand and not fall over. When I opened my eyes, immediately more information was delivered to my brain with regard to balance because I was now able to see all around me and everything was no longer reliant on my feet alone. What a huge difference it made.

When we move from merely standing to walking or running, the information that needs to be processed is coming in much faster the faster you go. Consider the information sent when the ground you are on is not flat, as a sidewalk, path or roadbed would be. Imagine you are now hiking a trail in the woods, and you have roots and stones to contend with. Now consider what happens when it's raining, or the ground is simply soft or muddy because it has rained. Throw in a hill or a pothole or depression of any sort in the ground and the whole scenario is different. When you are young and have no physical liabilities to contend with, these things appear minuscule on the surface (pun intended) but in fact, they can present real challenges and, quite literally, danger if you are struggling with your balance. The greatest fear I faced was falling. It was the greatest fear in the hospital, and it continued to be the greatest fear when I left. Particularly early on, if I go down, the chances I'd be back in the hospital are very high. Therefore, I work to avoid that at all costs.

I had no real idea when I was still in the hospital that my

strength was almost completely gone. What I did comprehend was I had a difficult time talking and it took me a bit to sit up in bed, but I would kind of rock myself up, or attempt to grab something that would help me pull myself up. What I didn't fully comprehend was just how weak I was because I had a bed that moved up and down at the push of a button and that got me started. One can't fully understand until one physically must try to stand and find they can't. Attempting to walk can be the most frightening thing one can imagine because there is no strength to do it, and one fears they are going to fall without someone being right there to catch them or hold their belt. It's a long process to get strength back. Since I have already relayed to you what they had me do to start the process of building back while I was in the hospital, I won't go into it again here. What we will discuss is what I had to do on my own.

First, I had to establish a baseline to work from. I had moved so far backwards; it was discouraging at first. That was so until I reminded myself of something I always say, "You can't take the second step until you've taken the first."

One of my first bright spot days, during physical therapy as an out-patient, was when I asked my lead PT doctor, Dr. Brian when I could go back to the gym. His response was, "Yesterday!" I couldn't have been happier. I was now going to start the process of real strength recovery. Little did I know I would have so far to go.

Regarding strength and balance, which go together, I feel it necessary to make some comments about aids used for balance. There are four basic aids that can be employed to help with balance as you regain your strength. The first is the wheelchair, employed when there is just not enough strength yet in the legs for any other device to be used. This helps build upper body strength, targeting the arms. It can also aid lung recovery. When a body moves faster in the chair the heart rate goes up, which is good for the heart and increases the breathing rate, thus pulling in more air and expanding the lungs. It might not seem on the surface that it is helping your balance. It isn't directly, but indirectly it is building the support areas around walking again and thus indirectly helping regain balance.

The walker provides direct support for balance as it aids confidence to take steps. They are strong and give four additional legs for support. Sometimes bright yellow tennis balls are placed on their front feet to help them move more smoothly across floors.

Another tool is the cane. It is used either when progressing from a walker until one can walk unassisted. The nice thing about canes is they come in varieties that help the psyche while being an aid. I was determined not to have to use a cane; however, I wasn't going to let vanity get in the way of my safety or my progress.

Having been in such great shape before COVID has made the recovery much easier in some respects and much harder in others. Easier, because I had a good base of muscle memory to work from; harder, because I kept feeling I should be so much further along. To be blunt, I honestly didn't know how far I had slipped. Notes in my medical charts kept repeating that I didn't understand my disabilities. I didn't perceive myself as being in such peril. I very often must replay the words of encouragement from my PTs, both in the hospital and out. "Jonathan, you are doing great, so much further than the others I work with. Jonathan don't be discouraged; I'm purposely giving you very hard things to do. Just keep going, keep doing everything you have been doing."

A phrase I've often heard is, "Getting older isn't for the faint of heart." When I was young and full of sass, I thought, "I'll never get old, I'll never be like that. I work out too hard, I eat right, I take care of my health." And suddenly, in the blink of an eye, I was there.

In the critically acclaimed movie *On Golden Pond*, Henry Fonda and Katherine Hepburn portray an elderly couple visited by their daughter, portrayed by Jane Fonda. The father and daughter have been estranged for some time. The daughter leaves her thirteen-year-old stepson with them for the summer. The boy and Henry Fonda's character form an endearing friendship, but not before going through some very rough spots. At one point, Fonda's character snaps at the boy yet again, and the boy asks Katherine Hepburn's character, "Why does he have to do that?" Hepburn responds, and I paraphrase here a bit, "He's an old lion, sometimes he just has to roar to show he still can."

Many years ago, I asked my then-sixty-year-old adopted mom, Vivian Smith Crooks, what it was like to be sixty years old. She smiled and said, "I don't feel any different today than I did when I was thirty. I just can't do all the same things." How prophetic those words were. At sixty-six, I reflect on those words. How true they became for me post-COVID. Though I wasn't at sixty as I was at thirty, I still could do many things. Now, I am concerned about walking. What must I look like? Am I now an old man? Can I walk up that mounded hill, can I climb that embankment, can I take that path at the park? Maybe not today, but as I told you earlier, I will not accept "No" for an answer.

Perhaps you read this book now because you have had a similar experience as I, whether it was COVID or some other illness. Either way, we are now connected and will be forever going forward. Even though we are not physically together, I'll keep you in my prayers and ask you to do the same for me. Always remember, you can't take step two until you have taken step one, so keep stepping, and by God, keep roaring!!

Why Am I Still Here?

At some point, in every person's life, we find ourselves contemplating the meaning of life. "Why are we here?" Some people seem to have found their calling. They are doing exactly what they have wanted to do from the time they were young children. My children have been that way.

Vivian has always wanted to work with animals. She enjoys

them far more than people, and I can't say I blame her. For the most part, she has been able to do this work and continues to strive to have it be more central for her. She has worked for SeaWorld, Orlando on their rescue team. To date, that has been her most rewarding experience. COVID pushed her out of that. It's a very difficult field to break into and she had made it. She volunteers for the Georgia Aquarium, which keeps her hand in the field. Perhaps one day she will be working for the Georgia Aquarium full-time.

Kristine, from the time I can remember, has wanted to be in law enforcement. She came up through the Explorers program while she lived in Florida. She rose to the second-best shot in her Explorers group. She has worked in the field as a deputy sheriff and works as a probation officer now.

Gary is very definitely the technology kid in the family. He has run his own worldwide server since he was fifteen. He's always been great on computers, and anything associated with them. He works in computing technology.

I have wanted to be just about everything at one time or another. I'm one of those jack-of-all-trades, master-of-none people. I've worked in higher education, telecommunications, datacom, merchandising, sales and marketing, politics, and the list goes on. I'd rise to the top of whatever I was doing and then get bored. I never found what or where I should be. My parents always thought I should have been a history teacher. They were most likely correct.

What does all this come down to? Simple... purpose. Yes, purpose. My meaning of life. Why am I here? If I had passed away in August 2021, I wonder what my legacy would have been. How would I have been remembered? Have you spent much time pondering the question for yourself? If you were not to make it through one more day, what would people remember you for? I am still unsure about my answers. Mister High Average, remember? I have often said to those who might not remember me at first glance, "That's all right, I'm not that memorable." They will often immediately disagree with me. I'm very grateful for that. Finding your purpose in life is not an easy task, but it is an important one.

Almost everyone holding this book has lost someone to COVID, or knows someone who did. Every time I speak to people about my journey, I inevitably meet someone who has lost someone. Sometimes we'll pray together over that person lost, and most often we share memories about them. I have had the honor of having friends call me and ask me to speak to someone who has either come through a rough time with COVID who wants to know what I have done to cope or endure.

I can't help but ask myself, "Why me?" There just isn't anything special about me that I should be here and others are not. Virtually every time I voice this question aloud, I am met with a response like, "You have been kept here for a purpose." I know that, too. But finding that purpose is the hard part. I strive to be open to hear, see, and feel where I am to be and to see how I can help and where I can be of comfort. Perhaps that is my purpose. Perhaps this book and its messages are my purpose. Perhaps I will never fully know why I was saved when so many others were not. Then I ponder: is it truly important that I know specifically why or is it only truly important that I know there *is* a reason. When I move from this place to the next, whatever that is, wherever that is, perhaps then it will be revealed to me. Perhaps then I will have a true understanding.

Information

No one, and I mean no one, told me I had been in a coma for an entire month! Or at least I didn't remember anyone telling me I had been. My children didn't tell me, my doctors didn't tell me, and my nurses didn't tell me. At least not that sunk into me if I had heard it. It was the huge whiteboard at the end of my bed on the wall opposite me that "told" me when it finally did sink in. It had such a profound effect on me that the feeling revisited me in January 2022.

January 19, 2022, I walked back into the hospital I had spent that month in a coma to have my first colonoscopy. It was a bit surreal for me to enter the same hospital I had started my COVID journey in. When I came out from under the anesthesia, the first thing I asked the attending nurse was, "What time is it and what is the date?" I proceeded to tell the nurse that the last time I went under anesthesia there, I woke up a month later. I was pleased to be told it was only about forty minutes later than the last time I saw a clock before going under and the date was still January 19, 2022. I was extremely relieved. The attending nurse chuckled, seeing the humor in it all.

My advice is to keep an eye on your medications and track the side effects. That information may be key to how your body reacts down the road.

On January 20, 2022, I had my doctor check some reddish spots on my left hand. As it turned out, they were merely eczema, but the collateral conversation was interesting. I was informed the doctor suspected I had a heart attack during my coma. It was mild, according to the medical charts; however, I didn't recall hearing I had possibly had one. My children subsequently told me that it had been mentioned (like a sidenote) at an update meeting while I was still in the coma. They said the doctor mentioned it as they walked out the door. The notes in the cardiologist's records indicated that I had sustained one. There was no real damage, so no one seemed too concerned. I still felt the information was worthy of notifying the patient, mild or otherwise.

Swelling

Swelling was and continues to be part of my journey. The photo below (shown earlier in the chapter) shows swelling in my left foot.

I had to wear a compression sock on that leg, similar to the one you see on my right foot in the photo for quite some time. The left leg is the one that had the blood clot in it when I first came to the hospital. Movement and general use of my legs again is what eventually made the swelling go away.

Atrial Fibrillation - Heart

Since I was fifteen, I have been told about a little blip in my heartbeat. As I've had it for at least fifty years now, I don't pay much attention to it when it's mentioned. However, all doctors want to look at it in a stress test. After I realized they thought I might have had the heart incident while in the coma, I decided it might be best to take a look at my heart in a stress test. On Friday February 11, 2022, I went in for the test.

While taking the treadmill test, the technician said, "Oh!" which sounded like a surgeon saying, "Oops!" in the middle of an operation. "What's wrong?" I asked, somewhat afraid of the answer. She answered, "Well, you start going up to where we need you to be and then you just immediately recover down to 81 percent!" That sounded familiar; it is something the PTs told me while recovering.

The technician increased the incline and the speed of the treadmill until I felt like a mountain goat! Finally, she said, "Okay, we got it!" That was music to my ears at that point. The notes in my medical chart post-test indicated all was well. I suppose for me the best test would have been the type where they insert dye and watch it go through all the necessary portals; but for now, I'll take this one as a good thing.

Several weeks later I visited my cardiologist for the follow-up to the stress test. Though my stress test had gone extremely well, they had found a "flutter" in my heart.

Atrial fibrillation or heart flutter "is an irregular and often very rapid heart rhythm. An irregular heart rhythm is called an arrhythmia," according to the Mayo Clinic.[3]

When I met with my cardiovascular doctor, Dr. Achtchi, he said I had not sustained a heart attack, mild or otherwise, while in the coma (as previously feared). That was extremely good news. However, I required an outpatient surgery to fix "the flutter" and get my heart back in rhythm.

Dr. Kooshkabadi performed a procedure that placed my heart back into a regular rhythm. I have a deep appreciation for both my doctors, whom I have grown very fond of!

The Good

This update is from January 23, 2022. I have been out of the hospital for four months. My last blood pressure reading was from Wednesday January 19, 2022, after the baseline colonoscopy. I'm happy to report that everything was excellent - no polyps! On top of that, my blood pressure reading was 127/82, my heart rate was 77 beats per minute, and I've had it down to 66 beats per minute on occasion. My oxygen level was running 99 to 100. Can't get better than that.

My balance is getting better all the time. It's nice to get up at night to find the bathroom and feel very confident making my way through the dark and not be concerned about falling. I might be a

---

3. "Atrial Fibrillation." *Mayo Clinic*, Mayo Foundation for Medical Education and Research, 8 Mar. 2024, www.mayoclinic.org/diseases-conditions/atrial-fibrillation/symptoms-causes/syc-20350624.

little stiff when I stand up after sitting for a long period, but once I straighten, I move quite well. My drop foot is still there to a degree, but it is getting better all the time.

I am no longer required to wear the foot brace, and I can walk and drive fine without it. Being able to wear all my old shoes again is a real pleasure. The motion in my foot is increasing all the time.

MY WORKOUTS at the gym have come light years from where I began. I've moved from riding just a couple of minutes on the bike at level four to twenty minutes at a strong pace on level eight. Many of my weight stations have increased in the weight category. In most cases, I'm within twenty pounds of where I was before COVID.

I am back to my 3.3-mile hike/jogs outside again, though not as fast yet as I used to do, but it's still moving in the correct direction, so we'll count it as a win. I won't be running any marathons soon, but I didn't run them before, either.

My wind is good! I can pull in a full lung capacity of air, and that is extremely satisfying. I may not yet walk as fast as I would like, and I can still get a little winded at times, but I am way ahead of where I was. I'm now thinking of moving back into one of my old, side fun jobs leading the Roswell Ghost Tours. They have always been great fun, and I miss them and the people I work with. I was concerned about walking stairs without any railings, but even that has subsided. If you are ever in our city of Roswell, GA, come see us! David Wood, the owner, is a great guy, and he'll take care of you. If I'm leading, I'd love to meet you!!

My taste and smell are coming back. There are very few days now where it doesn't seem to be there. I have been told by many that the taste and smell normally come back in three to six months. My daughter Vivian, who had a very mild case of COVID, still complains about not having her taste back, and it has been a good seven months for her at the time of this writing.

My nails have almost completely grown out, removing the line that ran through each of them. It's nice to see them back to normal.

My hair is also coming back very well now. Just this morning, February 5, 2022, I felt that it was getting thicker again. I remember when there was a gap in the part of my hair if I didn't make the part go away. I can finally feel the difference. It's not quite as full as it always was, but it is getting there. I also felt little bumps on the back of my head. It almost felt like pimples or even small scabs. They are all but gone now, and the hair feels soft and smooth again. As of February 9, I no longer feel the bumps.

In summary, I'm coming back, more and more to normal than I have been in a long while. I keep increasing my weights at the gym, increasing the difficulty level of my bike rides, and feeling more and more like my old self. My hikes and jogs are getting closer to my old hikes and runs.

The next thing will be to get back on the dance floor. I can say I've been there once so far, with my dear friend Kimberly Giordano on January 11. It felt wonderful to move to the music again, particularly with such a beautiful long-time friend.

I attribute my recovery to my attitude, previous health, the faith of my friends and family, and the angels who were sent. Don't take "No" for an answer; there is hope, and there are miracles in store for those who seek them.

CHAPTER 8
THE INEVITABLE QUESTIONS

Since my survival through this ordeal, there have been a few inevitable questions put to me quite often, such as, "Now that you know what you know, would you have done anything differently?"

For thirty-some-odd years, I have delivered historical talks. I have also conducted first-person interpretations for nearly as long. First-person interpretations involve portraying someone from the past as the person in character. When I am playing that part, I am to act as that person and restrict myself to what that person would know at that time. For clarification purposes, let me relate a story.

Many years ago in Virginia, I was portraying a gentleman by the name of Theodorick Lee. He was an uncle of Robert E. Lee. The Lees were like the Kennedys of the 1700s. Theodorick's eldest brother, Henry, was known as Light Horse Harry Lee. He was the ninth governor of Virginia. He also was George Washington's calvary brigadier general and the person who described George Washington at Washington's funeral as "First in War, First in Peace and First in the Hearts of His Countrymen." Theodorick was also the younger brother of Richard Bland Lee, who was the first Congressman from northern Virginia. I portrayed Theodorick at his brother Richard's home for a Christmas event almost thirty-five years ago. I was chatting with a woman who wanted to talk about Thomas Jefferson. Now, you must understand we were portraying the year 1799. The person I was engaging with was talking about Jefferson and his famed University of Virginia, which he had founded. I kept saying I was very familiar with Mr. Jefferson but was not familiar with the university to which she spoke. After a while, she was a bit frustrated with me. I finally broke character (which is a big no-no in first-person interpretations), and I picked up my cane and removed my hat. I reminded her that we were portraying 1799. Jefferson hadn't even been president yet, and the University of Virginia had not yet been founded; it wasn't founded until 1819, a full twenty years in the future. With that explanation, she understood and said with a big smile, "I get it now!" I was then able to go back into character, and we had a lovely chat.

CONCERNING COVID, "What might I have done differently?" The question has no bearing in reality. I didn't know what was to happen in the future.

There is a wonderful line at the end of the movie *Sully*, starring Tom Hanks. Hanks portrays pilot "Sully" Sullenberger, who landed an Airbus 360 with 150 passengers and five crew members in the Hudson River on January 15, 2009. It was a bold maneuver, very dangerous, and the waters in January were frigid. At the end of the movie, the panel investigating realized there was no better option for the safety of all on board but to attempt the water landing. In closing, they asked the co-pilot, "Is there anything you would have done differently?" He replied, "Yes, I would have done it in July!" That's a wonderful answer, and it accurately mirrors my point.

When I deliver historical talks, I always begin by asking my audience to suspend their 2022 eyes and look at what we are discussing with 1853 eyes, 1799 eyes, or whatever time we are looking at. I tell them that true history is not always pretty. Some things were done that we would not and do not agree with today, but the acts were fully accepted and legal in their time. That can be hard to swallow but must be done to look at the period without prejudice, objectively. The same is true when looking at my answer to the question at hand: knowing what I know now, would I have done anything differently? If I'm going to lose you, this might be the place. Why? Because you may very well not agree with my answer, or with what I did coming up to contracting COVID.

I had not been "vaccinated" and still haven't been. However, to be fair, I have been counseled not to get the shots at this point.

What else did I do? Outside of the very first month when we were told to stay at home for a month, I did just that. The only time I left my home was one hour a day to go outside and get some fresh air, natural vitamin D from the sun, and some much-needed exercise. I was always very respectful of others, meaning I moved to the side of the sidewalk to give good clearance for anyone I occasionally saw in passing. I washed my hands frequently and still do, though not excessively. I have always done so in normal circumstances, as you most likely have as well.

I was made to work from home as most, or at least many of us, were. That was something I never personally cared for, as I like to separate home and work as much as possible. I also tend to be a very social beast, meaning I enjoy being around people and somewhat thrive on the interaction.

As time passed and the end continued to move out, I went back toward a more normal life. I went back to the gym when it reopened. I used my spray bottle on all equipment before and after use, and it honestly felt like I had my own personal gym as there were very few people there. I was in great shape working out twice a day, and I took all the vitamins necessary to boost my immune system.

I wore a mask when required to do so. I also gave people the "social distancing" outlined in CDC guidelines.

Would I have done anything differently? The answer is "No, I would not have," This seems to be such a personal disease. You put four people of the same age and the same basic physical and immune makeup side by side and inevitably one will never contract it; one will never know they ever had the disease; one will have mild symptoms; and the other one is at death's door. There doesn't seem to be any rhyme or reason to it, other than perhaps age and overall general health and known, or unknown, underlying medical conditions.

If I were to have done anything differently, I would have gone to the doctor at least a day or two earlier. I would have stocked up on the medicines that many people I know have worked to get their hands on that are becoming known to help in the early stages of the disease. That might have helped a bit. What I can tell you is, the doctors at the hospital stated that I was patient zero for the Delta Variant. They hadn't seen it before I came through the doors, though the floodgates opened with the Delta Variant after me. They also stated that everything they knew and had tried from their knowledge of standard COVID-19 did not work on Delta. All the doctors I have spoken with after I was released indicated that they were thrown back to square one when the Delta variant came along.

In an attempt to avoid politics, I will state some reasons I chose not to vaccinate. I subscribe to the belief that in today's age of technology and information availability, individuals can secure the information necessary to make their choice and an edict or command for all can cause as much harm to individuals as disobedience to the "remedy" for all. There isn't one answer that works for everyone. There has been research lately that supports the vaccine for COVID-19 has no impact on any of the variants, so taking the vaccine may not have prevented my illness in any case. Besides freedom to choose your medical treatment is a principle. I stand by my decision to not be vaccinated for the COVID-19 virus, and I believe the jury is still out on the overall effectiveness of the method and the long-term effects.

A second question that comes up quite often is, "Where did you pick it up?" I understand why people ask the question; however, honestly, that is like asking where you picked up the common cold. I suppose people can make a semi-intelligent guess, but who knows? It's not like you can see it. It isn't as if there is a sign that says, "Pick up common cold here, pick up COVID-19 over there." Honestly, I haven't a clue where I picked it up.

The part that amazes me is how did it happen that I was the first one to contract the variant the doctors hadn't seen yet? Now to be clear, I was the first one they saw at WellStar North Fulton hospital, not the first person in the country or the state or even my area to contract it. However, do understand, WellStar North Fulton is a very big hospital, very well known, and yet with all the patients they see on a daily basis, I was the first one they saw with the Delta variant.

The final question that has been put to me regarding the shots and my not having taken them is, "Was it worth putting your family and friends through the ordeal?"

In order to answer this final question, I want to relate a story to you. It is a very personal story and a very difficult story for me to recount. I'm letting you into some very painful family history here. The rest of my family may well have different recollections of the incident. This is fully my version and my version alone.

You may recall, in my opening to this book, I mentioned my younger sister Sheila. I mentioned her, even though she has been gone for over forty-five years now, because she is still my sister and I miss her dearly. Just because she is not with us every day, as she should have been, she is still very relevant to my family and lives on in our collective memories and our hearts. My niece, Becky, carries her middle name and even bears a bit of resemblance to her. I see Sheila in her smile and different expressions at times, and that makes me smile.

I am writing this piece in January 2022. We lost our sister in January 1977 when I was twenty years old. It was the morning after a snowstorm, and my father was taking her to a private high school in Albany, New York. Dad worked in Albany as well. As they were on the way in, normally about a forty-minute drive, they weren't more than five to eight minutes from home when my dad's passenger side tires caught in a separation of the roadbed from the shoulder. It shouldn't have been there, but it was enough, even at twenty to twenty-five miles per hour tops, to throw his car at a ninety-degree angle across the road. Another car coming in the opposite direction hit Dad's car on the passenger side. It was enough to throw my sister against the windshield. My father had three cracked ribs, cuts, and bruises all over his body. When I saw my sister in the hospital hours later, she didn't have a mark on her that I could see. She was in a coma and on a ventilator. By the time I saw her, the only thing working was her heart. She lived five days more, and then a decision had to be made. I still vividly remember sitting by myself in a stairwell of the hospital praying to God that he would take me instead. I was twenty, she was just fourteen. "Take me," I prayed. "She is so much better than me and deserves to live."

Dad was a fine driver. He had grown up in New Jersey and by this time had lived in upstate NY for years. He knew how to drive in the snow. He had done it countless times. The chances this kind of thing would happen were remotely small. He knew to take his time and extra care and did, but the accident still happened. It destroyed him for several years, and he continually tried to get over the blame he placed on himself. It nearly destroyed his marriage. The long-reaching effects on those who remained were deep and different for each one of us. I nearly flunked out of college, failing one course outright and getting several Ds. It ruined my GPA and kept me out of graduate school, which changed the entire course of my life.

I penned this poem several months after the accident:

With Me

Here comes Spring with all its warmth,
to surround a heart that once was warm.
'Twas frozen hard by winter past,
by winds and snow the sky had cast.
With all of this it brought that day,
now a girl will be laid to rest in May.

She lays in state in a tomb above,
away from time who pushed and shoved.
but if she had her choice to be,
I think she'd rather be here... with me.

— JONATHAN CROOKS
CIRCA 1977

I had been raised a strong Christian young man with five years of perfect attendance in Sunday School. My sister Nancy, of course, has seven! I almost completely left my faith behind. How could God be so unmerciful? How could this happen? I considered being an atheist, but it didn't make sense to be angry at something or someone you didn't believe existed. Therefore, I became an agnostic.

At the conclusion of a three-year court case, my dad found peace. A suit was brought against the State of NY for the road conditions that caused the accident. For my father it took something he held in high regard, in this case the courts, to tell him this was not your fault. He was then able to move forward in life and go back to being the man he had always been.

For me, reconciliation with my faith came in the form of a Franciscan priest at Siena College, from which I graduated in August 1978. Siena is a wonderful school in Loudonville, New York. I transferred there at the end of the spring semester in 1976 from St. Lawrence University, where I had spent my first two collegiate years. I no longer remember the priest's name, but I can tell you he was a funny little fellow, only standing about five feet six inches tall. He was very slight in frame, maybe weighing 135 pounds soaking wet and had a very funny, high-pitched gravelly voice. He neared the end of his teaching time when I was enrolled in his metaphysics course. I was carrying an A average until one day as he was defending what he labeled his "Sixteen steps to the existence of God." I was still very angry at the loss of my sister. I raised my hand and he called upon me. I rose and said, "Father, your argument is the strongest I have ever heard, and I thank you for it." He smiled encouragingly and then I dropped the bomb. I continued, "All you have to do is get me to step one. If you can get me there, I'm with you." I sat down.

His face turned red as a ripe tomato. As it happened, I ended up losing my A and finished the class with a C+, if memory serves. However, I have always credited him with putting me back on the path toward God and faith. You see, he always debated Bertrand Russell. Russell was known as "The" atheist of the 19th and 20th centuries. He lived to be almost 100 years old, passing away in 1976. The argument Father made that started me back down the path went like this:

> "Bertrand has been an atheist all his life, but even Bertrand was only 99% sure there was no God. I have been a priest my entire adult life, and I have followed all the lessons and teachings diligently these many years, but even I, as convinced as I am (I am 99% sure there is a God), I too have that 1% that nags me as Bertrand's 1% nagged him. However, when all is said and done for each of us, and they

put us both in the ground if Bertrand is correct, then the maggots will eat our bodies and we turn to dust (Father had a flair for the dramatic) and we end up even. But if I am correct, I win. I'd prefer to have the chance to win."

As a Presbyterian, I hold to a Presbyterian definition and doctrine of "predestination" as opposed to the Catholic interpretation that Father held to. The argument was enough at that moment, at the correct time I needed to hear it, to make me go, "Hmmm." It began the process of turning me around. That story may not be enough for you and that's okay as the point of conversion is going to be different for each soul. All I implore you to do is search a little deeper, if you are searching or if you have a little nagging voice inside of you calling to you.

DAD'S JOURNEY that fateful morning should not have ended as it did, and perhaps mine should have ended differently as well. In the end, here we are. They called me a "medical miracle." Perhaps I truly was saved by a miracle. I believe I was, and I believe, it means there are still things for me to do and messages to deliver. Therefore, as a message to the true powers that be, use me as your will desires.

CHAPTER 9
ANGELS OF PROTECTION

"Even when we don't see it, you're working, even when we don't feel it, you're working."

— FROM THE *WAY MAKER* BY NIGERIAN GOSPEL SINGER SINACH

The question most often asked of me is, "What do you remember, if anything, about when you were in the coma? Did you simply just wake up? Did you see a white light when you were so close to death twice during that time? Did you see deceased family members? Did you float above the bed and see yourself lying there?" All the above are different recollections of near-death experiences. I was informed that I was at death's door twice during the four weeks of my coma. My experiences were different from all the above. They were unique compared to any I have ever heard or read about. There are four in total, and they are all different. One of them, the last one, was quite funny really. The first and second are interesting, with some connection to what was happening to me at certain times. The third is life changing.

The most difficult time frame for me to relate was what was happening to me from July 25, 2021, to August 24, 2021. The cause for these lapses in my memory is the fact that I was in a medically induced coma. From my medical records, I can glean some of the information and have relied on others, mostly my family, to fill in the blanks.

To reset the stage, I entered WellStar North Fulton Hospital on July 25 in critical condition. I was almost immediately placed on a ventilator.

I TRULY HAVE no continuous recollection of anything until being asked to move my feet and arms and I'm guessing that is August 23rd. So, what do I remember from that month-long period? What you are about to read are the snapshots I have during that period.

I call these "snapshots' because it's the best way I can describe what I remember. I'm going to describe the four snapshots, and I will place them in order of my memory of them. From what I can tell, the first and fourth memories come from very early on and very late in my coma period, respectively. There is a fair amount of bleed- over from reality, meaning I was semi-conscious of what was happening around me. It is the second and third snapshots in the middle of my coma where I was deeply in an unconscious state.

Snapshot One:

This one is a bit bizarre. I'll attempt to tie it to what I can in my subconscious. I was at a pool with a woman I did not know or even recognize. We were submerging into the pool in a kind of diving scenario. The water was very blue, crisp, and clear. I was under the water seemingly with pins in me. I remember thinking I shouldn't be able to breathe, but somehow, I could. I remember being rather scared because of the fact I was aware I shouldn't be able to breathe, and I had no way of coming to the surface. I was being held down under the water for a long period of time. I don't mean that I was being physically held by someone, but more that I couldn't rise above the water. I remember the woman talking to me, but I don't recall what she was saying. I remember she was very beautiful and was in a two-piece bathing suit. (That part may very well be a dream).

I distinctly remember pins in me. They were in my neck and all around me. I don't know how long I was under the water, just that it seemed like a long time. Long enough that breathing would have been a major concern.

This first snapshot, I have placed early in my coma state. So, what was happening to me at that time that I might be able to tie it to? My children have told me that early in the time I was in the hospital, they were able to come to view me from the door of my room. According to my medical notes, I was in bed 255. My children told me I had twenty tubes going in and out of me. At that time, I was the only person in that section of the floor. There were liquid bags of different medicines all around my bed. Additionally, some lines crossed the floor of my room out the door to other devices I was attached to. This could explain the pins, meaning all the IVs I was attached to. The only thing I can tie the underwater pool scenario to would possibly be that I was just in the early stages of learning to scuba dive with my daughter Vivian and her boyfriend, Michael. The woman talking to me, I'm going to assume, was a nurse. Why she should have been in a two-piece bathing suit I don't know, other than the physical surroundings I was seeing myself in at the time were quite appropriate for that.

The concern about breathing, I am assuming, is tied to the ventilator. As you have already heard on July 29, just four days into the coma journey, they had attempted to bring me out of the coma, and I ripped the ventilator out of my own throat. This, apparently, is a fairly common reaction to the vent. I'm assuming that I was not deeply in an induced medical coma; therefore, I was not totally unaware of what was going on around me. One of the medical notes seems to indicate I had been consulted about the vent and I gave consent and understood what was going on. It also indicates one of my daughters had been consulted on the possible concerns. I have no recollection of any conversation to this effect. I'm not suggesting it didn't happen, only that I have no recollection.

The fear of not being able to breathe goes back twenty-five years to when I herniated a disc in my lower back at age forty. I used to do a lot of weightlifting in my garage back in those days. One day I was doing some deadlifts and suddenly heard a pop that sounded like a gunshot going off in my back. I dropped the weight bar and wondered if I would even be able to stand up. Fortunately, I was able to do so; it was obvious; however, I had done something that was not good for my back.

Eventually, I underwent an operation to attempt to fix my back and very distinctly remember waking up a bit earlier than the techs had planned. The tubes (I assume a ventilator) were still down my throat, and I recall trying to say, "I can't breathe, I can't breathe!" I was extremely frightened by the event. I even chipped a front tooth.

Although I don't remember pulling the vent out on July 29th, I can certainly believe I did so, because of the event twenty-five years earlier.

According to my medical records:

"Patient self-extubated during the SABT"
This was recorded at 11:21 am, the morning of 7/29/21.

Recorded in my medical records later that day:

"Intubation," which meant they replaced the ventilator. This was recorded at 5:57 pm on 7/29/21

For reference purposes, I'm going to include the information regarding my intubation. You may decide to skip over this part; however, take note of the parts I have highlighted, as I believe they are pertinent bits of information. Those of you reading who are doctors, nurses or in the medical profession to whatever degree, will most likely have dealt with the same or similar situations and understand what I was enduring at the time.

Medical recorders information:

Procedures by Absar A Mirza, MD, at 7/29/2021 5:57 PM
Procedure Orders
1. Intubation [986220580] ordered by Absar A Mirza, MD
Intubation
*Date/Time: **7/29/2021 5:57 PM***
*Performed by: **Absar A Mirza, MD***
*Authorized by: **Absar A Mirza, MD***
*Consent: **Verbal consent obtained.***
Risks and benefits: risks, benefits and alternatives were discussed (Daughter)
*Patient understanding: **patient states understanding of the procedure being performed***
*Relevant documents: **relevant documents present and verified***
*Test results: **test results available and properly labeled***
*Imaging studies: **imaging studies available***
*Patient identity confirmed: **hospital-assigned identification number***
*Time out: **Immediately prior to procedure a "time out" was called to verify the correct patient, procedure,***
equipment, support staff and site/side marked as required.
Indications: respiratory distress and hypoxemia

Intubation method: video-assisted
Patient status: paralyzed (RSI)
Sedatives: etomidate
Paralytic: rocuronium
Laryngoscope size: Mac 3
Tube size: 7.5 mm
Tube type: cuffed
Number of attempts: 1
Difficult intubation: noCricoid pressure: no
Cords visualized: yes
Post-procedure assessment: chest rise and ETCO2 monitor
Breath sounds: equal
Cuff inflated: yes
ETT to teeth: 23 cm
Tube secured with: ETT holder
Chest x-ray interpreted by me.
Chest x-ray findings: endotracheal tube in appropriate position
Patient tolerance: **Patient tolerated the procedure well with no immediate complications**

As I stated earlier, I have no recollection of any of this, but also want to be sure to say, I'm not challenging anything being said here either. I don't wish to leave the wrong impression.

The fact it says "patient states understanding of the procedure being performed" would indicate that I am somewhat cognizant of what was going on, even though I don't remember.

This would indicate to me that the first snapshot memory has some basis in the reality of this world. As we move to the next snapshot this changes somewhat.

Snapshot Two:

Though my medical records no longer indicate any substantive response on my part until August 22, I can still relate some of what I remember as being tied to reality to some degree.

Snapshot number two places me in a rectangular room, perhaps twenty by twenty-five feet. I am lying on what appear to be large pillows. My head and upper body were slightly raised in relation to my feet. The pillows are very comfortable, but I am unable to lift my arms as if they are being restrained. I am unable to rise, although I keep attempting to do so. I am trying to call out to the voices I hear off to my right. I can see figures, almost shadow-like, moving off to my right, and there are conversations that I cannot make out. What I can see to my right are openings that the shadows are floating through and by. The door-like openings appeared to be arches. There are several of them, at least three I recollect seeing.

I seem to have some voice, but it is very weak. I'm trying to reach whoever is off to my right to say, "I just want to go home." It is difficult for me to write this right now as the emotions are flooding back. I'm not afraid, I just want to get out of wherever I am. I don't know where it is, and I am afraid those who love me are trying to find me and they don't know where I am.

I feel as if I have been drugged and just arrived where I am now, with no idea how I arrived there.

Again, for reference purposes, so you can have a better handle on what my body was enduring, I have included all the medications I was on. I'm going to assume that unless you are in the medical field, most of this is Greek to you as it is me. For a clearer understanding, I have included medical definitions of all the medications in Appendix A in the back of the book. Please refer there for any you specifically want to know about.

Progress Notes by Madhu Reddy, MD, at 7/30/2021 7:51 PM

Patient Name: JONATHAN P CROOKS
Room :255/255-01

Length of stay: 5 days

Subjective/Interval History
No acute events overnight

Objective

Temp: [97.7 °F (36.5 °C)-97.8 °F (36.6 °C)] 97.7 °F (36.5 °C)
    Heart Rate: [61-96] 74
    Resp: [18-32] 23
    BP: (99-160)/(52-78) 115/65
    Arterial Line BP: (100-170)/(46-72) 156/67
    FiO2 (%): [50 %-60 %] 50 %
    MAP: [64 mmHg-107 mmHg] 96 mmHg

SpO2 Readings from Last 1 Encounters:
07/30/21 96%
GEN: self extubated, not in distress
CVS: S1+, S2+
RS: Coarse BS
Abd: Soft, BA+
Ext: no LE edema
Foley cath; clear urine

Medications

Medication	Dose	Route	Frequency
albuterol	2.5 mg	Nebulization	Q6H Resp.
aspirin	81 mg	Oral	Daily
balanced salt irrigation	10 mL	Irrigation	Q12H
balanced salt irrigation	10 mL	Irrigation	Q4H PRN
[Held by provider] carvediloL	6.25 mg	Oral	BID w/ meals
chlorhexidine	15 mL	Mouth/Throat	BID
Dexamethasone	6 mg	Intravenous	Daily
dextrose 40%	1-2 Tube	Oral	Q15 Min PRN
dextrose 50 % in water (D50W)	25-50 mL	Intravenous	Q15 Min PRN
doxycycline (VIBRAMYCIN) IV	100 mg	Intravenous	Q12H
famotidine Or	20 mg	Oral	Nightly
famotidine	20 mg	Intravenous	Nightly
fentaNYL (PF)	50 mcg	Intravenous	Daily PRN
fentaNYL (SUBLIMAZE) infusion And	300 mcg/hr	Intravenous	Continuous
fentaNYL	50 mcg	Intravenous	Q15 Min PRN
glucagon	1 mg	Intramuscular	Once PRN
heparin (porcine)	40-60 Units/kg	Intravenous	Q6H PRN
heparin (porcine)	0-50 Units/kg/hr	Intravenous	Continuous
hydrALAZINE	10 mg	Intravenous	Q4H PRN
ibuprofen	400 mg	OG Tube	Q6H PRN
insulin lispro	1-18 Units	Subcutaneous	Q4H
LORazepam	0.25 mg	Intravenous	Q6H PRN
ondansetron	4 mg	Intravenous	Q8H PRN
piperacillin-tazobactam	3.375 g	Intravenous	Q8H
propofol (DIPRIVAN) infusion 10 mg/mL And	0-50 mcg/kg/min	Intravenous	Continuous
propofol	10 mg	Intravenous	Q5 Min PRN
sodium chloride (NS) 0.9 % syringe And	3 mL	Intravenous	Q8H SCH
sodium chloride (NS) 0.9 % syringe	3-40 mL	Intravenous	Q1 min PRN
sodium chloride 0.9%	1-3 mL/hr	Intravenous	Continuous

Continuous Infusions:

• fentaNYL (SUBLIMAZE) infusion	300 mcg/hr (07/30/21 1500)
• heparin (porcine)	18 Units/kg/hr (07/30/21 1244)
• propofol (DIPRIVAN) infusion 10 mg/mL	20 mcg/kg/min (07/30/21 1929)
• sodium chloride 0.9%	3 mL/hr (07/29/21 2046)

PRN Meds:.balanced salt irrigation, dextrose 40%, dextrose 50 % in water (D50W), fentaNYL (PF),
Fenta NYL (SUBLIMAZE) infusion **AND** fentaNYL, glucagon, heparin (porcine), hydrALAZINE,
ibuprofen, LORazepam, ondansetron, propofol (DIPRIVAN) infusion 10 mg/mL **AND** propofol,
[COMPLETED] Insert peripheral IV **AND** Maintain IV access **AND** [COMPLETED]
INT **AND** sodium chloride (NS) 0.9 % syringe **AND** sodium chloride (NS) 0.9 % syringe

I wish I could fully understand all this information, but it's above my medical training, which is nil. What I can say is it sure looks like a lot to me. I'm now on eighteen intravenous medications and only four continuous infusions.

There are a few other memories from this snapshot worthy of note. At one point I recall wondering where my car was. I know I had been moved from the pool area of the first snapshot at some point and have arrived in the location I described above.

I felt that I was being treated for whatever happened to me in the pool. I also recall that it seemed I had been drinking a lot of something as well. I can't tell you what it was, just that I felt I had been drugged in some way. That's what I recall feeling.

At the front corner of the room, on the left side just before the corner, there was a window. I was looking down the twenty-five-foot-long side of the room (I estimated) and the window came right up to the corner of the room. I can see out the window. It is all in color outside. The room itself is more filled with shades of gray and is darker. Not colorless, but not as bright as the view out the window. Through the window, I can see my car across the street. It is bright outside. For some reason, I believe it is about five o'clock in the afternoon. Not sure why I would think that, yet that was my impression. My car is on the curb across the street facing an intersection of the streets. There is a sidewalk and then a tall red brick building. There are no windows in the building, simply a brick wall. I remember thinking, "There is my car. If I can just get up and out of this room, I can reach it and go home."

Now understand, my car is at home. I have been brought to the hospital in an ambulance. However, in my mind, my car is with me.

While I was in the room, a man came to me asking me to do some things. I believe it is a request to move my arms and my legs. This would certainly be consistent with the daily procedures to see if I am responding. This person is explaining things to me; however, I am completely unable to respond with my voice. He appears to want to help me, and I know he is giving me something, some type of medication. I want to respond but I am completely unable to do so. That was very frustrating, I recall, because I wanted to tell him I wished to go home and to please help me rise. I know I am attempting to form words, but they won't come out. Then he walks away, and I feel as if I have lost my chance to communicate what it is I want. I just recall lying there.

The other recollection I have from this snapshot is hearing, literally, repeatedly, a snap, like the sharp snap of fingers, and then feeling a pick to my finger. It's one after another, repeatedly. Snap, prick, snap, prick, snap, prick! The prick on my finger didn't particularly hurt, but I felt it.

I'm quite certain the man coming in to see me must have been one of the doctors checking to see if I was responding at all. I have no idea what the exact time frame is for this as it most likely happened once each day.

Angels of Protection

The "snap, prick" regimen was revealed to me when I came out of the coma. I believe I had been moved to the WellStar Windy Hill location at this point. I was moved on August 26; therefore, I'm guessing this next event happened sometime on August 27. A nurse rolled in yet another little cart of medical equipment. I assumed it was to retrieve blood from me yet again. My smart-aleck self wanted to say something like, "Go ahead Mrs. Dracula, take what you need, but I'm not sure there's any blood left!"

I always turn my head to the side whenever something new is being done to me - not so much because of fear, but I prefer not to watch the first one. I'll just experience it, and then I'll know going forward what is being done and what to expect. After the first time, I can just watch.

I turned my head and suddenly heard "snap" and then the prick on the end of my finger. My neck practically snapped off as I swung it around hard and fast. "There," I exclaimed out loud. "That's it! That's the sound and feeling I kept having over and over again." I finally knew what it was. The nurse explained she was testing for diabetes. She came back the next day, and just before performing the test again she stopped and said, "You don't need this, you don't have diabetes!" and she rolled the cart back out, never to return. I thought to myself, with a sly smile on my face, "I could have told you that!" It was so gratifying to have an answer to something. I finally knew what the "snap, prick" was!

The next experience, however, is far different and holds far-reaching implications. You're going to have to wait a bit to read that one, though. I'm certain it took place in the darkest time of my coma and the deepest coma time because of what happened. Truly, I was at death's door at that moment.

For the moment, let's move to snapshot four and then we'll return to snapshot three.

Snapshot Four:

Snapshot four I'm certain happened quite close to when I came out of the coma for good, which would have been around August 20 to 22. I believe this to be the case as it seemed a very short time until I was finally awake and reacting more alertly with the nurse who came to see me between five or six o'clock each morning according to my medical notes.

In this snapshot, I am again lying on something soft. I recall it being more like a recliner, the kind with a handle on the side that allows you to either sit up or recline. My arms are still pinned as they were in the second snapshot. I can't move them. I am still unable to rise, though I am attempting to. The room is not as large as it was in the second snapshot, as it seems to be more of a square versus the rectangle room in snapshot two. The chair I am in is in the center of the room. I can see a door off to my right. There are no windows in this room that I can recall. There are two other chairs in the room, the same type as mine. There is one to my left and one to my right. The chairs are lined in a row. I recall feeling that I was lying there for a good while, and initially, there were people in the chairs to my right and left. I don't know who was in the chair to my left, but whoever it was left at some point. The chair to my right had a female in it and at least, at one point, it seemed to me to be my sister Nancy.

Once again, as in snapshot two, people did come in and out of the room. At one point the person coming in was cleaning the room. I recall hearing a vacuum cleaning the floor. This is another reason why I believe this snapshot is very close to my awakening. Housekeeping used to come in and clean my room every day while I was in rehab. They would come in while I was out with my PT. They never came into the room to clean if I was in the room once I awoke.

I also remember trying to gain the attention of the person coming in, to see if I could get them to help me out of the chair. I never was able to get a response. I also tried to talk to the person next to me on my left, but I don't recall any connection in conversation with that person. I couldn't tell why I was there in that room, just that we were and that we were each connected to an IV. The room was not well-lit but was not dark either.

Eventually, the person to the right of me was also released, leaving only me in the room. The other two chairs disappeared. Intermittently people were moving around in the room, and there were conversations that I couldn't make out. I didn't recognize any of the voices.

I'm including the notes from the day before I began to be responsive, as I believe this is roughly the time I had the last snapshot of memory while in the coma. There was only one intravenous connection in my memory, and this is consistent with the notes below.

Progress Notes by Christopher W Nickum, PA, at 8/23/2021 6:04 AM

Subjective

On T-collar. Sleepy, not very responsive

OBJECTIVE

<u>Vitals:</u>
Heart Rate: [74-107] 89
Resp: [12-22] 21
BP: (119-159)/(79-106) 159/94
FiO2 (%): [40 %] 40 %
94%
<u>Intake/Output:</u>
Intake/Output Summary (Last 24 hours) at 8/23/2021 0607
Last data filed at 8/22/2021 1900
Gross per 24 hour

Intake 1150 ml
Output 600 ml
Net 50 ml
<u>**Respiratory:**</u> *T-collar*
<u>**Physical Exam**</u>*:*
Gen: *lying in bed, nad*
Head: *Normocephalic, atraumatic*
Neck: *supple, no significant adenopathy. Trached.*
Chest: *diminished bilaterally.*
Cardiovascular: *S1 and S2 normal, no murmur, click, gallop or rub*
Abd: *abdomen is soft without significant tenderness, masses, organomegaly or guarding.*

No hepatomegaly, no splenomegaly. Positive bowel sounds.
Extremities: *mild to moderate generalized edema. Right toe erythematous*
Neuro: *awakens, eyes open, makes eye contact, moves extremities to command but significant*
generalized weakness present
Skin Color: *no new rash*
<u>**Medications**</u>*:*

Scheduled Meds:

• acetaminophen	640 mg	OG Tube	Q6H PRN
• albuterol	2.5 mg	Nebulization	Q2H PRN Resp.
• ALPRAZolam	1 mg	OG Tube	TID PRN
• aspirin	81 mg	Oral	Daily
• bromocriptine	2.5 mg	OG Tube	Daily
• carboxymethylcellulose sodium	1 drop	Both Eyes	Q4H
• carboxymethylcellulose sodium	1 drop	Both Eyes	Q1H PRN
• carvedilol	6.25 mg	OG Tube	BID w/ meals
• chlorhexidine	15 mL	Mouth/Throat	BID
• clonazePAM	0.25 mg	OG Tube	BID
• dextrose 40%	1-2 Tube	Oral	Q15 Min PRN
• dextrose 50 % in water (D50W)	25-50 mL	Intravenous	Q15 Min PRN
• famotidine Or	20 mg	OG Tube	BID
• famotidine	20 mg	Intravenous	BID
• fondaparinux	2.5 mg	Subcutaneous	Q24H
• glucagon	1 mg	Intramuscular	Once PRN
• hydrALAZINE	10 mg	Intravenous	Q3H PRN
• HYDROmorphone	1 mg	Intravenous	Q4H PRN
• insulin lispro	1-18 Units	Subcutaneous	Q4H
• labetaloL	20 mg	Intravenous	Q4H PRN
• ondansetron	4 mg	Intravenous	Q8H PRN
• oxyCODONE	5 mg	OG Tube	Q6H PRN
• polyethylene glycol	17 g	OG Tube	Daily
• predniSONE	40 mg	Oral	Daily
• sodium chloride (NS) 0.9 % syringe And	3 mL	Intravenous	Q8H SCH
• sodium chloride (NS) 0.9 % syringe	3-40 mL	Intravenous	Q1 min PRN
• sodium chloride 0.9% (NS) bolus	250 mL	Intravenous	PRN
• sodium chloride 0.9% (NS) bolus	250 mL	Intravenous	PRN
• sodium chloride 0.9%	1-3 mL/hr	Intravenous	Continuous
• [Held by provider] ticagrelor	90 mg	Oral	BID

Continuous Infusions:

• sodium chloride 0.9%	3 mL/hr	(08/19/21 1205)

There is one other recollection from this fourth snapshot which is quite humorous. I distinctly remember someone coming in the room looking for extras for a movie that was to be filmed.

They were looking for Dwayne Johnson (The Rock) and Arnold

Schwarzenegger-type people for the extra roles. I remember them saying they paid a whopping seven dollars an hour for these roles.

I kept trying to raise my hand, attempting to say I could do that, all in the hopes of being able to get out of the chair I was in. I still was unable to raise my arms, and my voice was extremely weak as I tried to call out.

Snapshot Three:

I have no way of placing a timeframe for this snapshot, but I was deep in a coma at this point, and I feel that it took place at a critical time in my journey. The images in this remembrance are extremely vivid and quite profound. Though I can't attach a specific time to this, I will attempt to make an educated guess based on what happened to me at critical times. I am quite certain that it was placed at one of the times the doctors said I was "At death's door." For this information, I have had to return to the medical notes and ask my children about their conversations with doctors and nurses to better understand the circumstances.

According to the medical notes, there was a concern of "acute ischemia" in the middle

---

part

---

of August. It appears in the Infectious Disease Report dated August 14 and 15. In this case, the consideration is related to possibly using a brain MRI for evaluation. As discussed earlier in the book, acute ischemia is the sudden loss of blood circulation to an area of the brain.

Because of the concern of a possible stroke and the downturn that was reported to my children during this time, I am surmising that snapshot three took place somewhere between August 11 and August 14.

    This memory is most profound for me. It is the most dramatic and the most real to me. I lay in a reclined position on a very soft bed or recliner. I was in a well-lit room, not overly lit with an intense light. However, it was the whitest white I had ever seen, I was unable to sit up or move my arms. This was the first time I noticed that rising or moving was not at the forefront of my thoughts. I had no reason, nor desire, at that moment to want to move or to call out. There were no voices. It was extremely quiet with no sound at all. There were no other chairs or beds in the room, but I was not alone. They were unclothed, but I wasn't able to discern their being male or female. One entity stood to the left of me, another to my right, and one at my feet. All three looked directly at me. They did not speak to me but were merely there with me, watching me. It was extremely peaceful, not frightening in any way. It was comforting, I felt protected and that nothing would reach me that could harm me. They had rather broad foreheads, but the rest of their faces were long and slender. They were well proportioned with dark hair, either very dark brown or black. They had fine hair that looked soft. Their hair parted in the middle, and it gently framed their faces, curling slightly inward just above the shoulders at the base of the neck. The eyes were soft and almond-shaped with thin arched eyebrows the same color as the hair. Their noses were narrow and slender. Their lips were small and tender. The shape of the faces was somewhat triangular. The chins were rounded and slender. I couldn't see their ears under their hair. Their cheekbones were high, but not pronounced. The faces were soft. The cheeks themselves were soft and full, not sunken in any way.

    It is still very hard to contain my emotions when I think of them; they brought such peace with them. I know they were protecting me in my darkest hour. Nothing was going to get by them, nothing could. It was a peaceful silence coupled with a warmth beyond expression that surrounded us.

Some people who are close to death will describe a bright light or say they saw family members they knew were long gone. The light is a very bright white light. They often describe a warmth connected with that light. Occasionally, the person experiencing this will want to move on with the personages and are told, "No, you must go back."

"God sends angels with special orders to protect you wherever you go, defending you from harm."

— PSALM 91:11 (PASSION)

The verse describes how I felt... defended, encircled. There was a calmness. I wasn't going anywhere, and I was devoid of any desire to do so. I wanted to go home. Wanted to go back to my children, my family, and my friends, and they were there to ensure I did. I didn't need a bright white light, the softer white light was enough to know who they were and why they were there. It was obvious to me. They were there to be with me, to let me know I was not alone. We are never alone.

There is a purpose, and my purpose was and is still playing out.

So is yours, no matter where you find yourself. Keep looking for and keep finding your purpose.

I do not doubt that the beings that surrounded me were angels. Angels from a place we do not yet know, but strive to find and embrace.

Several weeks after I was released from the hospital, I spoke with my sister, Nancy. She was the first I talked to about what I had seen and experienced. She she relayed to me that her prayers for me were that angels would be sent to protect me, to keep me from harm, and to bring me back. For me, her prayers were answered.

I had originally asked my daughter Vivian to draw what I have described. Though she is a fine artist, she is, by her own admission, better at sketching animals than people, so she declined the ask. I then reached out to my friend April Caltabiano, whose husband Michael is an artist. I sent them the above description. Michael connected me to Angelika Donschke, Angel as she is known.

Angel is a German artist. She is an extremely accomplished scientist who holds several patents for her earlier work in science. She is now an accomplished artist and was the perfect person to bring my angels to life for you. I commissioned her to create the cover of this book and show you the face of an angel, my angels who protected me in my deepest hour of need.

CHAPTER 10
"THE EVIDENCE OF THE PAST GIVES US HOPE FOR THE FUTURE"

"The evidence of the past gives us hope for the future." This phrase was often recited by our former senior pastor from Roswell Presbyterian Church. I have been a member there for the past twenty years. Dr. Rev. E. Lane Alderman, Jr. was an incredible man of faith. He could deliver a sermon that would challenge you to a deeper sense of understanding while raising you so high as to peek into heaven itself. We lost him much too young in 2015 to male breast cancer.

The portrait is of the Reverend Dr. E. Lane Alderman, Jr. The portrait hangs in the narthex of the Roswell Presbyterian Church in Roswell, Georgia.

As we traverse our lives, it's hard to see what is really happening *as* it happens because we are so caught up in the moment. However, when we reflect, the timing of things and the connections become so real and illuminated that they not only give us pause but even blow us away. So much of what happens we write off as being "coincidence" or "luck."

I am not that lucky guy that every wonderful thing happens to. I truly am "Mister High Average." It's what makes this awakening to what happened to me and for me that makes my story one of magnificence - not just for me, my family, and friends, but truly for us all. It's the evidence we should all always be looking for. It's there! We simply must be willing to invest the time to find it.

I would also put forth that there are no coincidences in life. Everyone we encounter comes to us for a reason. We may not see it at the time, and it may be fleeting, but there is a purpose.

As I reflect on what happened to me, I see how people came in and out at the correct time to ensure I was here to relate this story to you. This section of the book and story is going to take you through a number of events not only during COVID but also through events in my own life. They are designed to lay out a road map for you to follow and then ponder on. The intent is to give you examples that you can take back to your own life for reflection.

The first such story takes you to my time at Epsilon. It is a period that led up to my COVID experience.

On May 15, 2020, I was released from Epsilon, where I had worked for five and a half years. Even with my seniority, I was not retained when the pandemic hit. It was devastating for me. With my hindsight and new perspective, I am no longer disappointed. It was a fine company, and I had many friends; however, I hadn't reached my full potential there. The loss of health insurance was disappointing, and I was without health insurance for nine months. I was eligible for Medicare before COVID struck me on July 25, 2021. Fortuitously, I had chosen the top tier of Medicare. Thank goodness I did. I had Medicare for a mere ninety short days before I was struck. Consider what could have happened if COVID had struck me ninety days sooner. Consider how devastating it would be to receive a bill in excess of $715,000. That was one of the billing statements I received for part of my stay in the hospital.

I CAN'T FULLY TELL the story of the miracles associated with COVID without sharing three occurrences in my life.

My own birth is the first miracle. "Why?" might you very astutely ask. Everyone is born. We aren't hatching people... at least, not yet. In truth, by human standards, I really shouldn't be here at all. At least not in the form I am. I was adopted. Nothing particularly unusual about that. Many children are adopted; I found out that little nugget of information when I was twelve years old. I had gone to the home of my best friend at the time, Hal Banker. I had stayed over at his house the night before. At the end of that Saturday, my dad came to pick me up. While Hal and I were upstairs gathering my things, the parents chatted. I was told later that the conversation went along the lines of Hal's parents asking my father if I looked more like my mother, because I didn't seem to favor him. My father replied that both my sister, and I had been adopted, as our mom was unable to have children. Nancy was adopted first in 1954 and then I was adopted roughly two years later in 1956.

The following Monday morning at school, my friend Hal exclaimed, "So, you're adopted!" To which I replied, "Excuse me?"

After school, my mom asked, "So how was your day?"

" Uhh, interesting day, Mom. Hal told me I'm adopted!"

She said, "Let's sit down," and she told me the story. I distinctly remember being completely lost for three days. It's an interesting time frame for those with a faith background. I remember thinking, why am I here? At the end of the three days, I realized that Mom was correct. She said I was there because they wanted me, and she was right. I decided at twelve that I was okay with that. I never had the motivation to seek out my birth parentage. But I did have some fun. I would tell people I had spent many years in the orphanage, sleeping in the attic with the other boys. It was hot in the summer and cold in the winter. We always asked for more gruel at dinner, and my best friend, Fagan, and I used to pickpockets in the street. Somewhere between the attic and Fagan, I am found to be a fraud and that I'm not *Oliver Twist*. It's still fun to say, but in truth, I was six weeks old when adopted.

Fifteen years later, when I was first married, my wife and I discussed having children, and she asked if I knew of any medical background that we should be aware of before starting a family. We asked my mother, and she assured me there was nothing in my background to be concerned about and that they had checked that out when I was adopted.

"Mom," I asked, " not that I have any interest in finding anyone, but what do you know about my biological family?"

She said, "Not very much. However, if I tell you what I do know, you must promise not to tell your father that I have told you." I promised, and I kept that promise all his life.

She told me they could have known the name of my parents but had chosen not to because of their proximity. I was born in Albany, New York. We lived in Cooperstown, New York, at the time, which was only forty minutes from Albany. My parents were afraid they would run into someone with the same last name and then they would wonder, could they be related? They chose not to put themselves through that, and I can't say I blame them. It was a wise decision.

You see, my biological parents were upper-middle-class, well-educated people who were married... unfortunately, NOT to each other. I was told I am at least partially northern Italian, which explains my great ability to tan so well. The most interesting and fun fact was that one set of my biological grandparents had been quite well-known for their dancing. They were semi-professional dancers, and they used to win dance contests up and down the eastern seaboard. This was of particular interest to me as I have always loved to dance and have always possessed natural rhythm. I, too, have won a dance contest or two over time and even done some 18th and 19th-century dancing. Throw on some good '70s to '90s music, and you can usually find me on the dance floor in my little world.

This photo of me was placed in my high school graduation yearbook.

Even this knowledge is not enough to stop me from occasionally thinking I wasn't supposed to be here, not by human standards. I really wasn't expected, planned for, or wanted by my birth parents. When speaking for a Dale Carnegie group several years ago, I sang part of the famous Supremes song "Love Child" to describe who I was. That is how I felt at times. I truly was a love child, never meant to be.

Although my adoptive family and my stepfamily are descended from some notable names in the history of our country, I'm not allowed to join certain groups because I am not a blood descendant. I get it, but it still bothers me because this is my family.

Regardless of that slight irritation, I believe it is a miracle because of where I could have ended up. I might never have been here at all, or I could have ended up with a family who wasn't as loving. I don't know my biological parents, but I am grateful for their strength to have me at all, not to abort, thus allowing me to be here to tell this story today.

COVID - Miracle One

Michael Drago had moved in with Vivian and me several months earlier. In truth, the setup goes even further back than that. To more fully understand the miracle here, we have to go back to when my daughter Vivian lost her position at SeaWorld in Orlando due to COVID-19 cutbacks, she moved from Florida to Georgia. Certainly not lucky for her, but it was lucky for me. Had she not moved here, Michael Drago wouldn't have been positioned to be part of this miracle. Vivian took a job at SeaVentures, now called Diventures. That is where she met Michael.

At the time, Michael had his own place. Instead, he chose to live with Vivian in our home. Had he not done so, he would not have been there when I needed him. Vivian had changed employers and worked in Cumming, Georgia, which was approximately twenty-five minutes away. On the day of my crisis, she wasn't scheduled to be done until seven o'clock. She normally doesn't arrive home until about eight o'clock. Michael was normally scheduled at work himself, but he was home because he had contracted a very mild case of COVID himself.

When the EMTs arrived, they found my oxygen level in my blood at 57%, when it should be at least 95% or better. I had passed that critical level. Had Michael continued to live in his own place, Vivian might have gone directly to Michael's house and not come to our home at all that night. It is likely she would have found me dead on the couch when she returned home the next day. Additionally, had Michael not tested positive for COVID and not been home, I would have had the same problem. I crashed so fast that I didn't have the wherewithal to call for help myself because I didn't realize what was happening. I have a faint memory of talking to Michael, but no real recollection of what I said or what was said to me at all. I have no recollection of the EMT's coming to my place or taking me out to the hospital. The next thing I remembered waking in the hospital bed a month later, at the end of August!

Let's be very clear about the point I had reached. I posed the question to my dear friend, Nurse Valary Anderson Dreyer, as to what the great concern was for me at that moment, with a blood oxygen level of 57%. The response was immediate... "Death." Certainly, that wasn't the only concern; however, it certainly is a great concern.

There are many possible scenarios that could have happened over the course of the months leading up to that fateful day that could have changed the outcome that afternoon.

I see these circumstances as a miracle. From my perspective, they were not mere luck. Michael had been in my home at the precise time required to ensure I got the medical attention I needed to survive.

A Second Journey Back in Time:

I grew up outside of a small town in upstate New York. I was very fortunate to grow up with horses on 250 acres of land. Along with the animals, I also had the opportunity to do some driving on the property much before I was old enough to secure a driver's license for the roads. Though we weren't farmers ourselves, we were technically considered one since we rented out acres of land to local farmers. They grew crops such as corn and alfalfa/hay, depending on the year. We would get a fair amount of that hay for our horses.

Having so many acres, we had a few farm vehicles. We had a dump truck I occasionally got to drive around the property as we moved different items back and forth. I had to learn to drive the stick shift it had. I didn't start driving that vehicle until I was fifteen years old, which was not long before I was eligible for a real driver's license. In those days, you were permitted to drive those vehicles on your property if you didn't drive on county roads. In addition to the truck, we had an older Ford tractor. It was one from the 1950s and very common in those parts of the country. It, too, was a stick shift. I used it to bush hog the fields that were not planted at the time. I started driving it when I was about eleven.

The photo above is me on the tractor at age twelve. This picture was not long before an incident occurred in 1968, on the dirt road we lived on.

One Saturday morning, my father and stepmom, Bob and Pat Crooks, had left for Saratoga for an event and my sister Nancy and I were at home taking care of the horses and other animals. I was twelve at the time. When the morning chores were completed, I jumped on the tractor and drove around the property a bit, as I often did.

Just up from the family home was an old railroad track that

was still in use. Originally there were two sets of tracks; however, over time one set had been removed. At one time, there was a station house for the railroad that was on our property at the point where the car roadbed crossed the tracks. For years we used the water out of the well at the old station to fill our inground swimming pool. There was a small turnaround area at that point.

The photo above shows the general area where the action occurred. If you look closely, you will see what looks like a white line going across the road, just before a rise in the road. Just to the left of the left-most side of the line is where the turnaround was. The family home is just to the left of the tree in the left foreground.

On the morning in question, I was driving the tractor close to its maximum speed, which, quite frankly, wasn't that fast, but I was in fourth gear and close to its top range. I came to the turnaround point and cut the wheel hard. The tractor turned, however the force of the turn was enough to throw me off to one side. I remember hanging onto the steering wheel, hanging half off the tractor and I couldn't pull myself back up. I remember hitting the ground and hearing the tractor right next to me. It was so loud. I must have momentarily blacked out because the next thing I remember, I woke up on the ground. I stumbled to my feet, a bit dazed. The tractor had continued moving, jumped onto the railroad tracks, and was driving along the tracks away from me. I tried to run after it, not quite sure what I would have done had I caught it. I stumbled, trying to regain my senses, and I finally gave up and walked back to the house and found my sister. It took her a good half hour to forty-five minutes to convince me I had not been run over by the tractor, for if I had been, I would be dead. I thought about what I was going to have to say to my parents when they returned later in the afternoon. I considered it might well have been better for me if I had been run over. It was 1968. There were no cell phones and no way to reach my parents.

You might be wondering what happened to the tractor heading up the tracks all by itself at this point. Can you imagine if a train had been coming the other way up those tracks at that time? I can almost hear the conversation between the engineer and whoever would have been with him. "Hey Zeke, what the heck is that coming at us? It looks like a tractor!" It would have been disastrous had it played out that way. Fortunately, it didn't. About three miles up the tracks, the tractor jumped off the tracks and crashed into a fence. The folks who lived just down from the tracks at that point found it and turned it off. They recognized the tractor belonged to the Crooks' and called. They said, "I think your tractor is up here." The tires were all beaten up and flat.

I'm sure you are thinking I was given a penalty much worse than being sent to bed without supper. I don't recall any penalty at all for that, shall we say, misstep. In the end, my dad decided I had suffered enough having to wait for their return to tell them what had happened. That, combined with my survival, must have been enough for Dad. My sentence was commuted to time served.

I have often thought about that incident and wondered how that tractor did not run over me. I honestly can give you no earthly answer. The back tires were large, standing about four and a half feet high. The tractor spun around me, and I had fallen off in the middle of the body of the tractor. By rights, it should have gone right over me, but it didn't. I had blacked out, and I believe I was saved that day, just like I was saved many years later. These things are not luck.

COVID - Miracle Two

I had just finished dinner with my Roswell Ghost Tour buddies when this photo was taken. I wasn't feeling the best that evening. I had a bit of a cough, but that was it. Because of all the COVID concerns, I was careful around my friends, but honestly thought, worst case scenario, I might have a touch of bronchitis. I ultimately went into WellStar Urgent Care on Wednesday, July 14, when the cough got worse.

The last text message I sent, before going down hard with COVID, was to David Wood, you see pictured below. I sent it on July 24. I let him know I had COVID and was concerned that I might have given it to any of my GT mates. Fortunately, none of them came down with it, as I found out later after release from the hospital and I had a chance to catch up with David.

I'm there on the left, Meghan Riley, David Wood, the owner, Alice Jankowski, Heather Nysewander, and Lauren Miller. Photo taken Monday July 12, 2021.

The first several weeks were very much touch and go. Just reaching the hospital at all, as you have seen, is fully the first miracle. The next two weeks were critical. As I arrived on the 25th, I was immediately placed in a medical coma and placed on a ventilator, as you already know.

The ventilator was particularly hard on me. I didn't fare well with it in these early days. On day four, which was July 29th, as you recall, they attempted to bring me out of the coma, and I summarily ripped the ventilator out of my own throat. This could have caused massive damage to both my lungs and my throat. I was kept off the vent for most of the day, but I had to be placed under the medical coma again, and in the evening of the same day was placed back on the ventilator. Reading through all the medical notes of the days from July 29 to August 11 there is an increasing number of times I am listed as *not responding* by the attending doctor. There is a darkening cloud settling over me in terms of how the chief medical staff is viewing where I am in terms of recovery. More and more they are beginning to believe I am not going to make it. The list of medications I am on, either every few hours or continuously, has grown to thirty to thirty-five plus, and I'm beginning to resemble a drug store.

They tested if I could wiggle my toes on command, move fingers, and follow their finger or a light with my eyes. The idea is to see if I am cognizant and can process the commands. More times than not, I am not doing so for the head physician, and it is being reflected in my medical notes. As each day passes, the longer I am on the ventilator, the worse it is. There is high concern for my kidneys and the clot that was found in my left calf.

There were moments of kidney failure, but fortunately, every time I reached a more critical stage with them, they came back online. At one point, doctors thought I was in full kidney failure but found instead that I was simply greatly dehydrated. It was a miracle that I had lasted this long - but I had. The *Eliquis* I had been placed on was taking care of the clot in my leg, and amazingly, my kidneys kept working. The loss of the kidneys was always considered the first step of complete and total bodily function shutdown. My kidneys were coming off and online. If the blood clot in my leg had moved suddenly through my system, it could have lodged in so many places and potentially could have caused a massive stroke or triggered a heart attack (the likes of which, in either case, I may very well not have come back from). Certainly, the work of all the medical staff around me at that time was vital to my survival. Never could enough credit be given to them as they struggled to find the correct mixture of medications to keep me alive and fighting. As you are already aware, the Delta Variant had thrown all knowledge of how to deal with COVID back to square one. It truly was a miracle, or as doctors and nurses all said, "a medical miracle." I was still alive.

There was also concern for my heart functions. At one time, there was even a thought that I might have sustained a very mild heart attack, as we have already discussed. However, I had it fully confirmed in a follow-up appointment with my cardiologist, Dr. Achtch. After my release, he was able to confirm to me that I never had one. Even though I had visited death's door in this period, I didn't walk through it. It truly was a miracle I was still here, but the darkest day was still ahead.

COVID - Miracle Three

The photo you are about to view will show you where I was in the middle of the deepest chasm of my life.

For those of you who know me well, this will be a very difficult photo to view. As I am writing this, it is the first time I have seen it myself. I can't describe my feelings right now. I am completely overwhelmed. It is no wonder Kristine said she didn't recognize me when she viewed me from the door. I can't imagine her feelings. It is devastating for me to look upon it now. (I wrote this piece in January 2022, and it was the first time I had seen this photo myself at that time, though you have seen it earlier in the book)

I've never sported a beard in my life. I don't recognize myself. The photo was taken the morning I was moved off the ventilator and placed on the trach, as you recall. Somewhere along the way, I had sustained the wound that you see on my chin. I have found a reference to it in the medical notes. The notes below discuss the wound:

"*Date First Assessed/Time First Assessed: 08/04/21 2000 Primary Wound Type: Pressure Injury Wound Description (Comments): stage III pressure ulcer chin Location: Chin Wound Location Orientation: Anterior*"

The following are notes from the next day August 5, four days before the photo below.

ECHO:
- *The left ventricular systolic function is normal with an ejection fraction of 56-60%.*
- *The left ventricular diastolic function is normal (based on LA volume index, TR velocity, medial and lateral e' velocities, and average E/e').*

- The left ventricular cavity, indexed to body surface area and gender is normal.
- There is mild concentric left ventricular hypertrophy present.
- The right ventricular systolic function is normal.
- The right ventricular cavity size is normal.
- The inferior vena cava demonstrates a high central venous pressure, 15mmHg, (>2.1 cm and <50% decrease).
- There is trace tricuspid valve regurgitation.

Assessment:
- Altered Mental Status/Delirium with agitation
- Acute hypoxemic respiratory failure/ARDS

As you can see in the notes above, I am in a delirium with respiratory failure. The notes also indicate "left ventricular hypertrophy." My research indicates this is *"a thickening of the wall of the heart's main pumping chamber."* That's how Google Research defines it.

A family meeting was held with Kristine, Vivian, and Gary on August 7, two days before the trach was placed and the vent was removed, as shown in the notes included below:

Addendum:
Met with daughters Vivian and Kristine in a family conference today. All questions answered. They requested Kristine be the point contact person instead of Vivian henceforth. They verbally consented to tracheostomy.
[My note in addition to Dr. Bhutta's. The change was made because Kristine was more accessible to reach by cell than Vivian was.]
Faisal M Bhutta, MD
WMG Pulmonary & Critical Care Medicine
8/7/2021 4:30 PM

You will recall this photo was taken on August 9, 2021, at 9:30

in the morning, the day the vent was removed and the trach placed. This photo must have been taken just before the "Bedside Tracheostomy" took place, as it is the first time it is noted anywhere. The report has a timestamp of 9:47 a.m. on August 9, 2021.

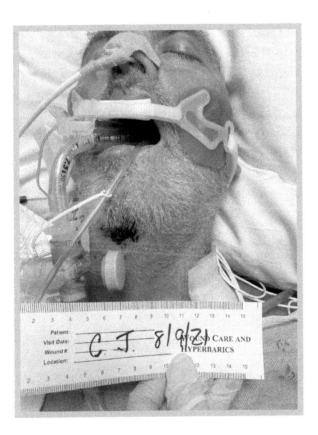

This was a critical time as they were greatly concerned about my condition before the trach was placed. The doctors felt this was the last step.

I responded to the procedure very well, and we progressed from there. Had this not worked, the discussion would have included making a very tough decision to pull the plug on me. There were those on the medical staff that felt we had moved far down that path. As I have been told by my daughters, it was the nurses who stepped in strongly on my behalf, telling them that there was still life here and that I was responding even though the doctors may not have been seeing it.

There was one nurse in particular who got to my daughters to tell them not to let them pull the plug on me. Kristine remembered that she had been The Daisy Award recipient. On a visit back to the hospital in April 2022, I asked my attending nurse about The Daisy Award. I wanted to know if there was a way to find out who the recipients were; was there a board or something of the like where they were listed? Much to my glee, there was. She directed me to the main hospital, and from there, I found a very helpful information desk staff person who directed me to the cafeteria area, where she believed there was a wall of "The Daisy" winners. Once again, emotions rose in me as I found the board:

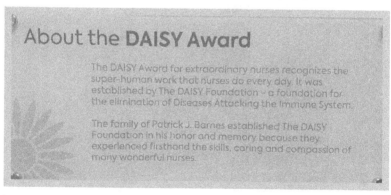

| Above is the plaque next to the winners' photos that explains its purpose.

Next to the above plaque were the photos of the winners over the last few months. As you see, there isn't a winner every month.

"The Evidence of the Past Gives Us Hope for the Future" 219

As I looked through the photos of these wonderful people, in the top right corner of the photos, there she was - my angel! The one who had grabbed hold of my children to make sure they knew their dad was still fighting and he was still there. There was still cognitive life. She let them know I was still responding. Below is my Angel Rebecca! She was the July recipient of the "Daisy Award," and she was on the ICU Critical Care Staff as an RN Nurse. She was there when I was there... when I needed her most. Once again, someone was placed in the path when they were most required.

In these situations, it is vitally important that you have an advocate for what you are going through. I could not do this for myself, and my children were not able to have access to me because of the COVID protocols at the time. Therefore, my miracle angels at that moment in time were my nurses. They were my advocates, and I thank God for them. Nurses so often do not get the credit they deserve for what they do and how strong they must be in the most critical of situations. Sometimes, most probably many times, nurses are required to stand up to the doctors who, through no fault of their own, must helicopter in and out and don't see the overall picture of what is happening with the patient. It's the nurses who do.

Nurse Rebecca had been placed there the day my daughters were there and knew the conversation that was taking place. Was it merely a coincidence she was there? Once again, simply a "lucky" break that was placed in the path of my demise? Remember who we are talking about, Mr. High Average. If you truly think it is a coincidence, I must beg to differ. She could have been off that week. She could have returned the next week to find I was gone, truly gone. I'd have been disconnected because she wasn't there to save me. Not there to have been my advocate. No one is as lucky as I have been.

I hope to have the opportunity to one day meet my nurses in person. I would cherish the opportunity to give them all a big hug. I'm fortunate to have two nurses in my family. My sister-in-law, Diane Keasbey, and my niece, Becky Keasbey. They are both BSN/RNs, and they were invaluable to my children during this time. The kids gave them access to my medical records so they could look at what was happening daily and help my children understand the process. They were invaluable to my brother Tim, who told me he would come home daily and ask Diane, "So, how is the patient?" Very often, she would say, "Well, I can either scare the shit out of you or can just say it's not looking good..." To have to deliver that information to my family could not have been easy. Having to somehow detach themselves and look critically as a medical person vs a family member was required.

Because of my good friend Jon-Paul Croome, who is president of WellStar, I hope to be able to track down and meet Nurse Rebecca. Jon-Paul told me when we sat together at a Rotary meeting in early May that he knew Rebecca well and that he would check her schedule and work to set up a meeting.

One Last Travel Back through Time

Six years ago, when I was sixty, I held a winning bid with a very close friend of mine, Tim Dunn. He and I had decided to bid together in a silent auction for a cabin up in the North Georgia mountains. It was a fundraiser for a great cause, and we managed to have the winning bid on the cabin. The plan was Tim and his wife, Liz, along with me and someone else, would go take the six-day, five-night stay together. As it would happen, somehow, we just couldn't quite seem to get it together to come up with a time we could all go. The package was only good for a limited period, and the end time was fast approaching. Only four possible times remained. Tim finally said, "We just can't make it during the time frame remaining, so why don't you just use it and don't worry about it? Someone should get to do so." At the time, my daughter Kristine was living with me with her dog Kit - Kitsune, to be precise. It's the Japanese translation of the English word fox. Kit is half Shiba Inu and half Pomeranian. He is a smaller dog, very smart, and loves his Grandpaw. You met Kit earlier when I had fallen. We, meaning Kit and I, headed to the mountains on a Wednesday evening in January with the idea of staying until Monday morning, the full length of the winning bid. Kristine was to follow on Friday after she finished her shift as a deputy sheriff in Cherokee County. She was to be off the weekend.

All started wonderfully well. Kit and I arrived with the basic food and liquid stock we had brought with us. The idea was we would go back out and get the rest of the supplies we needed once Kristine arrived. We were at the very top of the mountain in the most beautiful 5-bedroom cabin I had ever laid eyes on. It was three stories, complete with a pool table downstairs and a hot tub outside under the deck. It was paradise in the mountains.

Kit and I had wonderful walks in the woods the first evening and the next morning. The plan was I would work from the cabin on Thursday and Friday. Thursday went well until the afternoon, when I started to feel not quite right. It seemed I was taking on a bit of a fever. I had brought some ibuprofen with me, which helped with the fever.

As Thursday continued into the late afternoon, a rather heavy snowstorm blew in. I was able to get Kit out that evening and Friday morning, but conditions were getting worse, and I wasn't going to be able to negotiate the road down the mountain. Though I made it through the workday, I was feeling worse as the minutes passed. The snow continued to fall, and it started to be evident that Kristine was not going to be able to come up that night. The roads were not negotiable. Suddenly, the power went out, and my cell phone lost its charge. I had pretty well exhausted any fluids I had brought with me, as the plan had been to shop once Kristine arrived. The flu I had contracted was getting worse, and then a tree fell twenty feet from the cabin, completely blocking the road! Now, any escape route was gone. I am sitting on a mountain top, with barely any food (except for Kit's food, of course), deep into the flu, basically no water, no power or cell service, and now a tree blocking the road. I began to think the only thing missing from this very third-rate horror movie was Jason chasing Kit and me through the woods with a chainsaw!

I got into bed, shivering and feeling the worst I had ever felt (to that point) in my life. That little dog refused to leave my side. He knew his *grand-paw* was in trouble, and he was going to stand vigilantly with me. I woke up several times during the night with sweat racing down every inch of my body. I truly did wonder if I would make it through the night and felt very helpless. Little did I know, Kristine was working on a contingency plan with the sheriff's office. They were amassing the four-wheelers to get up the mountain and rescue us. Only once before had I experienced anything close to that type of sickness. I was eighteen at the time. Very seldom in my life have I ever felt I was in real danger from sickness or anything else for that matter. That night, I was afraid for my survival.

Come the break of dawn, I suddenly heard a chainsaw, which was music to my ears. My fever had managed to break sometime during the night and though the sheets were soaked, I was alive, and Kit was still right next to me. I got myself up and dressed, and out we went to investigate the sound. There at the tree was the president of the ten-home HOA of the mountain, chainsaw in hand. Instead of chasing us through the woods, he was cutting the tree, much to our collective delight. He had come up to inspect the power lines and power station which was just past the cabin we were staying in. All power to the mountain homes was out. He saw the car and the tree down and went immediately for his chainsaw.

It was only Saturday morning, and we had the place until Monday; however, in a unanimous vote (I raised my hand, and Kit raised his paw), we chose to cut it short and get ourselves home. Once again, disaster was averted.

COVID - Miracle Four

You will recall my final days at Cobb Hospital in Austell, Ga. That was the rehab hospital where I prepped for my return to normal life. I explained how I was supposed to have gone home on Friday, September 17. Everything was set for that departure date, and I couldn't have been more excited. It had been an incredibly long two months, even though I had been in a coma for the first month of it. It had been a long road back to learning to walk again and personal care.

All I had wanted to do at that point was go home! I knew how to take care of myself and just wanted to get to it. It truly was at the last minute that I was informed I was not going to leave that day. They were going to keep me until the following Wednesday, September 22. Though I was off the catheter in terms of it no longer being continually connected to me, I still had not reached a point of normal bladder evacuation. I was getting little dribs and drabs, but not a normal steady stream or anything close to a full emptying of the bladder. What this meant was, I would need to self-catheterize once reaching home, and I had been taught to do it. According to those who instructed me, it was easier to self-catheterize than to endure what they were required to do in the hospital. I'm sure that was meant to make me feel better; however, it didn't make the thought of the process any more comfortable.

You already know what happened that morning with the UTI and the bacterial infection that was discovered. Now let's look at what would have happened had I not been kept for the additional 5 days. I'd have risen that Saturday morning, September 18th, and tried to go to the bathroom. As I have stated, I had been able to go to the bathroom to a minor degree, so I am going to assume I would have gone a bit that morning at home as well. As I started to feel cold, I would have put on the sweatshirt, just as I had in the hospital. As I started to shake uncontrollably, there would have been no nurse to come in and recognize something very bad was happening. I'd have had no idea my blood pressure had reached 206/93. The doctors and nurses knew they needed to tap my bladder immediately, and then my blood pressure came down quickly. The problem for me being by myself was that I would have known *how* to tap my bladder but would not have known *to do it*.

If you do a Google search, you can see why this BP reading is a concern. The top number in the blood pressure reading is the systolic pressure. A systolic reading of 180 or higher can lead quickly to a stroke. I was already at 206. Let's keep in mind that this is only half the problem at this point. They had to run tests to see what was truly going on. I had a UTI and on top of that, I also had a second bacterial infection, which at that moment had not yet reached the bloodstream. The concern was sepsis and septic shock which can lead to all kinds of problems. Septic shock can lead to respiratory problems or heart failure, stroke, organ failure in other areas, and possibly death.

I was started on intravenous antibiotics. As they were unable to immediately identify and isolate the pathogen, my antibiotic drip was changed to a broad-spectrum antibiotic until they could figure it out. Eventually, they identified the "bug," and I was placed on the proper antibiotic to take care of both the UTI and the bacterial concern.

In the end, if I had not recognized that something very drastic was happening to me, there is a very good chance that when my friends Senator John Albers, Roswell Rotary President Terry Taylor, and fellow Rotarian Harvey Smith arrived later that morning to install handholds in the bathroom, they very likely might have found me with a stroke or even dead on the couch. No one would have been home with me at that point to call the ambulance if I became unconscious. It would have been disastrous! It was obvious in the hospital that, although they all remained very calm with two doctors and five nurses working on me, you could tell two things: one, they needed to figure it out and they needed to figure it out right then; and two, you knew they were saying, "We've brought him this far, we aren't going to lose him now!"

Let's say for a moment that I did manage to self-catheterize and started to settle down a bit. I may have thought I was okay and not gone any further. The UTI, and more importantly, the bacterial problem could have killed me, particularly if the bacterial infection had reached the bloodstream before it was found.

Being held in the hospital for those extra days was no fluke. I was held there to ensure I would be saved yet again. I've lost track of how many "lucky" things have happened to me by now in the story.

That was the fourth time in less than sixty days I had been saved from death. You may think luck or coincidence played in there. Had it been once, or maybe even twice, you might make a decent argument, but ten or so times, at least? Even the most stalwart believer in "luck" would have to think long and hard about that. They had already deemed me a "medical miracle" long before this final episode.

There was a fun movie brought out in 1994: *City Slickers II: The Legend of Curly's Gold*. It starred Billy Crystal, Daniel Stern, and Jack

Palance (as had the original *City Slickers*). They added in John Lovitz for this second one. There is a scene in the movie where the Crystal, Stern, and Lovitz characters are ready to give up the search after long days and nights for the gold they sought. They have been looking for a geographic formation that looks like a buffalo's back. Just as they are giving up, the Palance character points back to where they had crossed the night before in the dark. What was it? A mountain that looked like a buffalo's back. They had completely missed it as they came across it because it was dark. With the light of the day and fresh eyes, they were able to see it.

At some point you must look at events in your own life and realize you are, at least perhaps, being watched over and protected. You most likely won't recognize it while it is happening. Sometimes it takes a long time for it to set up as you need it, which further hides the tracks and traces. However, if you will take a little time to look back and reassess the events of your life, you might just find a bit more faith.

COVID - Miracle Five

There is no way I could leave this section of the book without speaking about all the people who followed my journey for so long. My daughters were diligent in keeping everyone up-to-date with what was happening with me over the month-long coma journey. However, before this, all three of my children talked about what they should or should not share with everyone. They didn't know if they should be quiet about it, meaning telling only those who needed to know and not the general public. Not because they didn't want to, but because they were unsure of how private I might want this to be. What they didn't anticipate was the response they would receive and how far friends were willing to go to find out what was happening.

As you have most likely gathered by now, I'm a pretty active fellow. I move in a great many circles. I have always attempted to get back to people very quickly when they reached out to me. Therefore, when all of a sudden (without any warning or saying something like, " I'm headed out of the country," or "I'll have limited access for a while,") no one saw me or heard anything from me, concern had begun to grow.

You have already read the story of my dear friend Jim Savage who went to the extreme to find me. It was at that point, the kids realized they needed to let people know what was going on. The word then began to go out. As you have already seen the FB message from my children I won't place it here again.

At the time of the message, I had been in the hospital in critical condition since July 25 which placed me almost two weeks into the coma. As you remember from the note, things are not going well. It was immediately after the note was posted and the prayer chains went forth that things began to change and the tide began to turn.

You will recall the photo from earlier of me on the ventilator with the ulcer on my chin. That is what is happening at the time of the note. On August 9th the tracheostomy took place, and the critical period of the next 4 days came and passed. It was the exact time when all around the country, and even beyond, people had started praying.

Let's not overlook the critical day of Saturday, August 7th, when my friend Leslie had organized the prayer vigil at the river. It was the exact day and nearly the exact time as the critical care meeting for my children, the same time nurse Rebecca was pulling Kristine aside telling her not to let them end this. Even the most ardent believer in "coincidence and luck" has to say that's quite a coincidence. Neither my children knew that the group was meeting at the river at that moment nor the gathering at the river knew that at that moment the children were meeting with the doctor. It was all happening virtually simultaneously.

All of the stories and situations of this chapter have been

included to help you understand that there is so much that happens behind the scenes that we so seldom see. Look for yours; they are there. I promise you that. However, you have to put in some effort to see them for yourselves. You have to look to connect the dots.

Always remember, "The evidence of the past gives us hope for the future."

CHAPTER 11
READJUSTING TO LIFE

I have finally returned home and now must readjust to living life. I'm a shadow of my former self. So skinny am I, I don't even recognize myself. I had been in such great shape, extremely healthy and full of life. I looked in the mirror and I saw someone ninety-five, not sixty-five. I had always looked so much younger than my years and now my skin was literally hanging off me and I just looked frail. I saw myself and just cried.

I put on a happy face for everyone I saw. "How are you doing?" I'd be asked. "A little better every day," I'd say, or "Outstanding!" I'm quite certain everyone inwardly was saying, "Oh my."

One of my dearest friends, Gia, had promised me that as soon as I was released she was going to take me to Marlow's Tavern - a favorite restaurant of mine, so I could enjoy a real hamburger. She, of course, made good on her promise. Below is a photo of us at Marlow's on September 26, just four days after my return home.

My hair is still long and shaggy as my friend and hair stylist Brenda, had not yet visited my home for my first haircut since July. Reviewing this photo now, I believe describing myself as death-warmed-over would have been a step up. Looking at this photo now, I still can't believe what I am seeing or that it could even possibly be me. But it is.

Though I had made strides in rehab in the hospital, I still had very little strength, and my balance was way off. I could walk because of the foot brace, but I couldn't drive myself and had many follow-up medical and rehab appointments outside the hospital to get to. I was fortunate to have my son, Gary, with me for five days, which was wonderful for my outlook on life. Kristine and Evan would come to see me; after Gary had to return to Florida, and I had Vivian and Michael to watch over and take care of me. So many friends brought me food and just came to chat. My friends Amy Andrews, Doc Torrance, and his mom, Janna Jannes, brought me food. When I was able to make the journey, I went to see my friend Joy Klan for a delicious lunch one day. All of them contributed to making me feel more like me. I just knew they were crying inside. They were all so glad I had made it and so glad I was home, but it was hard for them to see me this way. Not one of them said anything of how frail I looked. I only received smiles and hugs.

As soon as I was able, I returned to my Roswell Rotarian friends. It was a couple of weeks after my return home before I felt strong and comfortable enough to get back to our weekly meeting. I took my cane, even though I didn't want to. However, I felt I might be overwhelmed, and I was afraid of falling. The response when I entered our meeting room while transported by my dear friend Jim Savage was heartwarming. Rotary President Terry Taylor announced my arrival and welcomed me back. The moment brings tears just thinking of it.

I was determined to rebound and rebound with a vengeance. I was going to be me again, and look like me again, and have the energy of me again.

I attempted to do anything I could that would seem normal. I discovered I had very little strength and endurance; I found myself napping two to four hours every day in the afternoon. I'd sleep through the night no matter how much I had slept during the day. Because of the normal height of my bed, I was required to dismantle it and bring it down to just the mattress and box spring placed on the floor.

Attempting to stand from the bed's new position on the floor was a bit of a challenge. My daughter Viv was concerned about my ability to accomplish the task, but I wasn't going to be beaten by the challenge. I did my best to assure her I could do it and I would be fine. I could have moved around my room blindfolded, if necessary. I knew every inch of it. I wobbled a bit, but I successfully made every journey to the bathroom. It might take me several attempts to rise, but rise I did.

I had been instructed to not use my cane at home. I was to practice walking as much as possible. It was all part of the process of becoming self-reliant. It was also to aid the recovery from "drop foot." The more I could force my foot to move in a normal motion the better. Fortunately, at home, there were no stairs to negotiate, and the floors are all carpeted and flat, except the kitchen and the dining room which have wood floors. If I were to fall, my chances of avoiding serious damage were high. In the early days, I spent most of my time in my favorite chair.

I had accomplished my own goal of not requiring a wheelchair or a walker, and of that, I was quite pleased. I did require a cane when I left home. Still, I was determined not to use one whenever I could get away without it. When Gary and I made a trip to Target, I simply got a shopping cart and used it in place of the cane. It made me feel more normal, even if I didn't look normal.

The purchase of a foam pad to sit upon aided the wounds on my backside to heal as I sat in my chair for long periods of time those first few weeks after my return home.

One of the early highlights upon my return home was suggested by my son Gary. He suggested we take a little drive to get some fresh air. I was elated when he suggested we go to one of my favorite places, Bulloch Hall. Bulloch Hall is one of the historic homes in my town of Roswell, GA. It was the childhood home of Martha "Mittie" Bulloch, the mother of our 26th president, Theodore Roosevelt, Jr. I have spent many hours strolling the grounds and working on fundraisers for the site. "Perfect," I said at his suggestion. He knew I needed to get out and get moving.

The photo above is of "Teddy" and his grandparents, Major James Stephens Bulloch and his wife Martha.

Just driving around the town was enough to get my heart pumping. We arrived at Bulloch, parked and started heading to the stairs you see pictured below. I hadn't thought about the challenge I was about to face. I had walked a few stairs during rehab, however, what now faced me was more than a "few stairs."

They may not look like much, and today they are steps I climb easily again. However, on this first day of climbing, they were all the challenges I could handle. I was determined to do so though. I made it up five steps to the large landing before needing to stop and rest. My second attempt took me to the second landing five more steps further. The third attempt took me to the top. I knew my heart was pounding, and I simply had to rest for a moment and regain myself before I was able to move around the drive (not pictured) to the front of the house. I then had to sit for a bit. After a brief respite, I was able to walk around the property and soak in all the beautiful sites. By the time we reached around the property and back to the car, I was spent, but I was beaming. It was the first of many steps toward recovery, but what a great place to start.

Each day was a little better. The next big step was to get rehab outside the hospital. That was to take place at the medical building at WellStar North Fulton, where my COVID journey had begun. Dr. Brian was my chief physical therapist, and I came to look forward to seeing him every chance I got. He is bright, dedicated to his work, and someone I could easily relate to. I knew he knew what he was doing, and everything he was doing was aimed at making me better. He would challenge me in so many areas, and when he could see I was struggling he would always say, "Don't be discouraged, I am having you do hard things. You're doing great!" We'd walk the halls outside the PT room and walk the staircase as we moved through the process. Because there were so many patients, it was initially hard to get into the rotation schedule. I told the young lady doing the scheduling that I was fully in support of any opening first thing in the morning, as early as times were available. A smile crossed her face as I said that. She told me, "That will make things much easier getting you in. So many of the patients don't want to go early in the morning." They would text me as soon as something would open, and I took every opportunity. Our sessions were an hour long each time we met, and I couldn't believe how fast the time went by.

Regarding my foot brace: one of the biggest days for me came about three weeks after I had left my final hospital. I had been wearing the hospital-provided foot brace to this point. The call finally came, "Mr. Crooks, your custom foot brace is ready." Yes!

I'll be there tomorrow! I immediately called my good Rotarian friend, Jim Savage, and asked, "Can you take me to get my brace?" "Absolutely," came the response, and off we went at the appointed time.

This was a big day for a couple of reasons, not the least of which was the fact that the new brace would fit into most of my shoes. This would open up so many more normal-looking outfits for me. The brace would be hidden under my pants, and I would be able to get rid of the big bulky shoe I had been wearing. I had grown weary of the big sneaker worn on my right foot and one regular shoe on my left.

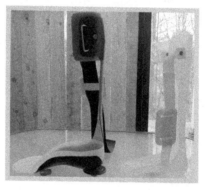

Pictured are the two foot braces side by side to provide a better visual of the difference between the two.

One can easily see, there is a huge difference in the size of the two. I was certainly very happy to have had the hospital brace while in rehab as it permitted me to get walking much faster than I was able to do with the ace bandaging discussed in the Cobb Hospital rehab discussion, or just attempting to walk with just a shoe on and no brace. The new custom brace felt so comfortable. I was able to walk right out of the office with the greatest of ease, and it was a huge step (pun fully intended) back toward normal life. I was able to get my shoes on easily now. However, the greatest gift was yet to come!!

When I left the hospital, I was instructed that I could not drive while wearing a brace. Therefore, for three weeks I had to rely on one of my children, one of my friends, or an Uber driver to pick me up and take me anywhere. It was painful since the last thing in the world I wanted to do was have to rely on anybody. Still, you do what you have to do. During my fitting of the custom brace the opportunity to ask the question I was dying to ask arrived.

As the attendant shaved a bit off here and a bit off there as he completed the fitting. I asked, in my calmest voice, "So can I drive now?" He looked at me as if I had three heads and replied, "Well, who told you that you couldn't?"

I replied , "They told me at the hospital I couldn't drive with a brace on!"

He retorted, "Well that's crazy! Look, you were here and now you are here." He was making gestures with his hands as if showing points on a graph. He continued, "Jonathan, I have people with full prosthetic legs who drive cars. It's a little different for them, but they do it. Of course, you can drive a car. Go home and drive around your neighborhood a couple of times and get the feel of it and you'll be good to go."

I nearly floated out the door to my buddy Jim's waiting car, jumped in, and said, "I can drive again!" Freedom at last! As soon as he deposited me back home, I went directly in and got my keys. I popped into my car and started her up. "Well, here goes nothing," I thought to myself and put the car in reverse. Would I be able to stop? I could! I drove around the community a couple of times. Stopped at the mailboxes and got my mail, and life couldn't have been better. I could drive again! I found that stopping was extremely easy and natural. You must lift your foot, move it over and place it on the brake whether you have a brace on or not. No difference. The only difference was how you stepped on the gas. Because the brace runs up the bottom of your foot, you can't push down with a flexing of your ankle. I was required to push down with my entire foot. I found that easily accomplished as well.

Once driving was reestablished, it was on to the next big hurdle. When could I go back to the gym and start building up my strength? When I looked at the photo with my friend Gia coupled with my inability to walk up the steps at Bulloch without stopping twice, it was obvious I had a long path ahead to regain my strength. As with everything I had faced to this point, I knew the only way to get there was to do it.

As my PT sessions started to become more regular, I finally asked Dr. Brian the question that had been on my lips for some time. "Dr. Brian," I said, "when can I go back to the gym?" The response was just what I had hoped to hear. "Yesterday," was his clear answer, and so off I went. Having been someone who had worked out my entire life, I knew how to approach the workout. What I came to realize very quickly was just how far I had slipped. If you are familiar with the bikes at the gym (I happen to work out at LA Fitness), I would ride for twenty minutes at a ninety to 100 RPM rate at level eight. I got on the bike for the first time in two and a half months and was barely able to ride at level four for three minutes. I was pushing it to just accomplish that. I simply had to tell myself: you have to start somewhere, and this is it. As I've stated before, you can't take step two until you make step one.

All the weight work I have now put in has paid off. Seven months later I am back doing almost all the weights I had done pre-COVID. Though I won't recount every milestone I'll share some of the equipment I used to help me strengthen and the people who helped me.

There were several different exercises used during my PT in the hospital playground and many of them continued to the playground after I left the hospital and moved to the PT outpatient work. All of this took place under the watchful eye of Dr. Brian and his trusted young intern. He was an outstanding young man, dedicated to the craft he was learning.

Photo of my intern, who has since graduated and should now be a full-fledged PT.

I'm disappointed not to show us without masks, but we were still required to wear them for our sessions. Hopefully, you can see the smiles under the masks.

The exercises were designed specifically around working on my "drop foot" and balance, which were the two biggest concerns. Very quickly I was scheduled for three days per week, this frequency certainly aided my recovery. One piece of equipment we used every time I came in for PT is shown below. The equipment is called a "neuromuscular electrical stimulator" machine.

The following definition comes from the "VeryWellHealth" website.

"Electrical stimulation is a type of therapeutic treatment that can serve many different purposes in physical therapy. It can be used to decrease pain and inflammation, improve circulation, and it can help your muscles contract properly. Electrical stimulation often is used to augment your physical therapy program after an injury or illness; it should not be the only treatment you receive when attending physical therapy."[1]

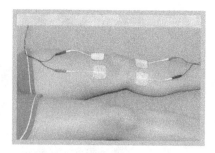

Photo comes from the same website. In my case, the pads you see deployed here were placed just below my knee and then again just above my ankle as opposed to what you see here.

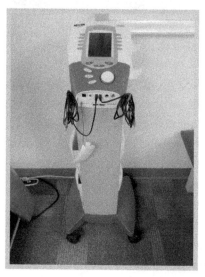

The specific machine you see is the one I used personally.

When we first began to use it, I could only feel a bit of tingling just below my knee. I was unable to feel it at my ankle and they had it set full throttle! My ankle and the top of my right foot had no real feeling. Even to this day, the top of my foot is still basically numb. However, over time, some feeling has returned.

The process is to send electronic waves down the nerves to help the healing and regenerate nerve impulses. Because of the damage to my back and down my leg sustained twenty-five years earlier that has never healed, we were starting the process behind the eight ball already. Still, it was determined that this process could help the overall drop foot problem, so we used the machine at every session. With each passing week, the tingling would travel further down my leg, and did so without the PT having to turn up the pulses to the top setting. That was progress and gave me hope I could overcome the drop foot problem. Dr. Brian would push my foot up as much as possible each session to get the full range of motion back. He was naturally incredibly flexible himself ; I, however, was not. I was lucky to get a 90-degree right angle. Still, by the time we ended our sessions together, I was able to get past a 90-degree angle and get the right foot to match the left foot. Once that was accomplished, we knew we had done what was needed.

Because I don't have a right calf to speak of due to the damage of 25 years ago, we needed to find alternative ways to strengthen my foot and ankle. Out came more equipment. The following are the different pieces of equipment employed to help me gain strength and balance and help offset the drop foot issue. We used different pieces of equipment each day, and they were indeed challenging. Much more challenging than what you might think. What I can attest to is, they worked for me over time.

I used the ball you see below by standing on it and rolling my ankle. It was difficult to get my balance on it initially, but eventually I came to master it well.

I would stand on it with both feet and then would stand on it with just my right foot, holding onto a counter to help balance me.

Below the ball, you see a long blue foam board. I had to walk on it, one foot in front of the other, and then turn to the side and move, left to right, to one end and then back, right to left. The idea was to give the effect of walking on uneven ground to help relearn balance. Additionally, it helped strengthen all the muscles around my ankle. I found it extremely helpful when I later walked on uneven ground versus a smooth, flat sidewalk.

The foam boards came in several different lengths, usually six to eight feet.

The next photo displays a wide variety of equipment that was available for rehab. We would occasionally use the square foam blocks. The cones were used toward the end of my time in rehab. When I was in Cobb Hospital rehab, my task was to bend down and pick up cones. Everything was designed to help me regain a total sense of balance: not just walking but performing every type of movement imaginable and to be able to do so with confidence. The goals were: one, that I could accomplish the move; and two, that I wouldn't be afraid of falling. This required doing moves at different angles.

The discs next to the cones were also used from time to time. They were like the ball, but flatter and had bumps on them. They gave a different feeling to the bottom of my foot. Remember, when your eyes are closed, which I was required to do with several of the exercises, you no longer have sight as part of the sensory information to use for processing whatever you are attempting to do. Remember the discussion of washing your hair in the shower? The idea, once again, is that your only sense of balance at that moment comes from the bottom of your feet. And these discs are not " stable ground." All these moves were difficult at first. They did get easier over time, but the practice didn't come fully into play until I walked in real life on uneven ground.

Also pictured are weights for ankles or wrists and ball weights for strength building. None of these were part of my specific therapy.

Over the course of my rehabilitation, I spent more and more time going to the gym to gain strength and this helped my PT sessions become better and better. I finally reached the point of asking Dr. Brian if he thought I could go without using the foot brace anymore. The main concern revolved around driving. Recalling that I had wondered if I would be able to drive *with* a foot brace, roughly three months later, in December 2021, I wondered if I would be able to drive *without* one. My concern was my ability to lift my foot normally, or at least normally enough to drive. Dr. Brian believed that day was coming, just wasn't sure exactly when we'd achieve it.

I began by not using the brace if I wasn't driving. However, if I was driving to for example to my PT session, I would wear the brace to drive, but then remove it to go into PT. I did my level-hearted best to walk normally and show this to my PT team. I wanted them to see we were making progress and how determined I was to regain my old gait. We achieved full success in just under three months from the time I received my custom foot brace. I put it aside for good just before Christmas, 2021.

Moving for a moment slightly backward in time, as October rolled around I thought it was time to write to all the wonderful people who had followed my journey while in the hospital. On October 7, two weeks after my release back into the world, I placed the following note via Facebook:

> *"Finally, a Note from the Patient*
>
> *Dearest, Dearest family, friends and wonderfully faithful souls I'd not had the pleasure of meeting before my incredible journey with COVID. It seemed it was time (actually, past time) that I write to you all and thank you for the wonderful support I received as I fought to continue life with you all. I tried to do so on several occasions, but FB didn't seem to want to cooperate with me. Each time I'd start to write I would get fairly deep and then hit some extraneous key, like backspace, and everything would just disappear. Finally, my daughters told me to just put it in Word and copy and paste, so that's what I am doing.*
>
> *I don't believe I can ever express in any real meaningful fashion what your loving support has meant to me. The prayer chains that went out through Rotary, The Lions, my Roswell Presbyterian Church, my High School Hoosic Valley, family, and friends leaves me speechless. The net was cast far and wide!! I heard from so many people, many of whom I don't even know personally, but have now become part of my faith family. Heaven must have been overflowing with the fervent prayers for me. Forgive the reference, but I guess it is kind of like "George Bailey", from "It's a Wonderful Life" (one of my personal favorites), "I guess we don't really know how many lives we touch in our everyday life." I have truly been blessed.*
>
> *I would be remiss if I didn't take a moment here to thank all my children for their diligence in watching over me, Kristine for sending out the updates to all of you (I have heard from so many who were so grateful for the updates), Evan for his undying support of Kristine in*

her support of me, Vivian for being here with me along with her boyfriend Michael to tend to, quite frankly, my every need and my son Gary for coming up from Florida, and postponing the start of a new job, to spend my first five days home with me. Gary, I personally know how difficult it is to be so far away and feeling so helpless. I had the same situation with your grandfather. I couldn't be prouder of my children as they handled it all with diligence and grace.

As an old seminarian, I'm not supposed to be "proud". I'm hoping for some special dispensation on that in this case. Speaking of my time as a seminarian and my faith background for a moment. My doctors called me a "Medical Miracle". As you probably know, I was patient zero. The first one through the door with the COVID Delta Variant at WellStar, North Fulton. They honestly didn't know how to treat it. I was told everything they tried from their COVID-19 experience didn't work on Delta. Therefore, when I went on the ventilator and my kidneys began to crash, there were those who felt it was game, set and match. There were those who said I was not responding. "Medical" Miracle? I think not. There were far too many prayers, far too many "coincidences" and miraculous restarting of my kidneys, nurses who stood their ground and said, "He is responding", to put my faith in "Medical Miracles". The whole story is quite amazing as it continued through my stay at "Windy Hill" and then on to Rehab at Cobb Hospital in Austell.

I am very aware that friends through Rotary and Church made sure I went to the correct places. I couldn't have been looked after, nor watched over better. Since this is my note, I can say this with complete confidence to those who can't see the hand of God in this, I think you might want to look a little closer.

Though I will write more in the future of my experience, some of which will no doubt make you chuckle, particularly those of you who know me to be a little bit of a, "Type A" personality, meaning I don't accept "No" for an answer, I will draw to a close here for the time being.

Know beyond all things, all of you are part of the reason I am here today, able to write to you and share my story with you. I can not tell you how glad I am to be able to share it with you myself, rather than have you hear it from someone else. May God continue to Bless each of you in whatever struggle you might personally face and know that you are held most dearly in my heart."

As with all the posts that went out from my family, the responses on this one were no different. There were 165 responses, 130 comments, and four shares. The following are a few of the comments I wanted to share as I have with the other posts.

> "Ginger Eatman
> Jonathan, what a joy it is for me to see your update. Praise Our Lord that He kept you here on Earth to heal you instead of taking you to Heaven to heal you. Obviously your work here is not complete. God bless you as you continue to heal."

> "Lynne Lindsay
> We are glad to have you back Jonathan. Prayers circled you and the Wellstar staff day & night. We knew you were in the best of hands & that the good Lord would provide."

> "Harvey Smith
> So glad you're back Jonathan P Crooks! Looking forward to seeing you at Rotary again!"

> "Bette Thompson
> Jon, I'm so very thankful to know that you are doing so well and that you are unbelievably able to put together such a beautiful post to assure all of us that you're here with us and planning to stay!! It puts a smile on my face to know this —a smile that replaces the concern I felt upon initially hearing of your situation! Prayer is a very powerful tool and was obviously extremely effective in your healing!! We'll continue to pray for you and your family while we look forward to your updates as you continue to heal! Take care Jon and know you're in my thoughts!!"

"*Valary Anderson Dreyer*
This is beautiful! No coincidences!
Can't wait for the rest."

"*Greg McDermott*
Jonathan P Crooks, I am so happy to read this post! Kathy and I have been praying for your wellness, and here we are. Too many years have passed, let's find a way to see each other. wishing you continued health and happiness!"

"*Kathy Alley*
I join your many friends in praising God for your miraculous recovery, Jonathan! It did my heart good to SEE YOU at church, talking so well, and so excited to be alive! Whew, it was a close one! It is agreed that God is not finished with you yet! Wonderful report; I look forward to more of them!!"

There are so many – actually all of them – I would love to share with you. They are so inspiring and uplifting.

Two weeks after this post I had the opportunity to share my COVID experience at our Roswell Rotary meeting of October 21, 2021. I shared the podium that day with two of my dearest friends, Senator John Albers and his wife Kari. John was relating his own story of donating one of his kidneys to his son Will. It is equally as inspiring a story as my own, and I was honored to share the stage with him. The photo below is from that day, with John at the podium, his wife Kari seated next to me, and our Rotary President Terry Taylor listening in on the left. You will recall Terry from my story about the hand railings being placed in my bathroom. It was he, John, and Harvey Smith (whom I quoted above) who placed those handholds.

The next photo is me at the podium that day relating the story. My sister Nancy said that I look like our father in these photos, and I can see that as well. It is rather amazing, as I was adopted, so the fact that I seem to favor him here is fascinating to me. The two photos were taken by my dear friend, Ian Mari, who takes most of the professional photos for Rotary.

Photo Credit: PhotoMari-USA/BlufftonPhoto

| Photo Credit: PhotoMari-USA/BlufftonPhoto

A WEEK AND A HALF LATER, Vivian, Michael, and I attended a fun Halloween Walk through the Chattahoochee Nature Center in Roswell, Ga. The photo below is from that evening in our attire. We had a blast hearing their stories and enjoying s'mores. It was a bit of a walk for me personally, but I made it.

Just a few days later, on November 5, 2021, I had the honor of attending Vivian's formal graduation from the University of Central Florida (UCF). It was pouring that day (as it can do in Florida). How much do you think we cared at that moment?

Vivian was radiant, and I couldn't have been prouder of her. We were able to keep her dry; me, not so much. Thus, the rain drops on my jacket. I couldn't have cared less. I was there, and I didn't have to miss it.

On November 20, 2021, I sent out my second update to all who had followed me on this journey. The following is that message. You will note at the bottom of it, in the second to the last paragraph, that I announced I was planning to write the book you are now reading. I honestly don't recall exactly when I decided to do so, but what I can tell you is many friends encouraged me to write the story as they felt it would be inspiring to many. My sincere hope is that it is inspiring for you all.

> "To all my dear, dear family and friends (both old and new) who followed me as I fought through my version of COVID. To all of you who prayed hard and long, who supported my family here in Georgia and Florida, up north in Schaghticoke, New York, and in North Carolina, I thank you, praise you, and send many good blessings to you!! I would not have survived the ordeal without you. Just know your prayers worked!!
>
> Again, it is past time for an update from me to you, sent with love. I continue to search for knowledge related to this nasty disease. It very obviously is a very personal disease, meaning it attacks each person

differently. If you were to grab three people of relatively good health and the same age, you could have three different results. One might never even know they had it, one may have very mild symptoms, and the other is at death's door. I survived it, and I pray all do.

There are so many side effects to this. So let me start with the pity party, crybaby stuff first and clear through it quickly. I'm finding I'm losing my hair. It has thinned quite a bit. What I have come to learn is that when one goes through high fever and long, deep illness, your hair goes through a shedding process. I'm going through that now. My hair is shedding all at once instead of gradually as it normally would. Here's the good news…in six to nine months, it should go back to a normal process, and it will come back. For the time being, it has stopped growing. Okay, enough of the cosmetic stuff!

Now for the medical things. I came out of the hospital with what is known as "Drop Foot" in my right foot. It is not uncommon with COVID patients. Particularly those of us who were in a coma state and lost much of our strength. I was informed by my nurses that you lose 50% of your strength per week if you are in a coma, medically induced, or otherwise. Therefore, after four weeks of being in one, I was down to about 6% of my strength. Drop Foot means your foot does not act normally. You may not be able to move it side to side; you can't push your foot down nor raise it up. In my case, I was able to move it side to side immediately but was unable to push down with it or lift it up. By the time I left the rehab hospital, I was able to push down; however, I was completely unable to raise my foot up. I was given a foot brace to wear that runs under my foot and up my leg so I can walk. I now have a custom-made version that allows me not only to walk, but I also can drive with it, making life far more normal!! I have been in Physical Therapy since leaving the hospital to work on the ability to raise my foot. It is slowly coming back!

Taste and smell are still an adventure. It's interesting how it kind of comes and goes. At times, only parts of the items can be tasted. For example, Sprite tastes horrible; Coke seems to be missing some of the taste elements, however, Ginger Ale tastes perfectly normal and good!

They say that should all come back over time.

Although COVID hit my lungs, it appears to have left my heart alone! My lungs are slowly coming back. I was on the stationary bike at the gym for the first time this past week, and I'm increasing my rides and levels. It really helps strengthen the lungs. I've also been walking 1 ¾ miles almost every day, with some slight hills to get the heart pumping and work the lungs. A long way to go to get back to where I was, but good progress!!

My weight has come back up to almost where I started. Funny, now I wouldn't mind losing 5 lbs. I think, however, I'll do it the old-fashioned way this time and just watch what I eat!! Losing 50 lbs. the way I did is not what I would recommend!

I often say to my children, "You can't do something the second time until you've done it once first." It's such a big day today! I accomplished my 1 ¾ mile trek today in just my running sneakers and no foot brace!

I discarded my cane weeks ago. Now, I'm working to get rid of the foot brace. They said it could be a year to eighteen months; I might have to use it. I was released from the hospital on September 22, and today is November 20th. Therefore, I'm getting close to losing the brace altogether in just two months!!! Again, a great testimony to prayer, good therapists, and hard-determined effort!

One last thing! I am in the process of writing a book on my experience through COVID, and you are all to be a part of it! A major part of it! The working title is "Miracles, Angels and Messages."

I have been collecting all the medical notes, contacting my doctors, and have already begun writing. There, I buried the lead!

May God continue to bless us all and bless each of you for being there praying for me through this…"

Once again, as with all before, the response was wonderful. Below are a few of the responses.

"Becky Stout
GOD IS GOOD…I thank God every day! Looking forward to

reading your book and hearing your story...who knows... we have wondered why your preaching process was stifled...maybe God will use your book as his messenger! Blessings. You will look great with or without hair and brighten the world with your enthusiasm and warm smile!"

"John Doyle
Thank you for sharing, and I'm so glad you're in the recovery process!"

"Linda Hahn Kent
Jonathan, writing your story will help countless people know how to pray for and minister to seriously ill COVID patients. God will use your words to His glory. Rejoicing with you for each milestone of progress."

"Cristi Coman Smith
You are an inspiring survivor, and believe your story will be a fantastic read and I look forward to it! So happy you're stronger and better with every new day."

"Hilda Downer
I am glad to hear of your progress – victory, really – and that you are writing a book. This will increase your healing manifold – from personal experience. My prayers continue for you."

On December 22, 2021, I wrote my last update, to date, on my progress. I should most likely write another one; however, I believe I will let this stand as the final update to all via Facebook and let this book be the final update.

The following is the update I placed on Facebook for all to see.

"Three Month Update – 12/22/21
Believe it or not, it's been exactly three months since I left the hospital. I thought it was time for the next update. I came out of Cobb

Hospital in Austell on September 22, 2021. Cobb Hospital was the rehab hospital.

COVID-19 is such an interesting (obviously an understatement) disease. It is so personal to each soul it hits. That's one of the biggest challenges for the medical community. You can have three people standing next to each other who are the same age same physical makeup in terms of health. One never knows he had COVID at all, the second has mild symptoms and the third is at Death's Door, as I was. The aftermath is just as confusing. I had the opportunity of being with some great friends this past Saturday laying wreaths for the "Wreaths Across America" program. We worked together in the Old Roswell Cemetery. My friends Tony Lay, whom I have known for years, Ron Cowan from Roswell Rotary, whom I met about six months ago through Rotary, and Jim (whose last name I need to secure). Jim is also part of the VFW, as are Ron and Tony. Great guys!! We all have had COVID; though my friends, all my elders, had it mildly. However, they indicated, as we sat at lunch at Lucky's after the wreath laying, they all have had some form of short-term memory loss from it, as well as the joy of some loss of taste and smell. For me, I'm not sure I have short-term memory loss (though my children might disagree). What I can say is I can't immediately grab words at times as well as I could up to five months ago. One of my greatest gifts is my ability to communicate "off the cuff." Hoping all of that will come back over time.

So, where am I now? What milestones have been reached since I last wrote to you all?

I'll start with the little downside. When I walk without my custom foot brace, I walk a little bit as a duck walks, with a slap of the foot. It is slowly getting better though, and that is the good news!

So where have we come in 90 days? Last week was a very big week. A week ago Saturday, I did something I hadn't done since July. I was able to complete my entire 3.3-mile hike/run! The hills I do are a bit challenging. I haven't been able to run up that type of terrain for a number of years because I only have ¾ of my right leg since herniating a disc in my back 25 years ago. I really don't have a right calf anymore.

So there is not enough push off with that foot to run up hills, but I can hike up fairly hard. I would then run down the back side of the hills and the straightaways. Saturday, I was able to jog parts of the runs I had been doing before COVID. I wasn't setting any land speed records, mind you, but I also didn't trip and fall as is always the fear. I had tried to jog a few weeks earlier and found I was still clipping my left foot with my right foot (the right foot is the one with "drop foot"), so it just wasn't safe yet. So, two big check marks...I could go out and walk at least 3.3 miles, and I was able to jog a bit, which works the lungs.

Two and a half months ago, you may remember, I was wondering if I could drive a car with a foot brace. Two and a half months later, I was wondering if I could drive a car without a foot brace. Well, as it turns out, the answer to both of those questions was an emphatic YES! As of Saturday, December 1, I no longer use a foot brace for anything. Hip, Hip Hooray! I was told I may have "Drop Foot" for up to a year and a half and might have to use a brace that long. Maybe even forever, though no one really thought that second statement would be true. I still have some drop-foot issues, but it's really more of just continuing to strengthen the foot and ankle. I do have some nerve issues in the ankle area, but it will not stop me.

The final milestone is the fact I had my last PT (physical therapy) session last Friday, December 17th. My chief PT doctor, Dr. Brian, said he didn't think there was anything else we needed to do together. I was basically doing it all and to just contact him if I needed him. After exchanging goodbyes and goodbye hugs, I bid all the staff who had worked so diligently with me fare-thee-well! Not bad, less than three months after my release from the hospital! Way ahead of schedule. As I had said to them all at the beginning, nothing on the table that needed to be accomplished had "No" as an option.

We now move to the next phases of recovery. Your prayers have worked to perfection. The "Powers that be" are listening to you more than you or I could possibly fathom. Please continue to pray for me to understand and employ the word "patience." Blessings to you all, and I continue to pray for you all as you continue to pray for me! With great

Love, Jonathan"

As with the other notes posted, the response was overwhelming. Below are a few of the responses.

> "Jennifer Lyons Alexander
> Wow, you are a miracle! With your attitude, you will be yourself again! You have always been a positive/half-full glass guy. I have admired that about you for years. You never give up. Good thoughts and prayers for you. Merry Christmas!"

> "Jenny Lynn Brewer
> This story amazed me last week...blessed to have had the conversation and for you to have such great progress! Positive vibes your way."

> "Andy Carpenter
> Enjoy your Christmas time! Much love to you & your family!!"

> "Bette Thompson
> Jon, I'm hoping that you and yours had a wonderful Christmas—your blessings were extra special this year!! So happy to hear of your tremendous progress and looking forward to the publication of your book documenting your journey! May 2022 treat you very well and know that the prayers for you continue! Take care and keep up the great job!"

AS TIME HAS MOVED ON, many other firsts have come my way. As you will recall, I sustained voice struggles as I came out of the coma. There were challenges related to the tracheotomy. I have always been a good singer, particularly in church. I do enjoy the old hymns and somewhat pride myself in my ability to sing them well. I also enjoy singing what I term my music - music of the '70s, '80s and '90s. As I have mentioned earlier in the book, I was an Area All-State Chorus singer while in high school. Because of my tracheotomy, it took a good while before my full voice returned, or at least close to it. Sunday, November 21, 2021, was a milestone. That was the day I was first able to fully sing the hymns at church again. Sounds like a small thing - I assure you it was not, certainly not to me. I was finally able to see that those abilities were coming back, and each little step was monumental.

Other "firsts" of note: Tuesday, January 11, 2022, was the date I had my first dance. It was with a dear friend, Kimberly Giordano. With glee, I can say she asked me to dance. It was a slow dance, and she knew I could handle the moves, though I was still struggling a bit with balance issues.

Less than two months later, on March 5, 2022, one of the most fulfilling events occurred. You will recall my daughter Kristine was informed on August 11, 2021, that a final decision about my survival was impending; it was the same day that she and Evan knew for sure they were expecting my first grandchild. March 5th marked the day of the baby shower, which I was here to attend.

| This is the invitation to that shower.

| Kristine, Evan, and me at that shower.

Little did we know at that moment of pure bliss and happiness that the road that was to bring little Jonathan "Henry" Lockstedt to us would be a rocky one. For that story, you'll have to wait for the final chapter. This day, however, was pure joy for the entire family!

As time continues to pass since my COVID experience, there have been some ups and downs. It's sometimes hard to pinpoint exactly what is an ongoing COVID aftermath and what are just normal life experiences of aging. For instance, on April 11, I underwent outpatient surgery for atrial fibrillation, or a heart flutter, as it is referred to. I mentioned this earlier in the book. It is a procedure in which a catheter goes into a vein in your groin area and goes up around into your heart. As the doctor explained to me, he, in essence, zaps some cells to slow the flutter and place the heart back in rhythm. It is 90% effective as opposed to an older method of shocking the heart, which is deemed 50% effective. I've spoken with several friends who have had one or the other. In my case, the method chosen was completely successful, according to my doctor, during the follow-up appointment two weeks after the surgery. When I posed the question, "Is this COVID-related?" The answer was, "Maybe." All I can tell you is I didn't have the flutter before COVID. Doesn't necessarily mean it came as a by-product, but it is difficult to exclude the possibility either.

I am finding I've had more extensive nerve damage since my COVID experience. I'm now experiencing numbness in both hands, on my middle fingers and index fingers, that comes and goes. I still have numbness in both my right and left ankles. Still, despite these things, I can use all my fingers fairly normally, and I can move better all the time with my legs. My balance is returning much closer to normal levels. That is extremely encouraging.

My strength is continuing to improve; I can best see that from my workouts at the gym. I am continuing to push myself to get back to pre-COVID levels.

On May 2, 2022, I completed my first two-a-day workout. I did my 3.3-mile circuit outside and then headed to the gym, rode the bike, and went through my weights workout. I have to chuckle a bit now as I have put weight back on and wouldn't mind dropping a pound or two.

Overall, things are going well, and I can't complain. There have been so many miracles, angels, and messages in my journey. As you have met so many of my family through the course of this book, I had to include one of my favorite family photos. I wish everyone was in it, but most are. Missing are my son, Gary, and daughter and son-in-law, Kristine and Evan.

I've always tended to utilize as many photos as I can in my historical talks. I do so because I believe the audience gains a much better appreciation for the subjects when they can look into the subjects' eyes. There is a much deeper connection that way. So, below is my family, who mean the world to me and who suffered through the journey. I am pleased to say we continue to live a full life as a happy family. This photo was taken at Thanksgiving 2017. Seems rather appropriate as we have given thanks so much in this book.

From left to right beginning with the top row and working downward: Top Row: My brother Tim; my sister-in-law Diane, married to my brother Tim; my cousin Kim; my brother-in-law Michael, married to my sister Nancy, who is standing next to me. Middle row seated: My nephew Philip, Nancy and Michael's son; my cousin Wayne, my stepmom of fifty plus years, Patricia; my nephew Jake, Tim and Diane's son. Front row: my niece Heidi, Nancy, and Michael's daughter; my daughter Vivian; my niece-in-law Thatiana, Philip's wife; and my niece Becky, Tim and Diane's daughter.

As I complete this chapter, we have traveled a full ten months since my COVID journey began. It is now May of 2022. The story continues, and so do the miracles. The final chapter in this journey, which you will read now, ends this book, but certainly not the journey. So read on one more time.

CHAPTER 12
IN THE END

"And in the end
The love you take
Is equal to the love
You make"

— JOHN LENNON/PAUL MCCARTNEY
"THE END"

A long way have we traveled, you and I. Our lives have become inseparably intertwined. This can no longer be undone. I can't express to you in words what it means to me that you have come along on this journey to this point. I thank you for doing so. Still, there are a couple of things I need to impart to you so that you grasp the full meaning of this book.

We have talked about so many topics. We've looked at miracles; we've met angels, both here on earth and those from above. I hope I have made you laugh at times, think of friends of yours who match the friends of mine, and I hope I have enticed you to reexamine your journey and have found that, in so many ways, it has mirrored my own. We are not so different, you and I. We aren't different at all. It comes down to awareness of all that is around us. That which is with us every day. Are we open to it? Do we see it? Can we hear it?

One of the benefits of writing a book over a period of time is the fact that new evidence can come your way as you write. New evidence has come my way that I can share with you here at the end of this journey.

I shared with you the fact that my daughter Kristine had her pregnancy confirmed on August 11, 2021. It was the same day she received a call from one of the medical staff saying that she and her siblings were close to having to decide to end my life. How much she had to process - being on the mountaintop of euphoria about her and Evan's impending first child, and realizing that this child might not have the opportunity to know one of its grandfathers, namely me.

So how did that turn out in the end? As you know, I am here, I did survive. However, Jonathan "Henry" Lockstedt did not arrive without challenges. You must hear this story to understand how miracles continue to the next generation.

Both my daughters, Kristine and Vivian, inherited a trait from their mother's side of the family. A trait their mother Kasie carries and her father before her carried. Fortunately, Gary does not manifest this trait; however, he could carry the gene. That remains to be seen. This trait causes one's immune system to attack its own platelets. It is not extremely uncommon but is far from common. Generally, most individuals will have 150,000 to 450,000 platelets in the body at any given time. I generally carry 250,000, and my son Gary runs about the same. Vivian and Kristine generally will carry around 60K to 70,000, as does their mother. Doctors my children have had over the years universally stated that my children can lead very normal lives. They will bruise much more easily than most, and the bruises can be rather dramatic in appearance. However, it simply becomes something you deal with and generally have to explain to people when they see an extremely dark bruise. As the doctors would often say, " I wouldn't recommend rock climbing as a profession."

Unfortunately, when it comes to childbirth this is where the condition often rears its ugly head most dramatically. The platelets plummet! I remember the twins' mother's platelets fell to 12,000 as their birth approached. This is dangerously low. The girls were delivered via C-section and the doctors needed to get mom's platelets to 50,000 to perform the major surgery. They infused platelets just before birth. The girls were just fine; however, Mom was not. I can't remember exactly what Kasie's blood pressure numbers were during the most critical time after the births, other than the top number was over 200. The bottom number wasn't much better. Fortunately, their mom did indeed survive the ordeal, though she very nearly didn't. I remember thinking, as I looked at their mom, that I might very well have to raise these two beautiful babies without their mother. The thought they would not know her was devastating to consider. Additionally, I would never have had my son Gary, who came three years later. As you are about to read, it was crushing to imagine that now my son-in-law Evan might have to face the same fate.

As it came time for Kristine to deliver, she encountered the same problem. Her platelets began to plummet. Just as they had with her mom, the doctors tried all kinds of methods to raise Kristine's platelet level. She had dropped down to 19,000 at her lowest; and though they were able to raise them to 31,000, they couldn't move them above that mark. She had entered the hospital on Thursday, March 31, 2022, to deliver, but because the platelets were so low, they kept postponing the birth. First, it was till Friday (when there were seventeen C-sections scheduled already), and then till Saturday. Finally, Sunday morning, they had to make the call. She started to go into labor naturally. She was at 31,000 platelets and the doctors said, "We'd rather you be at 50,000, but we're going to go with quality over quantity. Your platelets are really good and strong, though low." Jonathan "Henry" was born at 12:02 p.m. Sunday, April 3. He was pristine and beautiful, as C-section babies generally are. I was so thrilled that Jonathan "Henry" was here, but I was concerned for Kristine and asked Evan via text, "How's my baby?"

All was basically okay until about an hour after delivery. Then Kristine started to hemorrhage. She lost three liters of blood very quickly. That is approximately half the blood in her body! According to a nurse friend of the family (Laura, head nurse at Northside Hospital in Atlanta in the NICU where Kristine delivered), the hospital had very recently become certified for a new procedure called MIP (Massive Infusion Protocol). Kristine wasn't the first to receive it, but pretty close to it. They also used a "balloon procedure" called *Bakri*. Nurse Laura said that if they had not done these procedures Kristine most likely would have died.

Nurse Laura also told us that the lead nurse of the birthing team led the entire team in prayer just prior to the surgery, as they knew the concerns and potential dangers they were facing. I'm quite certain that isn't on the normal checklist. Thank God for them all and may they all be blessed.

We were all on our knees during this time waiting, praying that all would be okay. Once again, just as during my critical time, there were hundreds of people praying beginning with the family: Kim and John Lockstedt, Evan's parents; Kasie and Phil Escarsega, Kristine's mom and stepdad; brother and sisters of both Evan and Kristine; aunts, uncles, cousins, and friends around the country. Facebook notes were shared out to all the people who had prayed for me, letting them know that Kristine's critical time was imminent. We prayed that the doctors' and nurses' hands would be guided. They were. The skill employed by all of them is beyond thanks and gratitude for their work that day. They were wonderful to Kristine, Evan, and of course, little Henry.

How pleased I am to share with you these next few photos of

the newest addition to our collective family. The next generation. There is something magical in experiencing the next generation. Everyone who has experienced the birth of grandchildren knows the joy and it can't really be put into words. You truly have to experience it to fully appreciate it. All I can say is, it's euphoric!

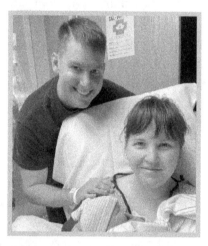

Pictured above: my daughter Kristine, and my son-in-law Evan, and the little bundle at the bottom is my first grandchild, Jonathan "Henry".

I am a proud Grandpa, "Pop Pop" as I'll be known to my grandchildren, and of course, once again Jonathan "Henry." He'll be known as Henry, which is his middle name. It's a tradition in Evan's family that the boys go by their middle names. You'll forgive my pride in the fact that his first name is Jonathan. A name, I know, he will carry better than his namesake has.

In the End

As I gaze upon my own face, I now see a man aging, something I didn't really see until my COVID experience. I had always seen myself through the lens of one appearing much younger than his years. It was always confirmed by others who would say, "I would never have guessed you were such an age." Still, the eyes are bright, the smile genuine, though the face is now no longer varnished and tight. How could it be anything different holding that little tike? A moment of pure joy captured forever. A photo I hope Henry looks upon years from now when we of my generation, when I, am long gone from this world. I hope it brings a smile to his face when he gazes upon it and says, "Yup, that's my Pop Pop. My Pop Pop and me," as he perhaps shows it to his own children and grandchildren one day.

What I have attempted to give you in this writing is not just a story of survival, but rather a story of hope, coupled with a road map of how to examine your own life. How to look for these miracles that engulf our lives? We have to learn to look for them. Some of them are obvious; most of them are not on the surface or at a casual glance. We miss so many of them because they are not obvious, and often happen over the course of time, which hides them from first inspection. However, when you see them, they are magnificent. They truly are holy, empowering and comforting when recognized.

Look once more for it here in my daughter's experience. With seventeen C-sections scheduled for Friday, it is easy to see how these might have delayed the attention of the doctors and nurses for Kristine which she needed at that critical time. They'd have done their best, I'm quite certain of that. They weren't delayed, however; they were able to be there, freed from any other responsibility at that moment. Having the birth on Sunday, when hers was the only delivery scheduled that day, was monumentally important. Then, to have these two procedures in place may seem like a lucky break or "coincidence." As you keep seeing these occurrences in your own life, over and over again, you begin to realize there are no coincidences. But you <u>must look</u> to see them. You may initially not recognize them because the situation may not have turned out exactly as you may have wanted it to. Why couldn't it be this way or that way instead of how it turned out? What I have to constantly remind myself is, that just because it might not be exactly as I wanted it to be, I must recognize that I was never allowed to fall. No, I don't have the mansion on the hill I always dreamed of having, nor have I traveled the world as I would have liked. Maybe I'm not as handsome or glamorous as I wanted to be. All this is true. But what I *have* is so far above all those things... I have my children, who are the joy of my life. I have a modest place to lay my head, countless friends who were there to support me in my hours of need over the course of my life, and now a new little life to call me "Pop-Pop." I expect there will be more of them over time, and each one will add to my joy.

There are two more stories I must share with you before we say fare-thee-well.

Earlier in the book, I mentioned how from time to time, because of my seminary background, I have been asked to speak at a memorial service on behalf of someone who has passed. I have always used one, or both, of these last two stories I want to share with you as we come to the end of our time together.

One of my very favorite poems was written by Robert Frost. He first published it in 1915 and then again in 1916, with two slight differences. The poem is entitled "The Road Not Taken." The final three lines at the end of that well-known piece are as follows:

> "Two roads diverged in a wood, and I—
> I took the one less traveled by,
> And that has made all the difference."
>
> — ROBERT FROST: "THE ROAD NOT TAKEN"

Frost never tells us if the road that was selected was the correct road or not. Did it lead the journeyman in the poem to heartache and ruin, or did it take them down a path to riches and joy? We don't know. That's by the design of the author. He didn't wish to tip his hand on that question, for it is really up to us how we will eventually evaluate the road chosen. One person's joy can be another's sorrow. The measure of one's success must come from one's own heart as opposed to the measuring stick of someone else.

I'll often use this poem to illustrate the journey of the person who is being memorialized. I'll talk about the person's life as I either knew it myself or through the lens of those who did know him or her and informed me.

The point of the matter is that we all must choose our own roads, and we must be comfortable with them, and we must take ownership of them. We will make some mistakes or missteps along the way. Every journeyman does. They are unavoidable, though hopefully, we learn from them when we do and do not make those same missteps again.

You, however, will make those choices on the road for yourself. Watch for the influences of others and evaluate their aid in deciding which paths to follow and which ones to avoid. I would implore you to call upon help from above as you make those choices. Take comfort and confidence in your own past as you discover aid given you from powers greater than ourselves, however, you may define it. Look hard for that evidence. Perhaps reevaluate that relationship and strengthen it as you take strength from it.

The second and final story I wish to share with you took place about fifteen years ago. I was working for Walton Communities at the time in the apartment leasing business. I was attending a company annual meeting, and the featured speaker that day was Dan Cathy. As I will often say, you cannot call yourself a good Georgian if you do not recognize the "Cathy" name.

Dan Cathy is the son of Truett Cathy, the founder of Chick-fil-A. At the time I heard Dan, his father was still alive and still chairman of Chick-fil-A, and Dan was the president. He was speaking to us that day about applying ethics in business, and he used a book he had written on the subject as the road map for his talk. It was an excellent speech, and I purchased his book when he was done and had him sign it for me. I must admit, I did not write a single note until he reached one point in his delivery to us that day. He quoted someone who had coined a phrase that has stayed with me these fifteen years, and I have quoted it many times myself. I have always given Dan credit for it as I don't want anyone to think I had coined it myself, though I wish I had. I honestly forgot to whom he gave credit for it before we even left the hall. For you see, it honestly didn't matter who said it. It was *what* was said that did.

He said, "Children are the messengers we send to times we will not see." Let me state this again for emphasis: "Children are the messengers we send to times we will not see."

When I use this phrase at a memorial service, I will say I am quite certain that the writer certainly means physical children. However, I have always expanded the use of the phrase to include all siblings, brothers and sisters, aunts and uncles, nephews, nieces, and cousins. I also include everyone who may have attended the memorial service that day and all those who wished they could have attended.

If we expand the sphere of influence to everyone we touch in the course of our lives, it means that everyone who is still here after we are gone from this world is, in essence, left behind to carry on and must be included in the definition of "children."

One last time, I shall reference *It's a Wonderful Life*. Clarence the angel reminds George that one life touches so many other lives in ways one simply doesn't know. It is true for each and every one of us. Every word spoken, every simple touch of comfort we bring. On occasion, we misstep with these things as well. It's okay; we are human, and sometimes we don't always do as we should or wish to have done. Ask for forgiveness, do what you can to correct it, and do better next time. Always remember we are sending a message with each act, both good and not-so-good on occasion.

For you see, in the end, there are but two questions each of us must answer for ourselves. The questions are easy; it's the answers that are complex and will be different for each and every one of us.

The questions are these...

What road will you choose?
and
What message will you deliver?
Amen

EPILOGUE

When you are writing a true story of life, you in fact never run out of material. The only way it can truly end is if the life itself ends. However, even then, your legacy lives on in the collective memories of those who love you. As this is a true story, therefore, the story continues and it has done so in two marvelous ways that must be shared.

I am writing this epilogue in late May 2022, and I now possess some additional information I didn't have when I started writing the book. The photos you will see below are part of the ongoing story.

After I came out of the hospital, a number of people asked me if I had received their card or letter. Because I had been in such a state and unable to get to the table in my room that held what I had received, I was not always certain I had received something, specifically from the inquirer. Not wishing to disappoint anyone, I would generally say, "Yes." and then thank them for having been so kind. Still, it bothered me that I was never really sure if I had received their particular card or note. I knew I had received balloons and flowers from certain of my friends, such as Miss Linda and Mr. James from "Great Oaks," where for years I had worked for them portraying the Reverend Nathaniel Pratt for weddings at their wedding venue. I had also received a lovely card from my friend Clint Johnson, who had prepared my taxes for years. That card had come to my home though, not to the hospital.

Imagine my euphoric surprise when I received a call from WellStar on May 5, 2022. They called to tell me that they had collected a number of cards and letters that had never caught up to me in the hospital. You will recall that I had begun my journey at WellStar North Fulton. I was there for one month, then moved to WellStar Windy Hill for two weeks, and then to WellStar Cobb Hospital for my final two weeks. The cards and letters kept moving through the system attempting to catch up with me, but they had not made it to me before I was discharged.

The kind woman on the phone said she was putting them in the mail to me and just needed to verify my address. On Thursday, May 19, 2022, the packet in the photo below arrived. The second photo is of some of the contents of the package. As you can see, I haven't yet opened them but will shortly. It will take me a while to get through them all. I want to savor each and every one. I'm sending a text to each person to show them I did finally receive his or her card.

I truly savor each one of them, just as I savor each one of you.

Epilogue

This final update is every bit as fascinating as how the letters finally found me. You will recall one of my angels was RN Rebecca Fabian. She was the "Daisy Award" winner from WellStar North Fulton, whom I said was instrumental in reaching out to my children when my lead physician wasn't very promising on the subject of my recovery. You may recall the story of how I had found her identity, or at least believed I had identified her based on the photo I had found by the cafeteria at WellStar North Fulton.

You will further recall that my friend Jon-Paul Croom was working to set up a meeting between Rebecca and me, if possible. Events of Sunday, May 22nd changed all those plans.

At ten o'clock on Sunday evening, May 22, I happened to be talking on the phone with my daughter Kristine. I'd had the pleasure of spending a couple of days earlier in the week with her and my grandson Henry, and I was following up with her. Suddenly a second call came in from my dear friend Russ Fawcett, whom you recall is my ninety-seven-year-old WWII veteran friend. I immediately said to Kristine, "That's Russ calling, at this hour it can't be good." So Kristine and I hung up and I immediately picked up Russ. As anticipated, it wasn't good. He was having a bit of a medical emergency and wanted me to drive him to the hospital. Fortunately, it wasn't bad enough to need an ambulance, but he did need to go. I immediately headed to his place, which was only two miles from mine. I picked him up and off we went. Finally, after roughly six hours in the ER, he was moved upstairs to the hospital and given a room. As it turned out, he had been taken to the ICU. He was placed in room 250, just around the corner from the room I had occupied, room 255. Russ spent the next few days there and eventually came home on Friday, May 27, 2022.

While visiting Russ in the hospital, I had the opportunity to see my former room. It truly was surreal staring at the room in which I had come so close to dying. So much had happened to me there that I didn't (and still don't) remember; I found myself standing just outside the door.

The photo you now gaze at below is one I took as I stood there - room 255 ICU WellStar North Fulton Hospital.

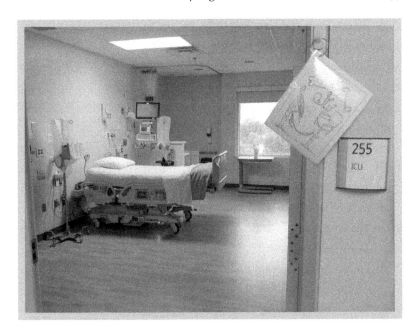

Standing outside that room I wondered, is it possible Rebecca could be close? Could she in fact be working on the floor right now? My heart began to race at the possibility. I pulled up the photo of Rebecca and asked Russ' nurse Leslie, if she knew Rebecca and was she there today? Leslie said that she didn't know Rebecca. My heart sank, but only slightly. I thought, well perhaps Leslie was fairly new in ICU and she just hadn't worked with Rebecca yet. Certainly a reasonable possibility. Everyone was so busy on the floor that day. I didn't want to bother anyone at that moment (though, in fact, that was exactly what I wanted to do). As I left Russ for the day, I thought, why not try the other nurse's station in the ICU. What did I have to lose? Worst case scenario was I'd go back to the original plan and let my friend Jon-Paul find her for me.

There were several nurses standing at the station when I approached. I pulled out the photo I had of Rebecca and gave the nurses a quick background of who I was and that I was trying to find the nurse in the photo. To my great delight, one of the nurses,

Kara, responded, "I know her!" She went on to say that Rebecca no longer worked there, but if I would like, she would take my information and pass it along to Rebecca; then if Rebecca wished to, she could then reach out to me. Though I was hoping to have a more direct contact myself, it was certainly an understandable approach, and I thanked her for helping me.

Off I went home and began the waiting game to see if Rebecca might reach out. This now appeared to be the only way I was going to actually find her. Since she no longer worked at WellStar, I wasn't sure how Jon-Paul would be able to help anymore.

In the evening of Monday, May 23rd, I received the following email in my inbox:

> "Kara from North Fulton said you had come by today and you were looking for me? :)"
> Rebecca Fabian

I was overjoyed! Not only had I found her, I was now connected to her! I was so excited, and I immediately responded:

> "Hi Rebecca,
> You probably don't remember me.
> I was in your ICU back in July and August 2021. I was, according to what my daughters were told, patient zero for the Delta Variant. Sat at death's door twice. Dr. B—— was ready to throw in the towel. You told my daughters there was still life.
> I'm still here now. You're one of the reasons why.
> I looked at room 255 today. A room I was in a coma for almost 30 days in.
> A room I ripped my vent out of my own throat in on July 29. Had a trach placed in on August 9, and a peg tube on August 19.
> A place I met someone I don't even know in. That person is now in the book I am writing about the whole experience.
> You are that person. I would really like to meet you. I tracked you

down and was able to find you because my daughter, Kristine, said the nurse who grabbed her was the Daisy Award winner in July. The one who saved my life.

The book is currently with my Editor and is entitled, "Miracles, Angels and Messages". You are one of those Angels.

If by chance you don't wish to meet, I had to at least say, "Thank You". Thank you for being who you are. Thank you for helping save my life. I needed an advocate. Someone who believed…

Let me know if a meeting is possible.
With gratitude and love,
The patient in room 255
Jonathan Crooks"

I felt I needed to give her as much information as I could in hopes she would remember me. With all the patients nurses have to see and take care of, I wouldn't have been surprised if she didn't remember me. Imagine how I felt when the following response came back to me the next morning.

"OH MY GOODNESS YES!!!!! I DO REMEMBER YOU!
(Followed by three crying emojis)

This is absolutely crazy!!! I remember everything now. You self-extubating. The meeting with your daughters and Dr. B—. All of it. I would be absolutely honored to meet you!…… I'll give you an interview and anything else you need. I came to see you one day after you were better. You had the trach and PEG. You were miserable and discouraged, but I introduced myself and told you how great you looked. (laughing emoji) How you'd been so close to death multiple times. How I had taken care of you when you were on life support and how happy I was to see you ready for rehab! I remember!!

When are you available?
Rebecca Fabian"

Rebecca and I went back and forth several times, looking at

times and dates and settled on Friday, May 27, 2022. We were to meet at 11:00 a.m. at a favorite place of her husband's – *Rock n Taco* on Canton Street in Roswell. The day couldn't come soon enough for me. Finally it arrived. I got to the meeting place about fifteen minutes ahead of time. I wanted to be inside so I could see her walk in. I told the waitress who I was waiting for and a bit of the story. I related to her how I was waiting to meet the person who saved my life when others were ready to give me up for lost.

Finally, the moment arrived. In came Rebecca and her husband, David. David videotaped the initial meeting on his cell. With my biggest smile and best hug, we met. I didn't want to let her go, and emotions just poured out of me.

I began by recounting the entire story of how I had found her. As we enjoyed a wonderful lunch, Rebecca talked through the whole experience from her side. She told me how I had become known as "The Wild Man in room 255" by the nurses on the floor. The designation was not an endearing one. I was in a total delirium. That phrase was something written in my notes that I never understood until that moment. Rebecca first came on the scene for me the day I had ripped out my vent. That was her introduction to me. She told me how I had to be restrained in my bed, which explains why I was unable to raise my arms or raise myself up in "the snapshots" I shared with you earlier in the book.

We talked about the meeting with Dr. B— and how he and Kristine had an obvious dislike for each other. How Dr. B—- had received text messages during the meeting with my children. She explained how he had received an important text that he was indeed needed for. Such a shame he didn't have the presence of mind to explain that to my children at that moment, which would have averted the confrontation.

Side note: Rebecca had explained to Kristine after the meeting that Dr. B—- didn't have the best bedside manner... after Kristine had gone after him in the meeting for seemingly not being attentive to the subject at hand - me- when the text came in. Dr. B

— was indeed taken back by it. I'm sure he's not used to being "called out"!

I said to Rebecca, "So you were there, there at the meeting?" She responded, "Yes, I was there." I hadn't known that until she told me. Rebecca went on to say she had to be quiet in the meeting. It was the way it was with Dr. B—-. The nurse doesn't say anything in his meetings. This is just my own thought here, but he sounds like a bit of a narcissist. I told Rebecca that if I were ever to meet him, (and I didn't think he'd really want to meet me) I wouldn't go after him, but I would certainly be pointed. I would simply say to him, "I understand you were ready to pull the plug on me. What do you think now Doc, what do you think now?" Then I would walk away. To say anything more would, I believe, simply fall on deaf ears. And to be honest, I couldn't care less what he would have to say. I simply hope he might at least think on it a bit.

The purpose of the "care" meeting described above was to determine if I should be placed on the trach or not. There was danger as it was a surgical procedure and I was already in a weakened state. Rebecca told me that Kristine asked her this question: If it was your father, what would you do? Rebecca's reply: I would go ahead and have the trach put in and give it two weeks. The trach was placed and although I did have a downturn at one point a day or so later, I turned it back around as you already know.

It was at this point that Rebecca shared something extraordinary with me. She said in her four years as a nurse, only twice had she told the family NOT to do what was being suggested by the doctors. The first time she had done so, the patient recovered within a couple of days.

I was the second time. The rest is now history (that you already know as it pertains to me). I asked her why she did it. She said, "I just had a feeling." Somehow she had been moved to do it, and she was correct both times.

As we finished our time together that day, I told Rebecca that it was no accident, no coincidence, that she had been there with me during my time at Windy Hill. I wasn't "lucky" that she was in the meeting on what could have been a tragically fateful day with a doctor who was indicating I shouldn't move forward. It wasn't some random feeling that she had experienced. Neither for me or the other individual. She had been placed there and had it placed upon her to speak up and not ignore the feeling. In the universe of faith, we call these things Providence. She was the correct person, at the correct time. Placed there to do a deed.

For me personally, it was yet another miracle. She was my miracle that day and every day she was with me.

The bill was paid that day just as a far bigger bill has been paid for each of us. However, before we rose to say our goodbyes, I asked David if he would be kind enough to take one more photo. It's the photo you see below, of me and my angel, Rebecca Fabian... nurse.

My closing thoughts to you, as you finish reading this true story, are to be vigilant in finding your miracles, connect your dots, and find and thank your personal angels. All these things are all around you. I promise you they are there. Deliver your messages. And may that which is greater than ourselves, however you define it, always lead you, guide you, and be gracious unto you. Amen

APPENDIX
MEDICATION DEFINITIONS

Definitions provided by MedlinePlus, Wikipedia, Drugs.com

Albuterol - Albuterol is used to prevent and treat wheezing, difficulty breathing, chest tightness, and coughing caused by lung diseases such as asthma and chronic obstructive pulmonary disease (COPD; a group of diseases that affect the lungs and airways). Albuterol is in a class of medications called bronchodilators. It works by relaxing and opening the air passages to the lungs to make breathing easier.
Balanced Salt Irrigation - A salt water rinse.
Chlorhexidine - An antiseptic used in wipes to cleanse an area.
Dexamethasone - This medicine is given through the vein (IV). Dexamethasone, a steroid medicine, to help reduce an overactive immune response in the body.
Dextrose - Dextrose is a simple sugar made from starch. Starch is a naturally occurring complex carbohydrate found in many plants, including corn, wheat, rice, and potato. The most common source of dextrose is corn starch.
Dextrose, when used as a medication, is given either by mouth (orally) or by injection. Dextrose is also known as D-glucose. Dextrose is also used to provide carbohydrate calories to a person

who cannot eat because of illness, trauma, or other medical conditions.

Etomidate - A short-acting intravenous anesthetic agent used for the induction of general anesthesia and sedation for short procedures such as reduction of dislocated joints, tracheal intubation, cardioversion, and electroconvulsive therapy.

Famotidine - Prescription famotidine is used to treat ulcers (sores on the lining of the stomach or small intestine); gastroesophageal reflux disease (GERD, a condition in which backward flow of acid from the stomach causes heartburn and injury of the esophagus [tube that connects the mouth and stomach]); and conditions where the stomach produces too much acid, such as Zollinger-Ellison syndrome (tumors in the pancreas or small intestine that cause increased production of stomach acid). Famotidine is in a class of medications called H2 blockers. It works by decreasing the amount of acid made in the stomach. Clinical trials have reported that a high dose of famotidine was found to decrease inflammation and alleviate symptoms of COVID-19 earlier. Two reviews in 2021 found famotidine to have "no significant protective effect in reducing the risk of developing serious illness, death, and intubation for COVID-19 patients", calling for further studies.

FentaNYL - Fentanyl is used to treat breakthrough pain (sudden episodes of pain that occur despite round-the-clock treatment with pain medication) in cancer patients at least eighteen years of age (or at least sixteen years of age if using Actiq brand lozenges) who are taking regularly scheduled doses of another narcotic (opiate) pain medication, and who are tolerant (used to the effects of the medication) to narcotic pain medications. Fentanyl is in a class of medications called narcotic (opiate) analgesics. It works by changing the way the brain and nervous system respond to pain.

FentaNYL (SUBLIMAZE) - See FenyaNYL

Glucagon - A glucagon blood test measures the amount of a

hormone called glucagon in your blood. Glucagon is produced by cells in the pancreas. It helps control your blood sugar level by increasing blood sugar when it is too low.
Sold under the brand name Baqsimi, among others, it is a medication and hormone. As a medication, it is used to treat low blood sugar, beta blocker overdose, calcium channel blocker overdose, and those with anaphylaxis who do not improve with epinephrine. It is given by injection into a vein, muscle, or under the skin. A version given in the nose is also available.
Heparin (porcine) - Deep vein thrombosis (DVT) is a condition that occurs when a blood clot forms in a vein deep inside a part of the body. It mainly affects the large veins in the lower leg and thigh but can occur in other deep veins, such as in the arms and pelvis.
Also known as unfractionated heparin (UFH), is a medication and naturally occurring glycosaminoglycan. Since heparins depend on the activity of antithrombin, they are considered anticoagulants. Specifically, it is also used in the treatment of heart attacks and unstable angina. It is given by injection into a vein or under the skin.
Insulin Lispro - Insulin lispro injection products are used to treat type 1 diabetes (a condition in which the body does not produce insulin and, therefore, cannot control the amount of sugar in the blood). Insulin lispro injection products are also used to treat people with type 2 diabetes (a condition in which the body does not use insulin normally and therefore cannot control the amount of sugar in the blood) who need insulin to control their diabetes. In patients with type 1 diabetes, insulin lispro injection products are always used with another type of insulin, unless it is used in an external insulin pump. In patients with type 2 diabetes, insulin lispro injection products may be used with another type of insulin or with oral medication(s) for diabetes. Insulin lispro injection products are a short-acting, man-made version of human insulin. Insulin lispro injection products work by replacing the insulin that

is normally produced by the body and by helping move sugar from the blood into other body tissues, where it is used for energy. They also stop the liver from producing more sugar.

Midazolam (VERSED) - Midazolam injection is used before medical procedures and surgery to cause drowsiness, relieve anxiety, and prevent any memory of the event. It is also sometimes given as part of the anesthesia during surgery to produce a loss of consciousness. Midazolam injection is also used to cause a state of decreased consciousness in seriously ill people in intensive care units (ICU) who are breathing with the help of a machine. Midazolam injection is in a class of medications called benzodiazepines. It works by slowing activity in the brain to allow relaxation and decreased consciousness.

Norepinephrine (LEVOPHED) - Norepinephrine is similar to adrenaline. It is used to treat life-threatening low blood pressure (hypotension) that can occur with certain medical conditions or surgical procedures. Norepinephrine is often used during CPR (cardio-pulmonary resuscitation).

It is used mainly as a sympathomimetic drug to treat people in vasodilatory shock states, such as septic shock and neurogenic shock, while showing fewer adverse side effects compared to dopamine treatment.

Piperacillin-tazobactam - Piperacillin and tazobactam injection is used to treat pneumonia and skin, gynecological, and abdominal (stomach area) infections caused by bacteria. Piperacillin is in a class of medications called penicillin antibiotics. It works by killing bacteria that cause infection. Tazobactam is in a class called beta-lactamase inhibitor. It works by preventing bacteria from destroying piperacillin.

Antibiotics such as piperacillin and tazobactam injection will not work for colds, flu, or other viral infections. Taking or using antibiotics when they are not needed increases your risk of getting an infection later that resists antibiotic treatment.

Its main uses are in intensive care medicine (pneumonia,

peritonitis), some diabetes-related foot infections, and empirical therapy in febrile neutropenia.
Propofol (DIPRIVAN) - Diprivan is an intravenous general anesthetic and sedation drug for use in the induction and maintenance of anesthesia or sedation
Marketed as Diprivan, among other names, is a short-acting medication that results in a decreased level of consciousness and a lack of memory for events. Its uses include the starting and maintenance of general anesthesia, sedation for mechanically ventilated adults, and procedural sedation.
Rocuronium - An aminosteroid non-depolarizing neuromuscular blocker or muscle relaxant used in modern anesthesia to facilitate tracheal intubation by providing skeletal muscle relaxation, most commonly required for surgery or mechanical ventilation. It is used for standard endotracheal intubation, as well as for rapid sequence induction (RSI).
Sodium Bicarbonate - Sodium bicarbonate is an antacid that neutralizes stomach acid.
Sodium Chloride (NS) - Sodium chloride is the chemical name for salt. Sodium is an electrolyte that regulates the amount of water in your body. Sodium also plays a part in nerve impulses and muscle contractions. Sodium chloride is used to treat or prevent sodium loss caused by dehydration, excessive sweating, or other causes.
Vancomycin - Vancomycin is an antibiotic that is often used to treat these infections. Antibiotics are medicines that are used to kill bacteria.
An antibiotic medication is used to treat a number of bacterial infections. It is recommended intravenously as a treatment for complicated skin infections, bloodstream infections, endocarditis, bone and joint infections, and meningitis caused by methicillin-resistant Staphylococcus aureus.
Vasopressin - Vasopressin is used to treat diabetes insipidus,

which is caused by a lack of a naturally occurring pituitary hormone in the body.

Vasopressin is also used to treat or prevent certain conditions of the stomach after surgery or during abdominal x-rays.

Vasopressin is used in emergency settings to raise blood pressure in adults who are in shock. This is caused by a lack of a naturally occurring pituitary hormone in the body.

Vasopressin regulates the tonicity of body fluids. It is released from the posterior pituitary in response to hypertonicity and causes the kidneys to reabsorb solute-free water and return it to the circulation from the tubules of the nephron, thus returning the tonicity of the body fluids toward normal.

Vasopressin concentration is used to measure surgical stress for evaluation of surgical techniques.

ACKNOWLEDGMENTS

The thought that any work is the sole manifestation of one person's mind and efforts is so vastly removed from the truth it is almost laughable to think or utter such a statement. This work is no different. Without acknowledgement of the many people who have shepherded me through this long arduous task would be just shy of criminal. Without each and every one of them this shared journey would have been impossible.

I couldn't possibly list every soul who contributed to the work. However, what I must do is acknowledge the main artists who made this story come to life in a way that would not have been possible without them.

First, my sister Nancy T. Chesney was my first editor, saving me from the embarrassment of appearing illiterate. Though that admission may not be true in the whole, it is certainly true in part. Thank you for your dedicated effort and your undying encouragement.

Thank you to my entire family and friends for your unwavering support and for giving me the courage to tell this story and for being there through my many months of recovery. They are all listed in the dedication and throughout the work itself and the roles they all played.

Thank you to my dear friends at StreetStudioCreative.com, Lisa Weltsch the CEO and founder, and Ashlan Riess the Director of Brands for their unwavering commitment to ensure the look and feel of this Book on the Website and corresponding materials was professional and portrayed in its best light.

Thank you to my editor, Stacey Smekofske, publishing coach and Editor of Edits by Stacey for patiently waiting for me to complete all the tasks I needed to accomplish for her to provide me with the best presentation of the work and story.

Thank you to my three readers who provided critical insight and thought related to how the story would touch the reader. Senior Pastor, The Rev. Jeffery Myers of Roswell Presbyterian Church, Georgia state Senator John Albers, and dear friend former EMT Krissie Sullivan.

I would be remiss if I did not thank all the dedicated doctors and nurses who waged the battle with me through thick and thin. They are all in the book as well, however I must call out specifically ICU Nurse Rebecca Fabian and Nurse Valary Anderson Dreyer without whom I would not be here today.

And to my now dear friend Angelika Domschke, artist and scientist, of Angelikart.com who brought my Angels to life for all to share and see.

ABOUT THE AUTHOR

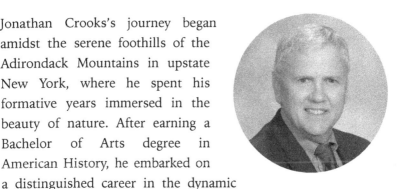

Jonathan Crooks's journey began amidst the serene foothills of the Adirondack Mountains in upstate New York, where he spent his formative years immersed in the beauty of nature. After earning a Bachelor of Arts degree in American History, he embarked on a distinguished career in the dynamic realm of telecommunications. He swiftly ascended the ranks to national director roles in sales and marketing. This trajectory culminated in the establishment of his own consulting enterprise, collaborating with prominent national and international telecom entities such as Northern Telecom.

During his early professional endeavors, Mr. Crooks also contributed significantly to the field of higher education while pursuing graduate-level studies towards a Master of Education degree, with a specialized focus on Elementary Education. His specialized focus played a pivotal role in shaping his journey of learning and personal growth. Later on, he further enriched his academic pursuits by enrolling in the esteemed Master of Divinity program at Columbia Theological Seminary in Decatur, Georgia.

Follow Jonathan at MiraclesAngelsandMessages.com

www.ingramcontent.com/pod-product-compliance
Lightning Source LLC
LaVergne TN
LVHW041043180125
801576LV00006B/9/J